THE JOHN DEWEY LECTURE

The John Dewey Lecture is delivered annually under the sponsorship of the John Dewey Society. The intention of the series is to provide a setting where able thinkers from various sectors of our intellectual life can direct their most searching thought to problems that involve the relation of education to culture. Arrangements for the presentation of the Lecture and its publication by Teachers College Press are under the direction of D. Bob Gowin, Chairperson.

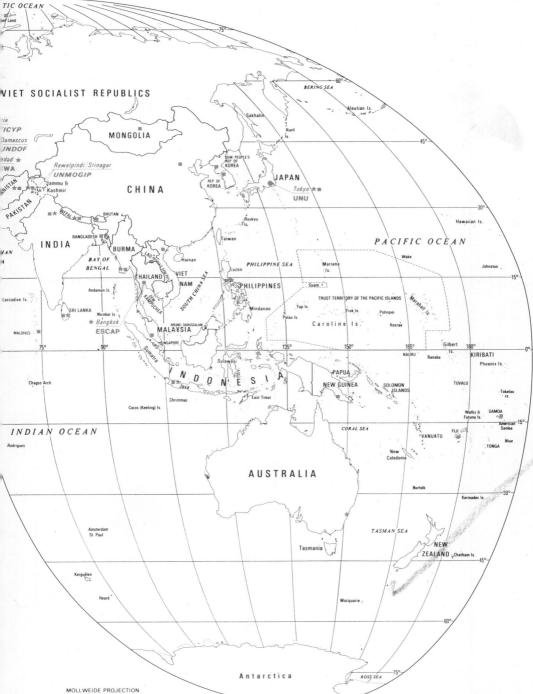

ARCTIC OCEAN

VIET SOCIALIST REPUBLICS

UNICYP
Damascus
UNDOF
Baghdad ★
UNIIMOGWA

Rawalpindi Srinagar
UNMOGIP
Jammu &
Kashmir
PAKISTAN

MONGOLIA

DEM PEOPLES
REP OF
KOREA

REP OF
KOREA

JAPAN

Tokyo ★★■
UNU

BERING SEA

Sakhalin

Kuril
Is.

Aleutian Is.

CHINA

Ryukyu
Is.

Hawaiian Is.

BHUTAN

NEPAL

BANGLADESH

Taiwan

PACIFIC OCEAN

Wake

Johnston

INDIA

BURMA

BAY OF
BENGAL

Hainan

LAO PEOPLES DEM REP

PHILIPPINE SEA

Luzon

Mariana
Is.

Andaman Is.

THAILAND

VIET
NAM

SOUTH CHINA SEA

PHILIPPINES

Guam ●

TRUST TERRITORY OF THE PACIFIC ISLANDS

Marshall Is.

Laccadive Is.

Nicobar Is.

KAMPUCHEA

Mindanao

Yap Is.

Truk Is.

Pohnpei

SRI LANKA

★ Bangkok

BRUNEI DARUSSALAM

Palau Is.

Caroline Is.

Kosrae

MALDIVES

ESCAP

MALAYSIA

SINGAPORE

75°

90°

Sumatra

I N D O N E S I A

Sulawesi

135°

150°

165°

180°

NAURU

Gilbert
Is.

0°

KIRIBATI

Banaba

Phoenix Is.

Chagos Arch.

Java

Christmas

East Timor

PAPUA
NEW GUINEA

SOLOMON
ISLANDS

TUVALU

Tokelau
Is.

Cocos (Keeling) Is.

CORAL SEA

Wallis &
Futuna Is.

SAMOA

American
Samoa

INDIAN OCEAN

VANUATU

FIJI

Niue

TONGA

Rodrigues

New
Caledonia

15°

AUSTRALIA

Norfolk

Kermadec Is.

Amsterdam
St. Paul

TASMAN SEA

NEW
ZEALAND

Chatham Is.

Kerguelen

Tasmania

Heard

Macquarie

Antarctica

ROSS SEA

75°

MOLLWEIDE PROJECTION
Scale 1: 70 000 000 (approximate)

(Map continued on inside back cover)

Building a Global Civic Culture

Education for an Interdependent World

ELISE BOULDING

Teachers College, Columbia University
New York and London

For reprint permission, grateful acknowledgment is made to the United Nations, for permission to reprint UN Map No. 3105, Rev. 7; Union of International Associations, for permission to reprint material from the *Journal of International Associations* and from the *Yearbook of International Associations;* National Center for Atmospheric Research, for permission to reprint the polar projections centered respectively on Delhi and Washington, DC; Mershon Center, Ohio State University, for permission to reprint from Feld and Coates's *Role of International Nongovernmental Organizations in World Politics;* Westview Press, for permission to reprint from Paul Wehr's *Conflict Regulation;* Nuclear Free America, for permission to reprint the 1986 listing of nuclear-free zones around the world.

Published by Teachers College Press, 1234 Amsterdam Avenue, New York, NY 10027

Copyright © 1988 by Teachers College, Columbia University

Library of Congress Cataloging-in-Publication Data

Boulding, Elise.
    Building a global civic culture: education for an interdependent world / Elise Boulding.
        p.   cm.   —(The John Dewey lecture)
    Bibliography: p.
    Includes index.
    ISBN 0-8077-2867-5
    1. Intercultural education.   2. Internationalism.   I. Title.
II. Series: John Dewey lecture (Columbia University. Teachers College Press.)
    LC1099.B68   1988
    370.19'6—dc19   87-28593
                                                                  CIP

Manufactured in the United States of America

93 92 91 90   2 3 4 5 6

FOR MY GRANDCHILDREN
whose world this book is about

Contents

Foreword

Social imagination, seldom explicitly taught in American social science, is nevertheless a necessary ingredient in social intelligence. Imagining how events could be otherwise than they are is a hallmark freedom and power of human beings. Making social imagination work involves us in new concepts and principles, in new ways of using our minds to grasp complexities we do not yet comprehend. Thinking this way helps us construct new social realities both locally and globally. Social imagination is not merely for the sake of academic knowing; it must include our feelings, and it must include our acting. Thinking and feeling and acting can be integrated. And when this integration flourishes, we remake ourselves and our world. "We want to act, to help build this more peaceful world civic culture that will ensure a better life on all parts of the planet," writes Professor Elise Boulding.

In a moment of idle speculation, we may ask why we need "civics" and reflect on the sad fact that civics is not taught any more in most of our public schools. Indeed, the very word *civics* has a somewhat old-fashioned tone to it. One cannot major in civics in most colleges. And World History, which was a standard eighth-grade public school offering before World War II, is not often taught as a history course any more in junior high schools. The world has changed so much in only fifty years that the idea of "history" and "civics" as something to be taught and learned seems curiously out of date.

In this finely crafted book, Boulding writes in a new way about civics and an emerging world civic culture. She gives the idea of "civics" a new meaning, and offers an idea of history as a greatly expanded sense of the present. She proposes we learn to live comfortably in a "two-hundred year present." People are alive today who were born 100 years ago, and some people born this very day will celebrate their centenarian birthday in 2088. In this span of 200 years the nature and meaning of civic culture comes alive. Boulding thinks of a large family of five generations meeting together to recall values of the past and to project present values into the future. Making this gathering educative (more then merely ceremonial) requires us to use our minds in new ways. Our present is a continuously moving moment, stretching out 100 years in both directions from here and now. This expansion of our time perspective is a useful way to get a grasp on the complex events of our world, and helps us to think about ourselves as if the future mattered, and to recognize, as John Dewey did, that the present is always a present-of-the-past, the future a future-of-this-present. It is all here, he proclaimed.

History taught in schools and colleges often has been dominated by military history, the recounting of wars, generals, heroes, and dates of battles. Such history serves a narrow patriotism, and tests of truth are not always made explicit. Indoctrination and socialization through propagandistic curriculum materials occur commonly. Perhaps this sort of history as the basis for civics is better not found in schools today. Professor Boulding, in this book, eschews such negative appraisal for the positive planning of our future.

One of the new ideas deriving from her large view is the concept of INGOs: International Nongovernmental Organizations. These INGOs are significant alternatives to the dominating nation-state system, with its alignments of wars, treaties, and power struggles begun with the drawing of arbitrary border lines. Boulding cites the facts that 167 nation states now exist, over 61,000 treaties have been contracted, 93 countries have standing armies for "security," and one out of three countries today are aligned with either the USSR or USA. In sharp contrast to this sort of order, Boulding notes that there are over 120 nonaligned countries, and over 18,000 active nongovernmental organizations. She believes this substantial demographic/political/organizational base can, with the help of new concepts and principles, build a new civic order for the world.

Resources for new thinking come from new perspectives on educating not found in schools today. Today's schools, like today's hectic short-lived currencies, are limited to a severe technocratic rationality. This high-tech culture produces restricted, procedurally driven thinking. Boulding's alternative is to use the mind in new ways. Her book is rich with examples, techniques, and workshop plans for building skills of thinking, feeling, and acting. The social imagination, when put into action, is a marked antidote to despair. Can you "imagine a world without weapons"? What would such a world feel like? What new thoughts might you think if war and weapons, arms control and disarmament, and nationwide power struggles were totally absent from daily news reports? Boulding presents a strong case for peace praxis, for "doing peace." Peace making takes time. And space. And world enough. And ideas.

Facts and concepts, generalizations and principles, and new events we can make happen, are expertly woven together in this book. We can think anew about time and space, location and causality. If you will, Boulding sketches a "metaphysics of civics"—a way to arrive at a world view and to anchor such a perspective in reality. There is also an educational epistemology here as she describes how to use our minds in new ways. First we think with new ideas and then change our minds and actions, as we become familiar with a set of new concepts and principles, and what they mean for constructing new social spaces.

Another key idea presented is that people around the world are much more alike than different. Boulding describes this concept as "species identity." We are all of one species. That fact will help us cope with the alien and unfamiliar cultures of the world. What can be shared within a culture locally can be shared globally, because all such sharing is in the first place an educative process of "grasping what is alien and unfamiliar." Culture itself carries the alien and unfamiliar. Consider algebra, quantum theory, DNA, microchips, Picasso, fractals, quarks, and strangeness. To upcoming generations these will not be at all familiar. In every culture the same problem exists: The older generations must educate the younger generations.

Valuing, Dewey argued, is a process of seeing in what is, that which would be better. From these direct experiences of value events, we come to learn to appreciate, understand, interpret, and make instrumental use of existing value to imagine how and why it could become better. This view, as Boulding also argues, is transformative. And both conservative and progressive elements of the social order, indeed all diversities to the fullest extent, participate in the transformation of value into as yet unimagined new goods.

This book is meant to be used as a primer of civics. Its validity derives from the actual changes it will cause in our experience. It goes a long way to help us envision a newly imagined connection between education and culture.

D. Bob Gowin
Professor of Foundations of Education
Cornell University
Chair, John Dewey Society Lecture Commission

Acknowledgments

Many people have contributed to the making of this book, beginning with my parents, Joseph and Birgit Biorn-Hansen. By raising me as a Norwegian-American, they helped me to understand from a very young age that identities cross national borders. Then there is my husband, Kenneth Boulding, with whom I have shared a mind-stretching intellectual and spiritual journey for nearly 50 years. Next, my mind turns to the many dozens of children, from toddlers to teens, including our own five, whom I taught and learned from between 1950 and 1966 in the First-Day School of the Ann Arbor Friends Meeting. It was in the freshness of those no-holds-barred interchanges that I began to understand the highly individualized process by which each human being forms an identity that can include the world. When the children reached high school, their leadership in civil rights and peace movements in the Ann Arbor High School classes of 1964 to 1967 showed me new ways to act in the world we had taught them about.

Then there were the college students in those same years. First, the founding members of Students for a Democratic Society (SDS) who joined us in midnight worship at our 1961 New Year's Eve party. They stayed on that night, into the wee morning hours, soberly discussing the difficulties of handling the violence that had been meted out to them by police (and police dogs) during the voter registration drives and civil rights demonstrations in the South in recent months. Their effort to respond in a spirit of love taught me lessons I will not forget. Later, as I watched some of the SDSers turn from nonviolence to violence in the face of an obdurate, uncaring society, I came to understand how difficult are the disciplines, how fragile the bonds, that hold us together in a common human identity.

I also learned never to underestimate the creativity of young people. Standing with students one memorable night in front of the University of Michigan Union waiting for candidate John F. Kennedy to arrive and promise to support the ideas of the Peace Corps, watching the students who formed Americans Committed to World Responsibility travel across Europe gaining support for the idea of a world university (which laid the groundwork for the present United Nations University), I saw firsthand how creative new institutions can be shaped by the imagination and willingness to act of youth.

Even faculty had their creative moments, as on that memorable night of March 24, 1965 when the world's first all-night teach-in took place at the University of Michigan. Professors met the challenge of applying their scholarly knowledge to the problems of making peace—all night long. That was before women's liberation, and my role was to serve coffee from dusk to dawn, but I was proud to be part of a new intellectual movement.

Those were action-filled years. I saw how each generation found its own role in working for a peaceful world. There were the young mothers across the country, nervous but firm, who wheeled their baby carriages to their local courthouses in public support for the Women's Strike for Peace in 1962, and there were the older generations from the Women's International League for Peace and Freedom (WILPF) who had been working for the same goals since 1915. They were all my colleagues, my sisters, and I learned from them all. My years as international chairperson of WILPF gave me my first important lessons in the workings of international nongovernmental organizations (INGOs), which feature so prominently in this book. I can never thank enough my WILPF sisters from Europe, Africa, Asia, Latin America, and North America, for all they have given as teachers and friends. I will single out only three names: Mildred Scott Olmsted, who was trained by Jane Addams herself for her peacemaking tasks; Dorothy Hutchinson, my mentor and traveling companion in memorable journeys to the Soviet Union and Poland; and Edith Ballantyne, untiring International Secretary of WILPF who has given me a second home in Geneva.

I owe a special debt to the University of Michigan faculty who, together with Kenneth Boulding, founded the first Center for Conflict Resolution. My work at the center as a volunteer, and as newsletter editor/networker for the emerging international community of peace research scholars, was a crucial apprenticeship in the task of building a global civic culture. I had splendid teachers (including Robert Angell, Dan Katz, and Charles Moskos), and eased very gradually from the role of volunteer/housewife to graduate student to professor. Fred Polak, the author of *The Image of the Future* (1972), which I translated from the Dutch, played a very important part in that transition.

The colleagues from all continents who worked with me in the founding and development of the International Peace Research Association from 1965, and of the North American Consortium on Peace Research, Education and Development from 1971, have all been my teachers: my own husband, and Johan Galtung, Mari Ruge, John Burton, Asbjorn Eide, Raimo Vayrynen, Yoshikazu Sakamoto, Chadwick Alger, Berenice Carroll, and Betty Reardon are a few among many. So have my colleagues and students at the two institutions where it has been my privilege to teach, the University of Colorado and Dartmouth College. My learning experiences in working with international networks in the International Sociological Association and the World Futures Studies Federation have expanded my ideas of how tasks can be accomplished across national borders. Here Andrée Michel of Paris and Eleanora Masini of Rome have been especially important to me.

My apprenticeship in the United Nations goes back to the early 1960s, when I first became a consultant to UNESCO's Division on Human Rights and Peace. Colleagues at the UN Institute for Training and Research (UNITAR), the Geneva-based UN Institute for Disarmament Research (UNIDIR) (here I must make special mention of Liviu Bota), the UN Disarmament Division (Swadesh Rana has been a valued woman colleague there), and the Dominican Republic-based Institute for Training and Research for the Advancement of Women (INSTRAW) (its director, Dunja Ferencic, has been a keen-witted advocate for women in decision-making sectors), have all helped educate me about the workings of different parts of the international system.

Last but not least are my colleagues at the United Nations University in Tokyo, including the council with whom I served for six years, and the professional and support staff of the university. Council meetings and research trips to the UNU have always been tremendous learning opportunities. I especially want to thank retiring Rector Soedjatmoko and Vice Rectors Kinhide Mushakoji (a very old friend indeed), Alec Kwappong and Miguel Urrutia, and Secretary to the Council/Professor Jose Abueva. Ivan Kanterovitz of the UNU Liaison Office at the UN in New York has been of very special help in the preparation of this book, arranging for the use of the UN map and identifying hard-to-get information.

Colleagues in projects I am currently involved in have all, mostly unwittingly, contributed to this book. In particular I wish to thank Saul Mendlovitz of the World Order Models Project/Committee for a Just World Peace; W. C. Ferry of the Exploratory Project on the Conditions of Peace (EXPRO); and Leonard Rieser and Gene Lyons, co-founders of the UN Institute of the Dickey Endowment at Dartmouth; as well as Dennis and Dana Meadows of Dartmouth. My work with Warren Ziegler over the years on the Imaging a World Without Weapons Project has profoundly influenced everything else I do. This influence shows up particularly in this book in the chapter on the uses of the imagination.

Two people who don't fit anywhere else but who have affected my thinking about the global civic culture very profoundly, as well as being important personal role models, are Alva Myrdal and Margaret Mead. Their recent deaths have made me realize how important it is to carry on the work of making us all into more complete world citizens.

Finally, I wish to thank those who have made this book possible in highly concrete ways: the John Dewey Society, for asking me to give the lecture that grew into the book; Bob Gowin, for a thoughtful reading and constructive feedback on the manuscript; Lawrence Senesh and Zome Thomson, neighbors in our happy "retirement" condominium in Boulder who provided other helpful suggestions; Stephen Schneider of the National Center for Atmospheric Research, who had the polar projections used in Chapter 1 drawn in his office; the editors at Teachers College Press, with whom it has been a pleasure to work, Peter Sieger and Guy Owen; my splendid copy editor, Susan Keniston; Marty Gonzalez, my fine research assistant (and Laurel Schneider, an earlier research assistant during my Dartmouth days); and Judy Fukuhara, who typed the final manuscript with patience and unerring accuracy.

The scholar-activist dichotomy has never been an issue for me. Theory is nothing without practice, and data is useless without experientially grounded models that can show how facts interrelate. I will therefore close by thanking all the neighbors and community groups I have ever been involved with, for what they have shown me about how the world works. I hope this book will be a useful guide for them as well as for teachers, scholars, and policy makers, in the shaping of a world community in which we can all live with hope and joy.

Prologue

What is civic culture, and what does it have to do with thinking about the planet? Civic culture represents the patterning of how we share a common space, common resources, and common opportunities and manage interdependence in that "company of strangers" (Palmer, 1981) which constitutes The Public. It has to do with the interactions that create the sense of a common public interest. Although most of us in that shared civic culture will remain strangers to one another all our lives, we nevertheless have a common interest in maintaining a public framework within which we can live our private lives as individuals and families, within our circles of intimacy. The price of not maintaining that public framework, of not developing a common public interest, is that society comes to be seen as alien and public spaces as dangerous. We have already seen how public spaces—city streets, parks, public squares—have become dangerous to the very young and the very old in our midst, and sometimes to middle-years folks as well. The more we try to retreat into our personal privacy, the more dangerous those untended public spaces become.

Public space is not only physical space, however; it is social space, that temporal realm in which we interact with one another in carrying on the business of life. Social space is action space, where we can tend to the arrangements that enhance our mutual well-being as a society. Our schools, our precinct polling places, our town meetings, and all the hundreds of voluntary organizations of any town—from the Chamber of Commerce and service clubs through Girl and Boy Scouts, athletic associations, women's organizations, and churches—are all important action spaces in our society. The time we invest in these organizations keeps our community alive as a caring, sharing microsociety. When not enough people invest enough time in these activities, the sense of trust and neighborliness is lost and levels of violence rise.

When we think about civic culture, we are usually thinking about our own society. Yet there is also a larger company of strangers—the 5 billion residents of the planet. Can we begin to perceive a common interest in maintaining a public framework for the world community, within which we can live our lives as members of national societies? Generally we do not see ourselves as having a civic role in the international system. In fact, the term *globalism* has come to have a negative meaning for some Americans, as if it represented a way of thinking that devalues and belittles our own country. Can we love our country and also the community of countries of which it is a part? Others try to deal with that problem by thinking of globalism in terms of a simplistic conception of one world family; that is, since we all live on one planet and are therefore to a degree interdependent, all we have to do is acknowledge that we are all one family.

Such metaphoric devices, while valuable, do not help make a world civic culture a reality. The ingredients are there, but we know very little about them. The 167 independent countries and associated territories of the world contain literally thousands of ethnic groups, each with their own language and cultural identity. The civic culture has to be forged out of these identities. In the Northern Hemisphere we think we have solved the problem of that common civic tradition through the development of what we think of as a universal culture. It is based on the Greco-Roman-Judeo-Christian traditions, albeit with both communist and capitalist versions of that culture. The two great alliance systems of the North, centered on the United States and the Soviet Union, would each like to invite the rest of the world to join its system and make it truly universal. Between them they represent the 50 nations that founded the United Nations in 1946. But the other 117 countries—the new countries born since World War II with the dismantling of the colonial empires of the North—have other ideas. If there is to be a world civic culture, they want to make their own contributions to it.

We sometimes talk of these different groups of countries as different worlds: The First World refers to the countries of the North which see representative democracy and free-market capitalism as the way to a peaceful international order. The Second World refers to the countries of the North which see socialism and a centrally planned economy as the way to a peaceful international order. The Third World refers to the countries of the South who generally prefer a mixed economy and are struggling to evolve their own political formulae for a unified state made up of competing tribal groups. Their concept of the international order is considerably different from that of both First and Second World countries of the North. They have called for a new international economic order. What that means is not yet clear to many, but it has caused anxiety and hostility in the countries of the North. Communication on the subject is confused.

Most writing on international conflict focuses on the North–North conflict between the First and Second Worlds, or the "Western" versus the "Eastern" blocs. Since that subject matter is so well covered elsewhere, it will not receive much attention in this book. The assumption here is that the gap between North and South is greater than the gap between East and West, or at the least that the former gap does not receive the kind of attention it requires. Both Northern blocs are competing for the allegiance of countries of the South, and both are to some degree exploiting the South. In the long run, the development of civic culture has to take place across both sets of barriers: North–South and East–West. No one knows how the twenty-first century will look, but it will be different from what we know now. The different conceptions of what the international order should be like among the "three worlds" will work themselves out over time. In the process a new civic culture will also work itself out. One thing we know is that this process can either take place peacefully through dialogue, negotiation, and diplomacy; or it can be pushed (and slowed down) by military force. In this century military force may mean nuclear war. This would be a very costly detour at best on the road to the peaceful planet we seek.

What this book is about is how we are going to approach this complex confrontation about our future world. How will we go about extending the concept of civic culture to the planet itself and developing a sense of the world public interest? How will we find ways to occupy the common space and share the common resources and the common opportunities in this company of strangers which is the human race, without obliterating differences or doing violence to deeply held values? Can we stay rooted in our own communities, retain the best of our own national ways, and still develop cooperative strategies for meeting human needs everywhere, in a linked system of mutual aid that respects the integrity of other ways of life? What kind of education would we need to prepare us for that?

The "we" means you and me. The learning task is a large one, and the time may be short. This means that it won't do to think in the ordinary curricular terms of waiting until new sets of learning materials have been developed and new specialist teachers have been trained. As it happens we are all learners and all teachers, all of our lives. Learning sites are everywhere—at home, in our neighborhood, in the places where we work and play and talk and act. School is only one of those learning sites. By drawing on our own life experience, with a little help on how to make the linkages, we can begin to map the outlines of the emerging world community, with all its diversity and challenge. We can also begin to develop the skills of communicating and functioning in that larger world community, skills that will facilitate the development of a world civic culture.

To do so we need to develop a learning community. An important feature of this community is not only that there are learning sites everywhere but that every age in the lifespan must be represented in order to have enough of the relevant kinds of experience and insight to draw on in the learning process. Depending on which decade of this century we were born in each of us has a special view of how the world works. That is because the special public events of our childhood become the lens through which we see later events, whether these be wars and catastrophes such as the assassination of a president, or times of great celebration such as the ending of a war or walking on the moon, or times of great invention such as the electronic age has been. From about the age of four on, decade by decade we each build up our interpretation of the world as new events come into our lives, both personal and public. If we only stay with our own age group, then we come to think that the world is really like what our particular age group perceives, and we miss a lot that is going on.

To understand the possibilities for the twenty-first century we need to know how the world looks to those who were born in the beginning of the twentieth century as much as we need to know the perceptions of today's kindergartners. We will have to be inventive about teaming up with people of different age groups from elementary school age to senior citizens. Each of us will be a teacher about our own cohort's world view (a cohort consists of all the people born in the same decade) and a learner about the views of other cohorts. What the world is really like is a synthesis of all those insights. It won't be as hard as it might seem, because each of us carries deep inside of us an inner child-person and an inner wise elder, whatever our chronological age. That is what is being referred to when someone comments that a child is wise beyond her years, or that an elderly person is taking childlike delight in a new experience. That is what makes us whole persons and gives us our civic potential.

Of course we have just begun our task when we have developed these interactions and these relationships in our own community. Once we have learned how to make linkages with other parts of the world, we can go through the same interactive process again, with due regard for cultural differences. Moreover, we are not doing all this just for the sake of knowing. We want to act, to help build this more peaceful world civic culture that will insure a better life on all parts of the planet.

Does that sound impossibly complicated, as if life isn't long enough both to learn and to act? It would be impossible if we were so made that we could only learn one thing after another, one thing at a time, and only act after we had learned everything. But that is not how we are made. We have intuition and imagination as well as cognitive-analytic reasoning abilities. This means that we can grasp complex wholes from partial sets of facts. We are often discouraged from using intuition and imagination except in the privacy of our own daydreaming. We are told to "stick to the facts." But every great scientist and public figure uses intuition and imagination in dealing with facts. It is intuition that transforms available facts into whole new configurations of reality. That is the process of discovery, of invention.

In this book we will be discoverers, inventors. We will use our imagination to grasp apparently unrelated facts, to digest indigestible complexities. We will see how different peoples in different world regions with different aspirations (and also with some aspirations that are the same as ours) can cooperate in the construction of a new civic culture for the planet.

We will move back and forth between fact and imagination. In doing this, we will begin to develop our own individual visions of what is possible for us and for humankind. For some, this will be rooted in the understanding of the religious dimension of human life. For others it will be expressed differently, but for all it will involve getting in touch with our understanding of ourselves and of the nature of creation. I write as a sociologist with deep convictions about the fact that every human being is called to participate in the making of society, in a process of continuous creation. Like Dewey, I ask, "What kind of person is one to become, what sort of self is in the making, what kind of world is making?" (Dewey, 1922, 217). That does not mean that you or I should decide what the world should be like and then try to get other people to do what we think is necessary. Our own experience and insight are important, but they can only develop further as we dialogue with others and learn to work with others.

In order to become more fully aware of our own experiential knowledge relevant for developing a sense of relatedness to other parts of the world, some readers may wish to turn to Appendix 1 and complete the Portfolio of Global Experience. Going over one's own record of life changes, of experience with groups different from ourselves, and of people and events that have deeply affected us will help us assess our own capabilities as citizens.

Building on our own experience is particularly important for those of us who live in technological societies, because we spend so much time getting knowledge about the world secondhand—through books, television, and computers. So much information is processed and packaged by others; in fact, our whole world is processed and packaged by others. We live inside a shell, a technological shield, which insulates us not only from the vagaries of wind, weather, and temperature but from most of the rhythms of the ecosystem—that wonderful interactive system of biological and social realms. In the well-ordered city, who knows when the bees are out for honey? When the moon is full? When it's time to dance barefoot? Who is crying alone in the night? Who can't sleep for hunger? We can move through life without knowing these things. We can fly around the world and only see the insides of planes, airports, and hotels. The shell moves with the people it encases.

I have spent most of my adult life exploring the cracks in the shell, finding out what was outside. In my senior year at college my homeland, Norway, was invaded and occupied. Norway, to me, was the beautiful land of mountains and valleys that I had always imagined as a refuge if another war should come. The first crack in the shell was to realize that there was no safe place to hide. If there was to be peace, it had to be out there, for everyone. The second crack in the shell came with Pearl Harbor. The technological shield couldn't work, even when the army was on duty. The third crack in the shell came with the cold war, in the early days of the rearing of five children. There was much love and joy in our home, but, when air raid drills were held in the schools, I realized that love and joy alone could not protect children.

What was at work in the world out there that reproduced wars in every generation, in spite of efforts to identify world public interest through the League of Nations and the United Nations? What were the structures and processes that kept pushing us away from peaceful international problem solving and toward national military buildups? How did this come to be seen as providing "security"? What was lacking in the civic culture?

I became a sociologist in order to find out what was going on outside the technological shell and why people kept hiding inside it. Joining the field of peace studies, I found out a lot about structures and institutions. I also discovered that people hid because they felt helpless. They needed to be empowered with a sense that the future could be better and that they as citizens could help make it so. If I learned a lot from my sociological studies, I learned even more from watching our children create, half in play and half seriously, the environments they needed and wanted for growing, out of the materials we helped provide. Whether building microworlds in our back-yard sandbox, campaigning for the right to debate the Vietnam War in school, or fasting in identification with the civil rights pioneers in Selma, they were helping to shape their environment.

When I began teaching I tried to apply what I had learned from our children. I tried to lead students to an understanding that the materials for their learning were everywhere and that society and its civic culture were what they had to help build. I also tried to go on learning from my students, since by then our own children were adults and no longer at home to teach me.

In the new fields of peace studies, environmental studies, women's studies, and minority studies, I found colleagues who shared my concerns about the civic culture. Many of us found our way into transnational peace studies networks[1] where all these concerns were woven together in the concept of a world civic culture. What we all had in common was a refusal to accept a dichotomy between research—the finding out what is there—and teaching—the telling what is there; a refusal to accept a dichotomy between the classroom and the world or between teachers and learners. Finally, we refused to accept subject matter categorizations that separated the civic issues of the economy, governance, and security from the civic issues of the environment and human rights. Understanding the interactions among these factors is one key to empowering those made

---

[1]The International Peace Research Association (IPRA), a network of peace researchers and peace research institutes, was founded in 1964, and its Peace Education Network (PEN) was founded about 1970. A newsletter, an active intercontinental correspondence, seminars, summer schools, biennial congresses, and the publication of books in peace studies and peace education have kept the members of this transnational community closely in touch with one another over the years. Its North American counterpart is the Consortium on Peace Research, Education and Development (COPRED), a consortium of peace studies programs, researchers, and educators working from preschool through university levels. See Wien (1984) for information on peace studies programs, and the quarterly COPRED Chronicle.

to feel helpless by complexity. Whichever thread one picks up, it can lead to all the others.

Working with researchers and activists on various continents I came to understand more about the tools we had to work with in creating a civic culture within which international tensions could be reduced and conflicts could be negotiated. I experienced that civic culture in its emergent form in my own interactions with international civil servants and with colleagues in academic, policy-making, and activist positions. This book provides a means of sharing what I myself have learned.

There is no intention here of promoting any specific image of the future. Life is process, and growth and change will continue as long as there is life. Rather, the book is intended to help readers recover the feeling of the purposive, creative act; to recover the feeling of possibility, the feeling that things can change. The emerging civic culture implies the existence of reflective human beings who are making choices. It also implies a willingness to immerse oneself in empirical realities, to find out how things are for many different kinds of people. If the planet needs mending, carpenters must know their materials.

PART I

Mapping the World: New Perspectives on the Emerging Civic Culture

We will begin our exploration of global civic culture with a series of mental maps of the "sociosphere," or the sum total of social networks across national borders on the planet. These provide the ingredients for an emergent civic culture on a world scale. Chapter 1 gives an overview of the kind of time span I believe we can work with in grasping the nature of the social problems we face in the transition from the twentieth to the twenty-first century. I call this time span the "200-year present." It includes a review of the heritage of utopian dreams with which we entered this time period. Chapters 2 and 3 provide a mapping of the structural transitions that are crucial to a grasp of the empirical realities of an emergent civic culture. Chapter 2 considers structural changes from the perspective of the nation-state and the intergovernmental order during the decades of the 1950s, '60s, and '70s, during which time the intergovernmental order shifted from 50 to 159 participants. With so many new nation-state actors, some new views appeared on the subject of what the international order should be. Chapter 3 considers structural changes from the perspective of the nongovernmental or people's order, a completely new historical phenomenon that grew out of gatherings of scholars, scientists, and social welfare leaders from different countries at the great world's fairs of the nineteenth century. This is a key chapter for understanding the emergent world civic culture. Chapter 4 looks at the problems of conflict management in the face of the ethnic diversity of nation-states. Since no one society can impose a universal order acceptable to all other societies, the creation of a species identity that will encompass cultural diversity is a major challenge. We explore the skills needed to deal with the conflicts involved, skills drawn from all fields of knowledge. In the best-case scenario, continued intersocietal bonding will take place, leading to societal transformations we cannot now foresee.

1

CHAPTER 1

Expanding Our Sense
of Time and History

THE 200-YEAR PRESENT

If we find two adults in the midst of an intense quarrel and are asked to mediate, we usually try to find out what happened before we arrived on the scene. If it turns out that the quarrel is a replay of a familiar pattern of quarreling, it may help to go back to earlier situations to see what the root of the problem is. In other words, we are trying to establish a longer time perspective. Although our concern is actually with the present moment of the quarrel, that present moment turns out to be elastic when we realize that this moment's quarrel has been going on for a long time and will probably have ramifications in the future.

Expanding our time perspective is a useful way of understanding all kinds of events, not just quarrels. It becomes particularly useful when we are trying to understand something as complex as what is going on in the world at large. So many changes are taking place, in so many places on the planet, that looking at what is in this week's newspapers isn't much help in getting a grasp of events. Yet we are very oriented to living in the present in the United States, more so than in most countries. Our foreign policy seems made almost from moment to moment. Our personal lives are also frequently lived moment to moment. It is ironic that a sense of history was much greater among the ancients than it is among ourselves. The people of India could think in terms of *kalpas,* which consisted of four thousand million years of human reckoning. The Babylonian tradition, later adapted by the Greeks and by medieval Christendom, included the concept of the *Great Year,* generally used to refer to a 36,000-year cycle, after which history was thought to repeat itself.

On the one hand are such great sweeps of time that individual human events seem insignificant; on the other is such a brief present that it is gone before we know it. Between these extremes there lies a medium range of time which is neither too long nor too short for immediate comprehension, and which has an organic quality that gives it relevance for the present moment. This medium range is the *200-year present*. That present begins 100 years ago today, on the day of birth of those among us who are centenarians. Its other boundary is the hundredth birthday of the babies born today. This present is a continuously moving moment, always reaching out 100 years in either direction from the day we are in. We are linked with both boundaries of this moment by the people among us whose life began or will end at one of those boundaries, five generations each way in time. It is our space, one that we can move around in directly in our own lives and indirectly by touching the lives of the young and old around us.

If we use this approach to thinking about the transition we are in between centuries, and between the old and the new international order, we will have a better grasp of events that cannot be properly understood in terms of what is going on this year. And we will understand better why the countries of the South want to make their own independent contribution to the world civic culture.

What was going on in the 1880s? It was the heyday of colonial-style internationalism in the West. On the one hand, Belgium, France, Germany, Italy, and the United Kingdom were rapidly expanding their domains in Africa and Asia. On the other hand, Europeans were beginning to talk among themselves about eliminating war as an instrument of national policy and replacing it with diplomacy and arbitration. The Hague Peace Conference, called by Tsar Nicholas II and intended to outlaw war, lay just ahead. There was a general sense of the maturation of the civic culture, in no small part due to the heady experience of the recent world's fairs in Paris, London, and Chicago which brought together the world's intellectual elite to engage in discourse and continued association. A new breed of world citizen was in the making, and the new century ahead promised to distill the utopian visions of past ages into social reality.

From the perspective of Africa and Asia it was a different story. Traditional societies suddenly found themselves under alien rulers. In order to make colonies profitable for their new masters, European administrators removed land right out from under whole populations of settled villages "in the name of the crown." Resettled natives were then taxed for the right to build new homes. Highly evolved indigenous systems of government and laws, land tenure, and agriculture practices were brushed aside without ever being noticed. "The new ideas must be implanted to replace the old" was the colonialist motto. Curious tribal ways were documented by anthropologists before they should disappear. Individual natives were often brought to the mother country to be educated and, perhaps, even treated as "equals"; but the colonized society and its social institutions were on the whole treated with contempt. Well into the twentieth century, Africans and Asians were conscripted to fight for European causes.

Where are we now, at the midpoint in our 200-year present? Western-style internationalism is on the defensive. The 26 nations that participated in the first Hague Peace Conference became the founders (either as victors or as vanquished) of the League of Nations in 1919. Augmented to 50 nations, they became the founders of the United Nations in 1946. By then the West understood that colonialism and internationalism were antithetical, and so one by one the colonies have become independent states and members of the United Nations. The postcolonial era is now under way.

As newly independent states reexamine both their economies and their cultural traditions at this midpoint in our 200-year present, they have come to the conclusion that a redefinition of the international order is due. Development policies initiated in the West have been a disaster for many of these states, and the poorest are getting even poorer. Hunger and poverty are endemic. An important step in the direction of a new order was initiated by the Group of 77 (countries of the South) in the Programme of Action on the Establishment of a New International Economic Order placed before the United Nations General Assembly in 1974 and adopted without vote. Basically, this program commits the industrial North to the principle of indexation. This means the linking of prices of exports of developing countries to the prices of imports from developed countries, so that when the latter increase, the former will also increase. In addition, developed countries are asked to provide debt moratoriums and increased financial and technical assistance under more flexible conditions and also provide for developing countries a larger share in the world industrial production. A monitoring system for the conduct of multinational corporations is also proposed. The North has resisted all these proposals. Only the monitoring system for multinational corporations has come into existence. The gulf between civic expectations of the North and South remains wide and deep.

What happened to the outlawing of war? On the one hand,

steady progress has been made in developing the skills of negotiation and mediation. A whole new profession has developed around conflict resolution at all levels, from local to international, and several countries have now founded governmental peace institutes. The United States Institute of Peace was established in 1984, following on the establishment of the Canadian Peace Institute the year before. Sweden, Australia, and the Netherlands also have national peace institutes (see Smith, 1985). The phenomenon of international nongovernmental organizations, which scarcely existed in the 1880s, has now become a major reality, with 18,000 separate continent-spanning networks existing as voluntary transnational groups generally independent of governments. Measured in terms of problem-solving potential, the new civic culture would seem to be doing well.

Side by side with these developments, however, we find the rise of the world military system, with an annual budget of $800 billion, organized into a bipolar alliance system which has divided the 50 founders of the United Nations. The countries of the South, though trying to stay out of that bipolar alliance system, are themselves (with a number of exceptions) also heavily armed. War has not only not been outlawed, the arms race has reached proportions undreamed of in the 1880s.

What does the next half of our 200-year present hold? The basis for a world civic culture and peaceful problem solving among nations is present. So is the possibility of Armageddon. As we explore the institutions and structures that currently hold the most promise in leading us to a more peaceable future, in the remaining chapters of Part I, it might be useful to consider how these institutions and structures could be used. What can you, the reader, make use of?

We are not yet ready to explore the institutions at the midpoint of our 200-year present, however. Easy optimism must be avoided. It is a heavy burden to look for positive signals for a peaceable world civic culture in the face of the threat of nuclear war. Is humankind up to the challenges it faces? There are two bases for answering yes to this question. The first is our own daily experience of peaceable behavior—the constant negotiation that goes on in home, workplace, school, and community to get the ordinary business of life done without major confrontation or struggle. Here is a core experience of human peaceableness that ought to be expandable into larger public domains. The second basis for answering yes is the study of the "other side of history," which shows us that all warrior societies from Antiquity on had images of a peaceable civic culture, images that were never extinguished by the experience of the battle. It seems that there is a special human capacity for envisioning peaceableness, for conceiving utopia, which has stayed alive through the centuries. It is a part of our heritage and has been celebrated by the United Nations Educational, Scientific, and Cultural Organization (UNESCO) in the publication of its peace anthology, *Peace on Earth* (1980).

THE HERITAGE OF UTOPIANISM

Because our heritage of utopian concepts may be empowering to us in the present, we will spend some time looking at it before turning to the details of where we are in the present. This will be done in two parts. First we will look at images from Antiquity, both legendary and historical, and then at the utopian aspirations that evolved in our own American society from pioneer days onward.

Images from Antiquity

Even a cursory glance at the literature from Antiquity reveals recurring mythical images of human beings living peacefully together in a garden. In this garden there is abundance, sharing, joy. The nomads of the Middle Eastern deserts, the Greeks who farmed the stony soil of Attica, and the Norse who farmed even stonier soil by the North Sea all knew those images. What is interesting is that they all have in common an idea of human togetherness and sharing; fighting to kill or take captive is absent. The legends reflect the idealized social order of each imaging society. The fact that such images come from well-known warrior societies makes them all the more interesting. It is noteworthy that these images are describing warriors who have become androgynous beings, embodying both the nurturant and the assertive traits of humanity, the "feminine" and the "masculine."

The Greeks knew of a place to which warriors sometimes found their way. Menelaus, returning from the Trojan wars, was told by the elusive immortal:

You shall not die in Sparta, but the gods will take you to the Elysian fields at the world's end. There life is pleasanter than anywhere else, for there falls no rain, nor hail, nor snow, but always a fresh singing breeze blows from the sea and renews the spirits of men. (MacPherson, 1962, p. 123)

Aeneas, guided by a Sibyl, was actually taken to these groves, located in a spacious and verdant valley.

Here Aeneas saw the founders of the Trojan State, magnanimous heroes who lived in happier times. He gazed with admiration on the war chariots and glittering arms now reposing in disuse. Spears stood fixed in the ground, and the horses, unharnessed, roamed over the plain. . . . Here dwelt those who fell by wounds in their country's cause, holy priests also, and poets who have uttered thoughts worthy of Apollo, and others who have contributed to cheer and adorn life by their discoveries in the useful arts, and have made their memory blessed by rendering service to mankind. (Bulfinch, 1947, p. 271)

The Norse folk knew of such a place too, to be found in Asgard at the center of the universe. In the Plains of Ida was a great hall, Valhalla, with 640 portals. From here Odin would send forth certain women of Asgard, Valkyries, to bring in the fallen heroes from earth. Their life on the abundant Plains of Ida, where there was always plenty of meat and drink (from a boar that daily renewed itself as meat supply, and from a goat whose udders always flowed with mead) was a "compromise image" of the peaceable kingdom. The heroes did don their armor and fight each other by day, but they removed it by night and feasted, sang, and recited poetry together (Munch, 1926, p. 48).

In Hindu mythology, replete with many warriors and battle scenes, Vishnu appears as Kalki at the end of the present age of the world to destroy all vice and wickedness and restore humankind to virtue and purity. The theme of restoration of goodness on the earth is also the theme of the ancient Jewish prophecy that "they shall beat their swords into plowshares" (Micah 4:3). The Christian vision of the good place in Revelation centers around the tree on the banks of the River of Life, whose fruit and leaves were for the feeding and healing of nations (Revelation 22:1–2). In the Islamic vision, God has recompensed his people with a garden. The delights of fountains, shade trees, soft breezes, and abundant food change behavior such that "should an ugly word fall from someone's lips . . . the answer from the other shall be nought but 'peace, peace'" (Stang, 1975).

The fact that the peaceable civic space usually seems to be a gift of the gods in each tradition does not make the images meaningless. What is significant is that a peaceable way of life could be conceived in imagination in Antiquity, and that it was seen as desirable. Moreover, images of a peaceful civic space are not confined to legend and prophetic utterance. In every age there have been rulers and advisors to rulers who have seen as their political task the creation of just and peaceful relations with the peoples around them. Less celebrated than the practitioners of Realpolitik through history, they have nevertheless made their mark on every century.

King Hammurabi, ruler of Babylon from 1730 to 1685 B.C.E., issued a Code of Laws which stands as one of the earliest evidences of the responsibility of governments for a beneficent social order. Hammurabi described himself as one who caused "righteousness to appear in the land . . . that the strong harm not the weak" (UNESCO, 1969, p. 175). Ikhnaton and Nephretite, co-rulers of Egypt from c. 1375 to 1358 B.C.E., made the decision to withdraw their troops from conquered lands, leaving only ambassadors to represent them. All the lands were given autonomy, Ikhnaton and Nephretite retaining only advisory control in a structure that was essentially a federation. From 776 to 168 B.C.E. the Greek city-states made one effort after another to form leagues to control their own militarism, though they had limited success. Yet those struggles bore many fruits. Many centuries later a North African sheik was to quote Aristotle to his Sultan:

> The philosopher Aristotle drew for King Alexander a circular geometrical figure, on which he wrote: "The world is a garden, with the government for its hedge; the government is a sultan supported by the law; the law is an administrative basis, handled by the King, the King is a shepherd supported by the army; the army is an auxiliary made secure by plenty; where there is plenty, the subjects cluster around; the subjects are slaves led by justice, justice is a synthesis which rules the world, the world is a garden, etc." (UNESCO, 1969, p. 115)

While the Greek city-states sought to create order among themselves, and others sought to create order by conquest, China was undergoing a similar struggle. Out of the Chinese struggles came the writing of four great ancients, Lao-Tzu, Confucius, Mencius, and Mo Ti, each of whom questioned the need or validity of violence and warfare. They looked beyond a simple acceptance of human conflict to theoretical principles and actual behaviors that would lead to a just and peaceful social order.

Lao-Tzu in the sixth century B.C.E. warned against war as an instrument of social policy:

In the world nothing is tenderer and more delicate than water. In attaching the hard and the strong nothing will surpass it. There is nothing that herein takes its place. The weak conquer the strong, the tender conquer the rigid. In the world there is no one who does not know it, but no one will practise it. (quoted in Mayer, 1966, pp. 33–35)

Mo Ti in the fifth century B.C.E. recommended love as a political principle:

In considering whence any disorder comes, (the holy man) discovers that it comes from mutual non-love. . . . The lord loves his State, but not another State. That is why he invades that other State for the benefit of his own State. The disorder of the whole world is no more than that. . . . In regarding another State as one's own State, who will invade it? Thus grand officers causing trouble and aggressive lords will no longer exist. If the whole world adopts universal love, one State will no longer invade another State. (quoted in UNESCO, 1969, pp. 31–32)

India also struggled with acute problems of social disorder in these centuries. By the third century B.C.E. the Emperor Ashoka foreswore the sword as an instrument for implementing the right. In his edicts he announced that all people were as his children, and he wished for all peoples the good and the happiness that he wished for his children (Kalinga Edict No. 1); he valued neither gifts nor honor so much as "the promotion of spiritual strength among men of all religions. For this purpose are employed many officers of piety, superintendents of women's welfare . . . and other bodies of officers" (Rock Edict XIII). A living being, said Ashoka, "should not be allowed to feed on another living being" (Pillar Edict V). For the well-being of his people he planted banyan trees by the roads for shade, mango groves for food, herbs for medical care, dug wells for water, and built rest houses for travelers (Pillar Edict VII). In abjuring conquest after his earlier military exploits, he announced "that conquest can be regarded as having been really no conquest at all because it was characterized by killing, death or captivity of people" (Rock Edict XIII) (all quoted in UNESCO, 1969, pp. 241–242, 335, 403, 465).

The image of the world as a family, and of the relationships between states as ultimately resting on the mutual acceptance of familial responsibility among all human beings, is never totally absent from formulations about the human polity, from the sixth century B.C.E. on. The Roman Emperor Marcus Aurelius expressed it this way during his reign from 121 to 80 B.C.E:

If our intellectual part is common, the reason also, in respect of which we are rational beings, is common: If this is so, common also is the reason which commands us what to do, and what not to do; if this is so, there is a common law also; . . . if this is so we are members of some political community; if this is so, the world is in a manner a state. For of what other common political community will anyone say that the whole human race are members? (UNESCO, 1969, p. 554)

We have moved in this historical overview from god-given peaceable settings to emperor-given peaceable societies, to the enlightened conception of Marcus Aurelius that there is a common political community maintaining civic peace for humankind. Thus the responsibility for peace shifts from the deity to the emperor to the citizen. The idea of a civic culture with equally shared responsibility for the maintenance of peace evolved slowly from the concept of the civic responsibility of the warrior. What is important to remember from this overview is that the concept of living in peace was never absent. If in the time of the archaic states despotism was taken for granted, so was the legend of the peaceable garden. Both the legends and the political experiments are part of our heritage.

Now we will leap forward in time to our more recent Euro-American heritage in the creation of civic culture.

Utopian Imagery in the Euro-American Heritage

The optimism associated with the settlement of the American colonies by European immigrants was neither an empty nor a casual optimism. The West had experienced a steady increase in scientific knowledge, in travel and communication capability, and in institutions of cooperation, in the centuries since the Treaty of Westphalia had ended the era of religious wars in 1648. A spate of fictional utopias about faraway lands where people lived ordered lives of shared abundance brought Europeans and North American colonists back in touch with that ancient human heritage of visioning the good society, a heritage that had been quiescent during the so-called Dark Ages.

The flow of immigrants from Europe to North America in the nineteenth century was an exodus to the new Eden, the new garden of the new world, where life was to be shaped afresh without any of the mistakes that cluttered up the Old World. Most immigrants came for personal betterment, but not a few came to experiment with new forms of community living for which crowded Europe had no room. The sense of virgin lands to be settled (no one thought very much about the indigenous peoples who lived here already) and social experiments to be tried were soon coupled to the new technological adventures of railroads, steam engines, factories, and all the appurtenances of the industrial era.

The coupling of virgin lands with emerging industrialization led to a deep ambivalence about what sort of civic culture should be evolving. The metaphor of the machine in the garden (Leo Marx, 1964) came to express that ambivalence. Washington Irving's description of Edenic Sleepy Hollow, a quiet pastoral scene suddenly invaded by the thundering roar of a nearby passing train, is symbolic of the sense of invasion that machines bring, at the same time that they bring mobility, productivity, and progress. Contrary to general belief, machines did not come gradually to America. They erupted suddenly, noisily. By the 1870s cities were struggling with urban poverty, crowded living conditions, and all the human misery that led to the foundation of settlement houses such as Jane Addams's Hull House in Chicago. American writer-activists attempted to develop populist political movements that would preserve the human scale and community values in the face of the onslaught of the machine. The country life, community planning, and the garden city movements all developed as ways of dealing with the problem of the machine in the garden.

This struggle is mentioned to make it clear that American utopianism did not evolve in a simple, uncomplicated fashion out of unlimited opportunities in virgin forests. It is also true, however, that there were a number of migrations to the United States by religious and political minorities who lacked freedom to develop the kinds of community life they felt called to in the old country, and who created a whole series of settlements—religious and social utopias—in North (and also South) America. In each case, whether religious or secular, the ventures were conceived of as contributing to the reconstruction of society by setting up working models at the microlevel of a new social order. (For more discussion of this phenomenon, and for further references on utopianism, see Boulding, 1987.)

When Charles Nordhoff (1875/1966) did his survey of *Communistic Societies in the United States* in the early 1870s, he found that there were eight societies for the promotion of communes and 72 communes that had developed between 1794 and 1852. The oldest had been in existence 80 years, the youngest 22 years. Some are still in existence 100 years later. Religiously based, or with a doctrine held with religious intensity, they had differing patterns of communal ownership but a similar work ethic, high craft-skill level, and good basic schooling for their children. The standard of living was generally higher than that in the immediate neighborhood. Peaceable and with a high standard of morality, generous in sharing with the local and transient poor, communal lives were so well ordered that Nordhoff found the communes unutterably dull. The culture was very limited, and no one had higher education. But they were all good farmers and clearly enjoyed their life with its "tame" amusements.

What did such communes achieve? They provided a demonstration of a more serene and humane way of life, lived on a higher level of altruism than in the outside world. These utopias did not set out to change the world, only to show that it is possible to live differently in it. Economic forces should not be ignored in considering the founding of this type of commune. Its members were working-class people who frequently had a hard time making it alone. More new communes are founded during times of economic depression than at other times. Many single women who could not find a place in the economy joined these religious, primarily agrarian communities and prospered.

During this same period there were 47 socialist experiments studied by Noyes (1870), all of which failed in rather short order. Unlike the religious communities, the socialist utopians were out to develop a model that could change the world. Their founders were, as Noyes says, "high-minded, highly cultivated men and women, with sufficient means, one would think, to achieve success" (p. 407). Unlike their religious counterparts, the socialist utopians were rarely skilled farmers. Equally unlike their counterparts, they were highly individualistic. Brook Farm, New Harmony, Nashoba, and New Lanark were among the failed secular attempts at communes.

Yet they were not failures. Their stories, along with the stories of the religious communities, have been read and reread up to this very day. They were all, religious and secular alike, experimenting with a new quality of civic culture, a new level of mutual responsibility, and their efforts and their ideals have become part of the story of the emerging civic culture of America. Each generation since their time, consciously or unconsciously inspired by their efforts, has tried its own working models of a better society. Many utopian ventures started in the depression of the 1930s. Another wave of utopian communities was founded by conscientious objectors after World War II, who were returning to their homes determined that society should not keep repeating its mistakes of using force instead of persuasion. The most recent wave of communes in the 1960s and 1970s has been less oriented toward solving civic problems, but continues in the tradition of experimenting with ways of finding the good life. The high level of individual initiative required to found all these utopian experiments reflects the unique combination of individualism and sense of community responsibility that characterize American civic life.

The story of the heritage of initiatives in the creation of civic culture in the United States cannot be complete without referring to our love of forming and joining associations. De Tocqueville (1945) noted on his visit to the United States in the early nineteenth century that this was a nation of joiners, continually creating new voluntary associations to carry out common purposes. In particular, women's activism of the nineteenth century—middle class or proletarian, radical or reformist—was a new phenomenon on the world scene (see Boulding, 1976, Chapter 11). Ideas about the perfectability of society led women to many educational ventures, for the children of the poor, for young working-class women, and for the community as a whole. They founded many schools and institutes and many special-purpose helping organizations. The profession of social work emerged out of their voluntary activity.

Unlike in Europe, there was never a lady-of-the-manorhouse tradition in the United States, no aristocracy of leadership at the village level. Until 1900 most people lived in small towns, with few status gaps to be bridged. Women invented ways of working together to improve the life of their communities. They invented the women's club to give themselves identity and purpose, and, for all the fun poked at women's clubs, they were probably the backbone of the civic spirit of nineteenth-century America.

SUMMARY

This chapter has been dedicated to expanding our sense of time and history. We began with the 200-year present, looking at an expanded present moment reaching back five generations and beckoning forward five generations. We found that the first half of the 200-year present had been experienced very differently by countries of the North and countries of the South. The optimistic expanding internationalism of the North was experienced as the penetration of colonialism by the South. The civic culture of internationalism is therefore interpreted very differently by the two sets of countries. Now at midpoint in this expanded present, the North finds itself divided by its opposing capacities for peaceful diplomacy and for sophisticated and all-encompassing military action, and without a coherent civic path. The South, also struggling with the implications of military capabilities, would like to redefine civic culture in terms of a new international order, a concept much resisted by the North. How the future civic culture might be constructed is to be considered in future chapters.

Since the task of creating that culture is an enormous one, we have looked at the historical record to get glimpses of human aspirations from the past. What is the heritage on which we can draw? We have found that the capacity for visualizing a peaceable and sharing society is reflected in legends and teachings from the earliest warrior societies of Antiquity. The capacity to visualize peace has never been absent. The concept of a participatory civic culture, however, comes later.

From the records of Antiquity we turned to the more recent story of the aspirations, dreams, and utopian experiments that have taken place in America from the nineteenth century on. We have looked briefly at how contemporary civic culture has emerged from repeated experiments with utopian communities, from efforts to deal with the contradiction of the "machine in the garden," and from the inventive culture of voluntary associations, particularly women's associations. Equipped with a knowledge of past dreams and past achievements, we can look forward to new tasks.

SUGGESTED FURTHER READING

Boulding, E. (1986). Utopianism: Problems and issues in planning for a peaceful society. *Alternatives*, 11, 345–366.

United Nations Educational, Scientific, and Cultural Organization. (1969). *Birthright of man*. A selection of texts prepared under the direction of Jeanne Hirsch. New York: United Nations Publications.

———. (1980). *Peace on Earth: An anthology*. Paris: UNESCO.

CHAPTER 2

A Planet in Transition: The Intergovernmental Order

PICTURING THE PLANET

If we try to picture the world as a whole in our minds, we picture it as stretching out around us from the town and the country in which we live. Starting from where we are is the most natural way to conceptualize a whole of which we are a part. This does not mean that our own country is objectively a larger part of reality than other countries, but it is the location from which we experience the planet. What has to be remembered, however, is that other people in other countries do exactly the same thing. Their own country looms larger for them than the rest of the world, even if it is a small country, simply because that is where they live.

While we can never be inside the mind of another and know just how the world-picturing process goes on, we can ask a computer to make polar projections of the globe centered on the capital city of any country in the world. That gives us an idea of how the world seems if one is looking out at it from any given country. Figure 1 shows us the computer representations of a polar projection of the world centered on Washington, DC and on Delhi, India. The land masses we become aware of are very different in the two projections. In short, the world looks very different, even though the same objective data about the world are used in both projections.

If we move to an examination of the maps of the world studied by schoolchildren in different countries and on different continents, we will find the same general tendency to put one's own country or region at the center and build outward from there. Mostly, when we think of world maps, we think of maps of countries, and when we think of those countries, we may even remember them as certain colors. In our old family atlas (Hammond, 1954, p. 12) the United States is colored yellow, Canada and Great Britain pink, France green and so forth. My mental map is colored that way, too. Other atlases

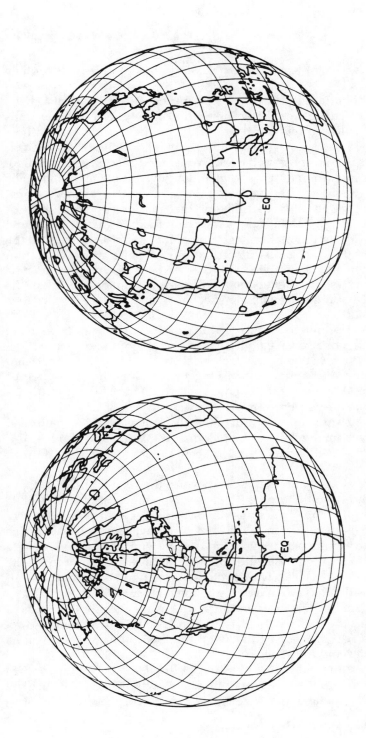

FIGURE 1. Projections Centered on Washington, DC and Delhi.

Source: National Center for Atmospheric Research

use different color schemes, particularly those published in other countries.

It is important to know about countries, and it is useful to have mental patterns for remembering them. But how can we ever communicate with our fellow citizens of the planet if we all have different mental images of where countries are, and if all we know about the world is country boundaries? We learned in elementary school that there are different ways to map the physical planet: relief maps showing mountains and valleys, rainfall maps, temperature maps. Then there are social maps, showing distributions of ethnic groups, languages, religions. But that is more information than we can hold in our minds, and it all becomes a blur. It is easier to go back to the yellow, pink, and green-colored countries, with our own nation safely in the middle. Yet we know that isn't enough, not for that new civic culture we are talking about. We need a common sensing of the whole, free of the personalizing effect of where we live. How can we achieve that?

What is proposed here is to think of the world map in terms of different sets of actors. The physical geography of the planet is taken as given: the geosphere (the geological structures of the planet) and the biosphere (the mantle of living things) together provide our base map. Now we want to know what social structures and organizations have emerged from it. We want to understand the sociosphere—the sum total of structures, thought ways, and patterned interactions among human beings on the planet. We want to understand them in terms of sets of agents, actors, shapers of human life.

The first set of units that act beyond the family and local community and have the capability of participating on a planetary scale makes up the familiar nation-state system. States do not of course exist in isolation, but in a series of intergovernmental pacts, alliances, and common markets. It is that system we will be focusing on in this chapter. A second, related set of units is found in the United Nations system, which consists of nation-state members but has bodies that have a separate, autonomous identity. These will also be considered in this chapter. Once we have a grasp of the kinds of things that these two sets of units can do, we will understand an important part of the existing civic culture of the planet, with all its possibilities and limitations.

The 1986 world map published by the United Nations, reproduced on the front endpapers of this book, will help us visualize the intergovernmental and UN activities being described. On the original map, Africa and Europe are in the center, with the Americas and Asia in the wings. In terms of land masses, this is an easily grasped presentation.

THE NATION-STATE SYSTEM

The nation-state system consists of 167 self-governing units, 159 of which are members of the United Nations. These nations are divided into two superpower alliance systems consisting of NATO with 16 members and the Warsaw Pact with 8 members, and what is referred to as the Non-Aligned Movement (NAM), which is composed of most of the remaining nations. As of 1986 there were 125 participants in the NAM; some of these states hold observer status, some (mostly neutrals of Europe) participate as guests. These 125 nations have in one way or another associated themselves with the concept of nonalignment, meaning they prefer not to be directly involved in either of the superpower alliances. In practice, however, a number of these countries have special agreements with one or the other of the superpowers regarding military deployment.

The military sector of the nation-state system includes a nuclear arms network that stretches into 56 countries, and foreign military bases in 93 countries maintained by the major powers and their allies. National armies vary in size, but there is one soldier for every 43 persons in the world. These estimates come from an internationally recognized, annually published source on overall global patterns of military expenditures and deployment over time (Sivard, 1986).

In addition to the military alliance system there is also a set of treaties binding nations to various cooperative activities in relation to common problems. In 1983 there were roughly 61,736 treaties in force (Rohn, 1984). The bulk of these treaties deal with such matters as boundary agreements (boundaries are the most common source of disputes between nation-states); special economic zones and common markets; scarce or potentially scarce resources in the global commons (in space, the world's oceans, the Arctic and the Antarctic); problems of transboundary pollution (acid rain from the United States and Canada falling in Europe and vice versa); and special regional problems such as control of drug traffic among the countries of North, Central, and South America.

Regional treaty making is one of the major peaceful activities of nation-states. Regional treaty-making groups are legion. The largest, best known, and most widely reported groups in terms of the daily press are the Organization of American States (OAS), the Organization of African Unity (OAU), the Association of Southeast Asian Nations (ASEAN), the Arab League, and the European Economic Community (EEC). The same negotiation processes go on within more specialized groups such as the Organization of Petroleum Exporting Countries (OPEC), the Contadora group (seeking peace in Central America), the African-Caribbean-Pacific Group (ACP, concerned with trade and transport), South Asian Regional Cooperation (SARC, trade and development), Gulf Cooperation Council (GCC, developing common services for tiny countries), Cartagena Consensus (11 Latin American debtor countries), the South Pacific Forum, (concerned with common problems of island states), and many more. Different groupings of contiguous states find different common problems, so new associations are constantly forming. Widely scattered countries may also have common problems, as in the case of the South Pacific Forum and the African-Caribbean-Pacific group.

Treaties and the Consensual Process

The treaty process can be considered a major factor in the development of a common civic culture across geographical distances and social differences. Treaty making is by definition a consensual process in which the interests of all parties must be considered. Treaties can be either bilateral or multilateral. Multilateral treaty making, in which these regional groups are mostly engaged, requires the greatest skill since the interests of a number of parties must be considered. Bilateral treaties, which major powers frequently prefer, need consider the interests of only two parties but frequently disadvantage small countries. Nonaligned countries try hard to maintain treaty relationships with both superpowers, although only about a third of them actually manage to do so. African and Arab states, as the most recently independent, are the least well integrated into the world treaty system. All other regions, including Eastern Europe, have high levels of international treaty activity.

It is important to note that studies of treaty partners indicate that diplomatic interaction crisscrosses major alliance blocs and regions, and thus creates opportunities for the further development of cooperative civic activity across social and political barriers.

Because of the unpopularity of the concept of multilateralism among the major powers, the problem of coordinating behaviors of sovereign nation-states in situations where cooperation is essential has led to the adoption of the concept of *regime* (Keohane & Nye, 1985; see also Johansen, 1986) as an alternative to multilateralism. International regimes are rules and procedures that define the limits of acceptable behavior on various issues (or a set of possible practices); they may or may not include formal organizational structure. The emphasis is on a decentralist self-regulation based on mutual self-interest. Because the concept of regime minimizes structure and gives the emphasis to interests and values, it provides a promising instrument for emergent civic culture in new arenas where it does not now exist. Space and the seabed are good examples of arenas where regimes can be effective as a transitional device in the face of the refusal of some governments to accept formal structural arrangements.

Consensus, which I shall explain shortly, is an important part of the process that moves nations toward more structured agreements. The Western tradition of majority voting runs counter to the consensual process, so many Westerners are uncomfortable with consensual procedures. Many Third World cultures, on the other hand, find the practice of consensus familiar and comfortable (see Selassie, 1980). Western and Third World political traditions have thus clashed both in intergovernmental interaction and in the United Nations. The Western mistrust of consensus stems from an awareness that consensus, when improperly exercised, can suppress dissent. When properly used, however, consensus allows for diversity of expression, political pluralism, and an active process of negotiation that can produce, not unanimity, but the willingness to go along with a certain course of action and not raise objections. This is how consensus is used in the UN and in the Non-Aligned Movement. When voting is not resorted to, an embittered minority can be avoided. This is particularly important in settings where there are deep divergences of views, as is true within both the UN and the NAM.

In the United States we would profit from more study of consensus as a problem-solving process. We do not have to go to the Third World or the UN to see it in action. The Religious Society of Friends (Quakers) has from its inception in seventeenth-century England done all its decision making by consensus. This is how it works. After presentation at a Quaker Meeting for Business of different points of view on an issue that requires action (presentations interspersed with reflective silence), the presiding clerk will "take the sense of the meeting" in the form of a written memorandum or "minute" which is read back to the group. If there is no objection, the minute stands as a decision. If there is objection, the discussion is carried over into future meetings, until a formulation has been arrived at that all members of the meeting are willing to go along with. This is not the same as unanimity, because individual Friends may disagree with the minute, but the process enables them to feel satisfied that they have been fully heard; eventually dissenters are usually willing to stand aside and let the group proceed. (The Quaker practice of consensus is analyzed in Cox, 1986, and in Pollard, Pollard, and Pollard, 1949.) This is exactly the process that goes on in the Security Council and other bodies of the UN, and it is the process used in the Non-Aligned Movement.

The consensual process as used in the NAM is worthy of more attention than it receives. The foreign ministers of most newly independent countries are acutely aware of competing tribal groups with competing interests at home as well as the competing interests of neighboring countries, when they enter NAM working groups. Arbitrary political boundaries drawn by colonial occupiers add to the possible sources of tension over the subject to be negotiated. Therefore there is a complex alignment of interest groups on any particular issue.

The NAM has 19 substantive working groups covering the whole range of economic, social, and technological problems NAM countries face, and each group operates by consensus. Some groups have as many as 15 countries in membership, others as few as 2. The Group of 77, another Third World group consisting of 120 members, focuses on issues of economic development and has 14 working groups within the UN Conference on Trade and Development (UNCTAD). These groups range in size from 15 to 33 countries. They work hard, meet frequently, and interact intensely, as the economic survival of each state is at stake. The skills of diplomacy are at a premium in their work.

To appreciate the meaning of all this diplomatic activity, one must be aware of the range of issues that Third World countries have to work through. First and foremost are the extreme problems of prolonged drought and mass starvation for countries of the Sahel and elsewhere. This and deforestation, soil erosion, and desertification represent basic survival crises for a number of states in the Southern Hemisphere. That is to say nothing of the survival crises generated by ongoing civil wars or boundary wars between neighboring states, as between Iran and Iraq. To this is added the phenomenon of religious fundamentalism, which is an issue in more than one part of the world. For Arab governments with differing proportions of

Shiite and Sunni Muslim populations, fundamentalism necessitates arriving at international agreements that will preserve political stability at home. Another recurring problem is the expulsion of ethnic minorities to their home countries in times of severe economic depression, a practice in Europe and North America as well as in countries of the South. This is a very touchy issue for neighboring countries on Third World continents and affects their willingness to negotiate other problems. What is significant is the level of negotiation that goes on among African and Asian states, and within the Arab League, in spite of the complexity of the conflict webs in which they are enmeshed. Overt conflict levels may seem high, but the wars that take place are relatively contained if we remember how intense the antagonisms are and how easily they could lead to total war.

Time and distance are needed to assess the eventual outcomes of these conflicts. Anyone observing Europe during the Thirty Years War, with its widespread slaughter, would not have predicted that three centuries later the antagonists would be sitting peacefully together in the Parliament of Europe. The civic culture of Europe was not easily achieved. There is much more that needs to be done to build up a comparable common civic culture within the Third World itself, let alone between countries of the North and South.

The Third World Looks at the Larger Picture

It should be understood that the Non-Aligned Movement, in spite of its internal struggles, has made a serious effort to think of the international system as a whole. From its very beginnings in the Belgrade Non-Aligned Conference Call, drawn up in Cairo in 1961, it articulated its purpose of "bringing about improvement in international relations, relinquishment of force as State policy towards other States and constructive settlement of pending world issues and conflicts" (Jaipal, 1983, p. 6). Messages were actually sent by the heads of state assembled at Belgrade to President Kennedy and Premier Krushchev asking for direct negotiations between them.

Because the countries of the South are for the most part poor, and the countries of the North for the most part relatively rich, efforts of the Third World, whether through the NAM or through the more economically focused Group of 77, are frequently seen as a rather simpleminded attempt on the part of the poor to get the rich to share their wealth and to avoid the more arduous tasks of developing the economies of their own countries.

In fact, the agenda of both the NAM and the Group of 77 is to set in motion a new "regime"—a set of rules and procedures that define the limits of acceptable behavior—for the world as a whole. Even within Europe itself, it is clear that countries ranging from certain members of the Eastern bloc in the North to Portugal in the South have been disadvantaged by historical circumstances and find themselves in a somewhat asymmetrical position in the world economy vis-à-vis the industrial leaders of the North, which now include Japan. The willingness of advantaged countries to adjust terms of trade, make debt management easier, and to provide technical assistance, while not high, is certainly more evident in dealing with sister countries of the North than in dealing with the Group of 77. The exception is when the North is able to tie aid to the South to involvement in military alliance systems. This weakens the concept of a new international economic order and is resisted as far as possible in the South. What they want is "development as equals," not manipulation.

At the same time, Third World governments have their own problems with corruption and greed and frequently agree to arrangements that advantage their own elites at the expense of the general population. When governments of the South speak of wanting development as equals, that may not mean equal development within their own societies. Idealism and self-serving behavior fight each other in the South as well as in the North.

Economics is only one dimension of the new international order as conceived by Third World countries. The goal for countries of the South is a common civic discourse with the North which includes values, traditions, and life ways that have up until now been written off by the North as "backward." The colonialist precept that "new ideas must be implanted to replace the old" still holds for many Northerners looking South (Mazrui, 1982).

On the other hand, there are many sensitive development specialists from the North who understand that development practices must fit local conditions and who have invested much time and energy in working with their counterparts in the South for what has been called "another development." The International Federation for Development Alternatives, the Dag Hammarskjold Foundation, and the Swedish and Canadian national development institutes are outstanding examples of Northern facilitation of a more autonomous development process in the South. The U.S. Peace Corps is another example. These projects are all based on a North-South dialogue, and on rural-urban dialogue in the country in question, rather than on one-way development planning.

In that dialogue about new development, the information and cultural dimensions are very important. The New International Information Order is one of the least understood of Third World aspirations in the North.[1] We in the North depend heavily on the elaborate infrastructure of information technology that feeds us information about the rest of the world and in turn sends out what we want the rest of the world to know. What we don't realize is that the near-monopoly of the North on information technology and channels means that we determine far too much of what information travels and where it travels. The ability to make that determination is what freedom of information means to us.

What freedom of information means to countries of the South is freedom to tell their own stories, to be the originators as well as the recipients of information, and to maintain independent and autonomous publishing sources in the South. Since resources are scanty and governments often have the only publishing capacity in a poor country, how this is to be implemented is very problematic. The responsibility of journalists to the welfare of the whole world community, which involves not participating in hostile opinion-formation between adversary nations, is another difficult issue the implementation of which cannot easily be visualized at this time. But the goals of fuller representation of the diversity of values, thought, and action in different parts of the world are clear. The interpretation of those goals as support for government censorship has been a sad if inevitable misunderstanding in the international community. The information dimension touches the very heart of the concept of the development of a shared civic culture. Much careful attention to and reading of materials not available in our daily press are required if misunderstandings are not to multiply in this crucial dimension.

A new cultural order is closely related to the new information order. A series of regional cultural policy conferences and national cultural policy studies, begun by the United Nations Educational, Scientific, and Cultural Organization (UNESCO) in the Third World but carried to the North as well, offers new substantive material for civic dialogue. The reading of some of the cultural policy studies for

---

[1]See the report on the new information order by the International Commission for the Study of Communication Problems, chaired by Sean MacBride (1980). See also the *Development Dialogue* Symposium issue, Towards a New World Information Order, published by the Dag Hammarskjold Foundation (1981:2). For an example of South-initiated information, see Khan (1985).

Africa and Asia will show how each formerly colonized country has listed as a major item of cultural policy some degree of reconstruction of indigenous culture destroyed by colonialism. (See, for example, Shore, 1981; also the series on national cultural policies published over the last two decades by UNESCO, Paris.) This is seen as essential for a development that can embody the best values of that country. Another contribution to that civic dialogue emerges from the increasing attention of countries of the South to the knowledge structures to be found in their oral traditions, to research methodologies for identifying and recording this oral knowledge stock, and to cultural practices that will insure continuing viability of oral traditions. This recovery of traditions provides the basis for mutual respect between North and South, as conceptions of values, life ways, and legitimate knowledge stock are broadened beyond exclusively Western ones. Furthermore, it opens the way for recovery of Western oral traditions and the knowledge stock they represent as well. The oral history movement in the United States represents such a development.

The new international order is an aspiration, not a formula. As long as countries of the North think of the international order in terms of their own history alone and of their own understanding of cultural and political universals, there can be no common civic culture. It is equally unthinkable that the countries of the South should try to shape the international order exclusively in terms of their own traditions. The common civic culture can only emerge out of dialogue and interaction. One of the key settings for that dialogue and interaction is the United Nations system, with all its associated bodies. We will therefore turn next to the UN itself.

THE UNITED NATIONS SYSTEM

The United Nations system can be thought of as an overlay on our world political map of nation-states. The UN is separate from nation-states but created by them, and the structures that embody its functioning are spread out across the nation-state system. The UN is the direct inheritor of the idealistic internationalism of the West that has characterized the whole first half of the 200-year present we spoke of in Chapter 1. The tradition of the international civil servant who carries an international *laissez-passer* instead of the passport of her country of origin, a servant whose responsibility is to the world community and not to any one nation in it, began in the

League of Nations. The United Nations took over and has continued many functioning administrative organs of the League, including the system of registration and publication of treaties of the League.

The children of that first generation of international civil servants at the League in Geneva attended the International School in Geneva, which developed a special international curriculum to prepare the next generation to become true world citizens. The present International Baccalaureate Diploma Program[2], which is used in a system of international schools around the world, is an outgrowth of that original program in Geneva.

The transition from the League of Nations to the United Nations was not a smooth one, however. An ugly world war intervened, in which many of the young men and women who had attended the International School in Geneva were killed. The preparation for a new kind of citizenship of the planet was lost, wasted—or was it? In fact, it was not completely obliterated. The Geneva School goes on, now in a network of international schools that includes the International School at the UN in New York, preparing the children of today's international civil servants for tomorrow's world.

The UN, the League of Nations's successor, also goes on. The heartfelt preamble to the Charter of the United Nations was written amidst the ruins of the old international order:

We the Peoples of the United Nations Determined

to save succeeding generations from the scourge of war, which twice in our lifetime has brought untold sorrow to mankind, and

to reaffirm faith in fundamental human rights, in the dignity and worth of the human person, in the equal rights of men and women and of nations large and small, and

to establish conditions under which justice and respect for the obligations arising from treaties and other sources of international law can be maintained, and

to promote social progress and better standards of life in larger freedom, . . .

Have resolved to combine our efforts to accomplish these aims.

---

[2]The International Baccalaureate Diploma Program (Route des Morillons 15, CH1218 Grand-Saconnex, Geneva, Switzerland) has 350 participating schools in 53 countries and works in three official languages: English, French, and Spanish. The North American Regional Office is at 200 Madison Ave., New York, NY 10016.

Accordingly our respective governments, through representatives assembled in the City of San Francisco, who have exhibited their full
powers found to be in good and due form, have agreed to the present
Charter of the United Nations and do hereby establish an international
organization to be known as the United Nations. (United Nations, 1945)

How do we describe the UN? The preamble begins "we the
peoples," but the UN was founded by nation-states. In a profound
sense it represents both peoples and nations. The map and legends
found on the front endpapers of this book give a sense of its scope.
There we see listed all the member states of the UN, its principal organs, and the location not only of those organs but of regional commissions and peace-keeping missions.

While the UN is a creation of its member states and can only do
what they permit, it also has an autonomous existence and provides
a continuously operating diplomatic and problem-solving capability
that increases the adaptability of the international system in the face
of continuing hostile criticism from the member states that created
it. We see from the map on the front endpapers that the UN system
consists of 6 major operating organs, 13 associated organs, 16 specialized agencies, 5 regional commissions, and 5 peace-keeping/ob-
server missions. In addition to the bodies listed, there are 20 other
research institutes, divisions, and special programs and a UN Peace
University not included on the map. These bodies together operate
about 50 worldwide information systems, 159 UN centers (one in
each member state), and innumerable regional and local offices to
administer the programs with which they are charged.

What travels over those 50 UN information systems? Almost the
sum total of data collected about the physical state of the planet—data
on rocks, minerals and soils, wind, water, weather, and on the trees,
plants and animals that make up the biota. Most of the data collected by the world scientific community on every continent pass into
these information systems. This means that every country, no matter how poor, can have the same high-quality scientific information
that is available to the richest countries. (Being able to use it is another matter, requiring local trained scientists.)

Similarly, most of the social and economic data collected by social scientists and demographers about birth and death rates; the
state of national economies, including employment rates; health,
education, and welfare services; schools, universities, museums, and
libraries; and the whole range of countable facts about how people
live, collected by governments, pass into these information systems. Most of these data are published in United Nations year-

books. In the United States, every state has one library designated as a UN repository, which maintains a complete file of United Nations yearbooks. This means that all the information collected by the UN is available to the citizens of every state in the Union. The world is literally at our fingertips. If you do not know which library in your state houses the UN repository, this would be a good time to find out.

Since the UN deals with the whole range of problems faced by the human community (and does so on a budget of $1 billion, compared to the world military budget of $800 billion dollars), there is no way to convey the substance of its activities in a brief space. As one new need after another has been identified, the UN has developed some type of program to deal with it. The result is an extraordinary array of problem-solving capabilities, and an extraordinary group of men and women who carry the UN *laissez-passers* to do the work member states ask of them.

If the organization sometimes seems to be a jumble of activities, it must be remembered that it was designed on the principle of "functionalism." There are things that need to be done in the world community that nation-states cannot effectively handle alone. Identifying those functions and providing the authority for carrying them out is the basis for the UN organization. That is what functionalism means (Mitrany, 1966). It assumes that technical problems can be isolated from political ones. Unfortunately this is not always the case, although UN officials try hard to make that separation. Since ad hoc growth also creates bureaucratic inefficiencies, including program duplication, UN machinery has many shortcomings. The redesign of the UN was a major topic during its fortieth anniversary year, 1985. At the same time, it represents a major resource available to governments for getting work done they cannot handle alone, and for resolution of conflicts with other governments. Failures in functioning tend to be publicized, while successes are ignored.

Because our major concern here is with the development of a civic culture for the peaceful management of conflict between groups and nations, it is appropriate to devote some space to one specific area of UN activities—conflict management (see Pechota, 1972, and Venkata, 1975, for helpful readings). One important and little-known tool the UN has available for conflict management is the Good Offices Missions of the Secretary General (Pechota, 1972). These involve a quiet diplomacy conducted by personal representatives of the Secretary General in the early stages of a conflict. When successful, these situations never reach the press at all.

The UN General Assembly itself spends a great deal of time on conflict management, specifically by focusing on disarmament policies. It has held two special sessions on disarmament, inaugurated two disarmament decades (the second from 1981 to 1990), and concentrated international efforts for disarmament by naming 1986 an International Year of Peace. While unsuccessful in the short run, the full impact of these efforts can only be known in future decades as the processes set in motion by the Disarmament Decades bear fruit.

The UN Department of Disarmament Affairs supervises the training of disarmament fellows, selected each year from the foreign ministries of member states. These fellows return to their home governments at the end of their nine months of training, but build up a rapport and mutual understanding during the months they are together. This rapport and understanding may stand the international community in good stead when these young women and men move into more senior policy-making positions in their respective governments. The Department of Disarmament Affairs also publishes detailed documentation on how arms policies and economic development needs interact negatively on each other, and how arms control can release resources for economic development. It provides any services on disarmament questions that member states ask for and also works with the UN Nongovernmental Liaison Services (NGLS) to facilitate the work of the NGO Disarmament Committee at UN headquarters. The NGO Disarmament Committee consists of representatives from over fifty nongovernmental organizations concerned with disarmament.

The UN Security Council, charged with implementing the decisions of the United Nations on the maintenance of international peace and security, has had a number of successes as well as failures over the years. Since the world's most intractable conflicts are turned over to the Security Council, its task has not been an easy one. A reading of Nicol's (1981) *Paths to Peace* shows the working of consensus in the face of deep ideological differences between the superpowers represented on the council. Since the chair of the Security Council rotates monthly, each member has a stake in being to some degree cooperative in dealing with difficult agenda items when other members are sitting in the chair, knowing that each will have a turn and will have to rely on a comparable willingness on the part of the others to be cooperative. One indicator of the success of the Security Council is that it still exists. Another is that there have been no permanent walk-outs.

The Security Council sends out special missions yearly, on request, to trouble spots; sometimes it succeeds in on-the-spot conflict resolution. The five observer missions and the seven peace-keeping forces the Security Council has sent out since 1946 have been an important part of postwar conflict management. The UN Blue Berets or, more recently, Blue Helmets, represent a new concept of the role of the soldier. Stationed between hostile forces, these soldiers' purpose is precisely to prevent fighting. They are only lightly armed and never fire themselves unless attacked. Their presence is intended to establish and maintain conditions under which peaceful negotiation between adversaries can take place, without fear of surprise attack. That their missions have not been more successful represents a failure at the diplomatic level to use the opportunities the stationing of the UN forces provide, not the failure of the soldiers.[3]

The Hague International Court of Justice, another associated agency of the UN, represents an ancient dream of justice between nations. The papacy in Rome was the nearest thing to an international court of justice in the Middle Ages. Popes, bishops, and sometimes emperors served as judges and mediators through the centuries until the late 1800s, when the first courts of arbitration were set up. By the time the first Permanent Court of Arbitration was established by the Hague Conventions in 1899 and 1907, there had already been a century of experience with special international arbitration arrangements. The present International Court of Justice at the Hague is a direct lineal descendant of the arrangements of 1899. It hands down decisions on cases, as it has done since 1899. Sometimes its jurisdiction is acknowledged, sometimes it is not. The historical record, however, shows a steady growth in the body of law developed by the court's decisions. The International Law Commission established by the UN General Assembly in 1947 continues the progressive development and codification of international law. Specific denials of jurisdiction, as recently happened in regard to the case brought against the United States by Nicaragua, in no way vitiate the existence of the court as an institution. The international community simply cannot do without it.[4]

The UN Institute for Training and Research (UNITAR) was originally established to carry out research on the structures and procedures of the UN and to provide training for UN personnel. Its

---

[3]Two outstanding accounts of UN peacekeeping are Moskos (1976) and Rikhye, Harbottle, and Egge (1974).

[4]For readings on international law and the international court of justice, see Larson and Jenks (1965), McWhinney (1984), and Rosenne (1965).

research reports and monographs provide one of the best documentations we have of how dispute settlement procedures work, and the conditions under which they fail. The Geneva-based UN Institute for Disarmament Research (UNIDIR), one of the newer UN institutes, collects arms control and disarmament data for member states, carries out studies of the problems of arms control and the dangers of accidental war, and helps train the UN disarmament fellows.

UNESCO is the UN agency most directly concerned with the long-run cultural factors that predispose countries to war or peace. The preamble to UNESCO's charter states that, since war begins in the human mind, it is in the human mind that peace must begin. Peace or the lack of it immediately translates into a number of political issues, particularly involving minority peoples seeking nation status. In these minority struggles, culture and politics become intertwined, and armed violence of disenfranchised peoples sometimes further complicates the issue. That is why UNESCO's cultural focus has made it harder for the organization to establish the objective domain of peace development apart from national aspirations than has been the case for other UN bodies. In spite of political difficulties, including the recent withdrawal (one hopes temporarily) of the United States and the United Kingdom, UNESCO has accomplished important work in the objective field of peace research. It publishes a periodically updated international directory of peace research institutes; supports the nongovernmental quarterly titled the *International Peace Research Newsletter*, and the *UNESCO Yearbook on Peace and Conflict Studies*; and gives the annual UNESCO Prize in Peace Education.

UNESCO has also supported investigative commissions made up of scholars and public leaders, which produce data on information flows and cultural policy that have been the basis for Third World formulations of the new international information order. Mentioned earlier, these have been regarded with mistrust by some Western countries, although scholars from the West provided much of the background research for the commissions. UNESCO's informational and bibliographical services in the natural, social, and cultural sciences provide a significant amount of the data that flow through the previously mentioned UN information systems. All these activities are important inputs to the development of a common civic discourse in the international arena. The fact that UNESCO runs into so much trouble is an indicator of the difficulties of establishing that discourse. The fact that UNESCO exists at all is, on the other hand, an indicator of the possibility of establishing that discourse.

The Tokyo-based UN University was established to conduct research on pressing global problems and train graduate fellows in various fields of expertise related to these problems. It has a program in regional and global security studies involving scholars working in both regional and global research teams. They study all the kinds of international and regional agreements and mechanisms that could provide security without resort to military defense systems. The Costa Rica–based University of Peace, mandated by the UN but not functionally linked to it, is developing a research-and-training program aimed specifically at expanding the supply of qualified peacemakers.

All other UN agencies, institutes, and programs have their origins in efforts to deal with problems that cause conflicts between member states. They are in effect increasing the substantive content of the world civic culture, and therefore increasing the world's problem-solving capacity. The organizational and human frailties of the UN—and, like all complex organizations, particularly of an international character, it has those frailties in good measure—will be dealt with over time. A crucial part of improving the UN is the preparation of another generation of internationally aware citizenry, scientists, scholars, and international civil servants who can participate in the improvement process.

SUGGESTED FURTHER READING

The Courier. A monthly journal published in 32 languages and braille by UNESCO, Paris, France.

Development Forum. A monthly periodical published by the United Nations Division for Economic and Social Information and the United Nations University.

Everyone's United Nations: A handbook on the work of the United Nations, its structures and activities. (1986). United Nations Publication E.85.1.24. New York: UN.

Jaipal, R. (1983). *Non-alignment: Origin, growth and potential for world peace.* New Delhi: Allical Publishers.

MacBride, S. (Ed.). (1984). *Many voices, one world* (abr. ed.). Paris: UNESCO.

McWhinney, E. (1984). *United Nations law making.* New York/Paris: Holmes and Meier/UNESCO.

Rikhye, I., Harbottle, M., & Egge, B. (1974). *The thin blue line: International peacekeeping and its future.* New Haven: Yale University Press.

Sauvant, K. (1981). *The Group of 77: Evolution, structure, organization.* New York: Oceana Publications.

Selassie, B. K. (Ed.). (1960). *Consensus and peace*. Paris: UNESCO.

Singham, A. W., & Hune, S. (1986). *Non-alignment in an age of alignments*. Westport, CT: Lawrence Hill.

Sivard, R. (1986). *World military and social expenditures*. Leesbury, VA: UMSE Publishers. (Published annually)

U.N. Observer & International Report. A monthly report published at 641 Lexington Ave., New York, NY 10022.

Venkata, R. (1975). *The ways of the peacemakers: A study of United Nations intermediary assistance in the peaceful settlement of disputes*. New York: UN Institute for Training and Research.

CHAPTER 3

A Planet in Transition: The Nongovernmental Order

PEOPLE'S ASSOCIATIONS

Let us return to the imagery of picturing a map of the planet, begun in Chapter 2. We are now mentally placing another overlay on the map of the nation-state system and the UN system. This overlay is of the 18,000 international nongovernmental organizations that span all continents and link households, communities, and nation-states in networks based on the common interests of their members. These transnational voluntary associations cover the whole range of human interests and include chambers of commerce; service clubs; scouting associations; YWCAs and YMCAs; churches; and associations of farmers, teachers, doctors, physicists, athletes—any type of group that seeks relationships with people of like interests across national borders. They may have national sections in as few as 3 or as many as 140 or more countries. You and your family are already part of this transnational network, through your local membership in the kinds of organizations just mentioned.

The idea of globe-spanning associations of private citizens is scarcely a century old and is one of the most striking phenomena of the twentieth century. It is based on a new-old perception that humankind has common interests. In 1909 there were 176 international nongovernmental organizations (INGOs). Today there are approximately 8,000 completely autonomous INGOs and another 10,000 specialized types of bodies that have substantial or exclusive participation by private citizens and that are also treated as INGOs. This makes up the total of 18,000 nongovernmental organizations reported in the 1985–1986 *Yearbook of International Organizations* (Union of International Organizations, 1985–1986). Another 2,000 intergovernmental organizations are reported in the same yearbook, for a total of 20,000 international organizations. With a ratio of 18,000 INGOs to 2,000 IGOs, we can see that the rise of people's associations as distinct from governmental organizations and activities represents a major shift in the nature of the international system. People's associations are small and poor compared to nation-states, but they represent a lot of human know-how.

Of the 18,000 INGOs, about 1% are federations of other INGOs, 8.5% are "universal," 17% are intercontinental, and 74%, the great bulk, are regional, (i.e., European, Latin American, Asian). While the purposes are international, the way of working, then, tends to be regional, with interregional federations linking groups as needed.

International nongovernmental organizations vary in character, and it must be recognized that many of them have highly specific, even technical interests; but the important thing is that these interests cross national borders. Some are exclusive to particular cultural groups; others are adversarial in nature. This is particularly true of those organizations that are made up of political exiles. Still others are simply humorous, such as the Worldwide Fairplay for Frogs Committee and the International Stop Continental Drift Society. It is important, then, to evaluate each people's association according to its purpose and ways of working.

The INGOs we will be describing and referring to belong to that body of people's associations that have come into existence because of some shared concern for human well-being that crosses national borders. These organizations should be understood as a phenomenon different from but related to that of social movements. Popular movements come and go, depending on whether the conditions exist for the mobilization of a somewhat fickle public opinion. INGOs represent longtime commitments to human welfare on the part of their members. Until recently they represented an educated elite that had leisure and means to pursue altruistic goals beyond national borders. The new grassroots activism of recent decades is gradually opening up the nongovernmental world to the local activist, while the long-term commitment remains. Success in one nongovernmental effort simply sets the stage for work on the next task.

Since INGOs have sections in all member states of the UN, they also have sections in countries that are members of military alliances. The 16 NATO states and the 8 Warsaw Pact states house a significant proportion of the national sections of INGOs. Since many of these organizations have sections in states belonging to both blocs, this helps reduce interbloc tensions. The ideal of loyalty to the larger community is never absent, but giving expression to that loyalty in a world divided by East-West power struggles and North-South economic asymmetries has required great ingenuity. It is the nongovernmental sector that maintains a steady flow of scientific and cultural contacts between East and West when governmental contacts are minimal. It is the nongovernmental sector that provides major programs of education, training, and social investment in human welfare infrastructures of the South while governments of the North denounce the new international economic order. (For helpful overviews of INGO activity, see Angell, 1969; Feld, 1972; Judge and Skjelsbaek, 1973; and White, 1968.

THE NATURE OF INGO ACTIVITY

State power is always a limitation on what INGOs can do. That is why the average person, looking at nongovernmental activity, tends to think of it as ineffective. However, these organizations are free to act in ways that nation-states are not free to act. It is necessary to understand both their limitations and their capabilities. What are the characteristics of INGOs that make them important in the nuclear era?

Looking at Time Horizons and Security Concepts

The state is always concerned with policy within a time frame of a few months; longer-term planning is always for maintenance of a position in the present. INGOs are by nature future oriented. They have some vision, however modest, of a world community in which their organizational goals are implemented, and they have their own repertoire of appropriate strategies.

Since a major INGO goal is international understanding, peace, and security for the whole world, not just for one bloc of nations, they work with more multidimensional concepts of security than do governments. The transnational networks each nongovernmental organization makes available to its members provide the means for this more multidimensional concept of security. These activity networks are in relation to specific human interests and needs, which may be in areas as diverse as science, sports, trade, and the arts and may be as specific as helping women farmers in countries of the South to improve their crop yields by giving them tools and credit. Network activity also provides the experience of interdependence across different cultural and political preferences, and of local-global linkage from hometown to hometown across continents.

The *International Peace Research Newsletter*, which I edited for the International Peace Research Association (IPRA) in the 1960s and again in the 1980s, provides an example of how this networking operates. IPRA members send in descriptions of their research activities and requests for help with obtaining data. These are published in the newsletter, and people correspond directly with one another on the basis of common research interests discovered through the newsletter. In addition, reports of research and teaching activities around the world (always with names and addresses) are carried in each newsletter. When IPRA members travel, they frequently carry with them recent issues of the newsletter, in order to find colleagues in the countries they are planning to visit. More will be said about how to use the opportunities offered by INGO networks in Chapter 7.

Interpersonal interaction at the international level should not be idealized. It can be difficult. Misunderstandings arise that produce sometimes painful but necessary learning experiences. Every international conference goer and every internationally performing athlete has experienced misunderstandings—some humorous, some not at all funny. But they go back for more!

Lobbying for Constructive Foreign Policies of Nation-States

INGOs provide a continuing lobby in support of constructive international policies—including human rights, trade policies, and arms control policies—directed at the governments of member sections and of the UN itself. They consider those policies in the context of the world public interest. They also develop models for new policies (this is what resolutions of INGOs at international congresses are often about) and consistently support emerging formulations of international law. Japanese people's associations, for example, have tried to further the idea of using their own peace constitution (which prohibits the development of military forces beyond strictly defensive forces confined to Japan) as a model for other countries. So have people's associations in Costa Rica, which has a similar constitution. These models become educational vehicles for the INGOs with which Japanese and Costa Rican groups are affiliated, as they develop foreign policy proposals for other governments.

Providing Education for World Citizenship

INGOs provide an educational program for world citizenship in the context of various specialized training programs in member sections. Such programs differ in character and coverage from the educational programs available in public schools. An outstanding example of this, reaching back to the last century, is the educational programs of the YWCA/YMCA. In many countries they pioneered vocational and literacy programs before public schooling was available. In each country they pioneered what was most needed in that time and place. In the United States they pioneered vocational education for young women before that was generally accepted. In Japan today the YWCA conducts an annual extracurricular nuclear war education program to compensate for absence of attention to this in the public school curriculum. Qualified volunteer teachers conduct the program, and bus trips are organized for children's pilgrimages to Hiroshima and Nagasaki.

In every one of the over 70 countries where there are national YWCA sections, "peace sites" are being established. These sites will be centers for peace education, symbolic nuclear-free zones affirming the kind of future world community the Y's world membership is working for. Many other INGOs have provided special publications, seminars, and community education on how to live in peace. The previously mentioned International Baccalaureate, providing a core curriculum of world history and geography, has been introduced to high schools on all continents by an INGO of concerned parents and teachers.

Expanding Conceptual Innovations and State-of-the-Art Expertise

INGOs in the social and natural sciences and in the humanities have provided significant conceptual thinking about the interaction between physical and social environments. This has led to an understanding of the linkages between development, environmental conservation, cultural autonomy, free two-way information flows, and disarmament. INGOs have played an increasingly important role over the decades in providing data and concepts relating to the functional issues of development, whether in terms of soil, water, and forestry practices in agriculture or in terms of economic development in the cities. This has become very important in an era of increasing politicization of government-to-government developmental aid. The knowledge stock represented by occupational and professional INGOs is at present a major problem-solving resource for governments.

Creating Opportunities for the North to Learn from the South

INGOs that have originated in the South provide an unusual opportunity for Northerners to learn new perspectives and new ways of doing things from traditional societies that are experimenting with a blend of new and old knowledge. These South-initiated organizations tend to link concerns for the environment, peace, and nonviolence with community development. Often spiritual wholeness is also present as an organizational theme.

Examples are Sarvodaya International, which began in India and Sri Lanka and now has a European network based in Geneva. It is a self-help community development movement that empowers villagers not only to improve agriculture and economic life generally, but to develop patterns of cooperation and mutual aid that reduce long-standing conflicts and tensions, including ethnic tensions. The Lokayan Save-the-Trees movement in India has evolved in ways that broaden its goals to human and social development at the community level, and its way of working has also spread to other countries.

Malaysia is the site of a new Third World consumer's cooperative movement which has peace and the environment as central themes, as does the older Japanese movement. This means that Asian consumer cooperatives have a distinctive character. Nairobi houses the INGO Environment Liaison Center, which again strongly links environment and peace for the many nongovernmental organizations which cooperate with it. African futurists have developed a new approach to futures studies and to social planning (World Futures Studies Federation, 1986).

Local sections of the Council of Indigenous Peoples, extending from an initial base in the Americas to include indigenous peoples on all continents, conduct camps, seminars, and conferences to research and further develop traditional knowledge in crafts, healing, and social organization. Latin America has a network of peace and human rights groups stretching from Central America to Chile, with a high degree of local activity and consciousness raising, made internationally famous by the work of Paolo Freire.

Many of these INGO activities are reported in the International Federation of Development Alternatives' multilingual bimonthly, the *IFDA Dossier*. This is an important source of information about the South for Northerners.

Creating and Maintaining Information Channels

Perhaps INGO's most important contribution toward a stable world order are the thousands of newsletters that travel the many INGO networks around the world, such as the *International Peace*

Research Newsletter mentioned earlier. These newsletters carry a range of information, from local "how-tos" to action alerts on important environmental, development, and peace issues. Local INGO members are provided with information and perspectives often not available through their own national institutions.

Offering Activity as an Antidote to Despair

The opportunity to experience interpersonal cooperative activity over time with colleagues in other countries on issues that have to do with improving the conditions of life on the planet, even when that cooperation is only indirectly related to the threat of war, helps replace despairing inactivity with feelings of personal efficacy. Certain aspects of INGO activity, such as local ecological and nuclear-free-zone projects, very specifically enable people to feel they can participate at the grassroots in reshaping the world.

HOW INGOs HAVE RESPONDED IN THE ATOMIC DECADES

At the close of World War II, public activity on behalf of peace-related issues was reduced to modest programs in the historic peace churches and organizations. Priorities for these traditional peace groups at that time were supporting the formation of the United Nations and strengthening its arms control capabilities. It took time for the general publics of the world to realize that the nuclear age was a totally different era and had to be dealt with in new ways.

The Pugwash group of scientists, which began holding international meetings at Pugwash, Nova Scotia in the 1950s, was the first of the new scientific INGOs to realize the urgency of postwar arms control issues. Not until the 1960s were INGOs generally aware that resumption of traditional activities on behalf of peace and disarmament was not enough, that the nuclear reality had changed the world. It was the scientific INGOs that brought about the awakening to that reality, through their testing of babies' teeth for strontium 90. As a result, Women Strike for Peace and other new peace movements emerged to respond to the dangers of nuclear fallout to the next generation. Lacking experience in how to organize and network, they were very much helped by those older organizations that were willing to put their organizational skills and information infrastructure to work for the new movements. A similar skill sharing between INGOs and social movements went on in the Vietnam antiwar movement and the nuclear freeze movement. As noted earlier, the movements come and go, but the INGOs stay.

The 1960s were not only a peace movement decade, they were a period of rapid growth and development for several thousand new international nongovernmental organizations concerned with science and human welfare. This was the decade in which the World Futures Federation and the International Peace Research Association were formed, and a host of developmental INGOs. The Stockholm Conference on the Environment in 1972 signaled the emergence of a new set of INGOs focused on the environment. They were not slow to discover the linkage between environmental preservation and nuclear arms control. Each new INGO represented the long-term commitment of a transnational community of scholars and laypersons to understanding the problems of preserving the planet in the atomic era. Many INGOs passed resolutions on nuclear weapons and disarmament, with gradually accelerating alarm.

A concept of the new international order was beginning to emerge among people's associations. As different organizations worked on different world problems within their spheres of competence, they came to see the significance of the interaction among economies, cultures, environments, information, and security systems. Since the 1972 Stockholm Conference, INGOs have been playing an increasingly important role at each major UN special-topic conference, including the Population Conference in Bucharest, the World Hunger Conference in Rome, the Technology Transfer Conference in Vienna, the Status of Women Conferences in Mexico City and Nairobi, and the Disarmament Special Session in New York. On these occasions, while the official intergovernmental conference often gets bogged down in political disputes, the nongovernmental tribunal being held separately in the same city is addressing the underlying substantive problems that need solutions.

At each conference the INGOs have become stronger, more competent, and more skillful. They have organized parallel conferences to represent the interests of local peoples, women, the elderly, children, small and landless farmers, and the urban unemployed. They have fed streams of information to each other, to participating government delegations, to the UN, and to the world's press. People's associations have learned to form coalitions to provide just that horizontal flow of local information to each other that is so lacking through formal communication channels. They have also learned to feed that information through a variety of systems to the larger world. The International Coalition for Development Action (ICDA), headquartered in Geneva, Switzerland, is an outstanding example of a group of associations pooling their energies to follow a number of critical global issues in which local input is crucial. Their networks report on special nongovernmental groupings such as Health Action International, which specializes in pharmaceuticals and is active at World Health Assemblies; they have produced a nongovernmental alternative version of the Annual Organization for Economic Cooperation and Development (OECD) Aid report; they follow closely European Economic Community negotiations with the African, Caribbean, and Pacific countries for a post-Lomé convention, and Nordic initiatives to create new relationships with Southern African countries. Examples of their development-related activities are published monthly in the *ICDA Newsletter*, and they are always ready with information concerning environments, resources, and needs of local target groups.

Another exemplary INGO is a new international alliance that was formed in September 1986 by the World Wildlife Fund, bringing together environmental conservation groups and the major world religious communities. The alliance was inaugurated at a public ceremony in Assisi, Italy, where religious leaders conducted an interfaith ceremony including rituals and readings from the Hebrew Bible, the New Testament, the Koran, the Bhagavad-Gita, and Buddhist sacred texts. Since there are ecological and earth stewardship teachings in all religions, this may provide a powerful new force of environmental conservation.

Similar coalitions on disarmament and human rights are gradually creating an environment in which it is no longer possible for decision makers, whether they serve a national government, the UN, or the multinational corporations, to make decisions in shielded headquarters that ignore the actual environments in which human beings try to survive.

THE IMPORTANCE OF INGO STAYING POWER: THE DISARMAMENT EXAMPLE

Nongovernmental organizations have a special role at the UN in regard to disarmament because they are the only group with a continuing historical memory of disarmament efforts going back to the pre—World War I era. They have watched the general lowering of aspirations of the international community from the earlier goal of general and complete disarmament to the present modest goal of regulating nuclear proliferation and the rate of weapons innovation. The older associations know what was considered possible in earlier decades and what may be considered possible again when political conditions change. Their technical expertise in arms regulation issues has been vastly extended by the expertise of newer scientific INGOs, whose studies on the impact of nuclear weapons use indicate that nuclear war is an unacceptable tool for national defense. That finding points to a fresh consideration of major reliance on political expertise in settling disputes—an approach considered indispensable by the leaders of the original movement toward general and complete disarmament.

The NGO Disarmament Committee, consisting of representatives of all INGOs with arms control and disarmament concerns, has existed from the earliest days of the UN. Today it has two active contingents, one in Geneva and one in New York. The First and Second Special Sessions on Disarmament in 1979 and 1982, and the present UN World Disarmament Campaign, have to a significant extent been INGO-powered, although this fact is little acknowledged. When the UN calls for experts, it sees them chiefly as individuals, rather than as members of special-expertise nongovernmental organizations. When INGOs try to introduce initiatives based on their expertise, however, they are dismissed as "only INGOs." Nevertheless they continue their research and their work with national governments, with the UN itself, and with public education through symposia and conferences in national capitals and international forums.

The continuity of attention to disarmament provided by INGOs is all the more important because mass movements have been fickle in their attention to the threat of war. After the partial test-ban treaty was achieved in 1963, nuclear war receded from public consciousness. The Vietnam antiwar movement was against one particular war, not against war in general or even against nuclear weapons in particular. By the time nuclear war again became a public issue as a result of political challenges to the SALT II process, the realization of the consequences of the 30 previous years of an unremitting nuclear arms race produced a new mass movement for a nuclear freeze. Since mass movements do not lend themselves to detailed education about the changed character of the international security system, the supporters of a clear but somewhat simplified weapons freeze proposal were defeated with relative ease. Thus, a vulnerable and frightened American public is now ambivalently considering the technological fix of "Star Wars." This happened in spite of serious efforts to give a strong intellectual underpinning to the nuclear freeze concept (Forsberg, 1984).

Current INGO Initiatives

The work of nongovernmental organizations has not been lost, however. The local groups that sprang up in response to the freeze movement are still there and are reported to be increasing in number. In 1985, the Institute for Defense and Disarmament Studies identified 5,700 national and local groups concerned with peace and environmental issues in the United States. The *Peace Resource Book* (Bernstein et al., 1986) is a compilation of such peace groups and identifies their activities along local, national, and international lines. What is of special interest about these groups is that they are linking disarmament, development, environmental conservation, high levels of local community participation, and world peace. This follows the pattern of the older INGOs. The process of skill sharing between people's association oldtimers and movement newcomers continues. Political alliances against nuclear weapons under the ecology banner are forming on every continent.

A related nongovernmental activity is the declaration of nuclear-free zones as a way of empowering individuals and communities to begin now with shaping the kind of life they want for the future. Every month more nuclear-free zones are declared. Nuclear Free America, which publishes *The New Abolitionist*, reported in the March 1987 issue that there are 20 countries that are nuclear-free zones by law or policy, and 3,572 nuclear-free communities (by declaration of cities, counties, and provinces) in 24 countries. There are a total of 38 countries in which INGO activity has led to some degree of public acceptance of the nuclear-free-zone concept. Representatives of these zones meet now every year in their own congress.

Many of the newer international people's associations are less formal than the older ones with their well-established international secretariats. The newer ones tend to be less hierarchically organized and more aware of local needs. Continuity has a special meaning when so much attention is given to strengthening the grassroots. The new style is to nurture the next generation of INGOs at the local level, giving less attention to international headquarters and more emphasis to skill and information sharing and local-global coordination.

Much of the new organizational energy for peace and environmental work comes from women. The rise of feminism and the entry of women into public life has meant that a whole new set of questions has been asked of the social order. Like the peoples of the Third World countries, women feel they are being asked to maintain an order they did not help create. If they are going to be participants in the international arena, they want it known that the old patriarchal order, which for centuries has meant the domination of women by men, has to go. They see patriarchy and militarism as closely linked. By introducing more participatory processes, more dialogue, and more listening in every setting in which they work, they are laying the groundwork for the replacement of power politics by the politics of mutual aid. Their message is resisted, but their skills are needed, and so the dialogue continues.

The Great Peace Journey is an interesting example of women's style in peace work. It began as an initiative of a local branch of the Swedish Section of the Womens International League for Peace and Freedom and resulted in the creation of a series of local teams of women and men who visited the heads of government of small and medium-sized countries in Europe in 1985 to pose five questions regarding governmental willingness to support peaceable foreign policies. The questions were on the willingness to shift to a purely defensive military, to eliminate production of mass-destruction weapons, to eliminate their trade, to share Earth's resources more equitably, and to utilize UN machinery for the peaceful settlement of disputes. At the close of the first stage of the European Journey, governments, peace researchers, and peace journey teams met in a "Yes Conference" to see how many governments were ready to say yes to all five questions. (Sweden, for example, was.)

On the basis of that Yes Conference, teams were formed to include locals from each world region, as well as international Great Peace Journey representatives, to put the five questions to each member government of the UN in turn. The local groups are charged with continuing follow-up regarding the answers given by their governments, and with continued networking with other groups in their regions. The results of this polling of governments have been presented to the superpowers and to the UN. The convening of a people's summit to discuss the government responses and decide on further strategies is the next step.

This is a highly imaginative way of doing local peace and foreign policy work on a global scale. It depends on strong local involvement, of course. Inevitably not all participants are equally comfortable with grassroots activity, so tensions between the more participatory new style and the more elitist old style will appear. Nevertheless, the women who have developed this project are helping create a new model of public activism.

One of the most striking contributions of the women's movement to the international peace movement has been the women's encampments at the sites of nuclear installations in different parts of the world. The best known are at Greenham Common in England and Seneca Falls in the United States. (See Chapter 8 for references.) There are at least a dozen others. More dramatic than the nuclear-free zones because they literally involve a live-in presence around the clock, they give the spotlight to women who are trying to demonstrate through the encampment communities what the world could be like without nuclear weapons.

The New Professionalism

The new localism of international people's associations is accompanied by a new professionalism as well, which bodes well for future nuclear-age problem solving. While the atomic scientists were the first to organize to make their knowledge available for public discussion, and social science peace researchers were second, now every profession is so organized. Physicians, lawyers, businesspeople, teachers, social workers, architects, and artists all have peace-focused associations. Most of these have moved from the purely local stage to become international nongovernmental organizations, meaning they have identified themselves with a transnational community of like-minded persons working for the same goals.

The cumulative mobilization of professionals has led to an all-time high in the rate of exchanges and visits between countries of the Warsaw Pact and NATO (particularly between the United States and the Soviet Union), in spite of an official policy of limiting contacts. The International Council of Scientific Unions has played a particular role in that exchange, since it has active member sections in both blocs. The Nuclear Winter Project, carried out by the council through its Scientific Committee on Problems of the Environment (SCOPE), has had many scientists working together on international teams doing the complex calculations required to model world meteorological phenomena as they would be affected by nuclear explosions. Not only have they shared their findings with governments and the general public, but they recently initiated a joint meeting with members of the world community of faiths—East, West, North, South—on the prevention of nuclear war.[1]

Religious institutions represent one of the oldest of all professions, the priestly profession. Furthermore, churches themselves account for a substantial part of the INGO structures of the world. Most denominations of each of the world religions are represented in local churches in the countries of every continent. Since churches have had a historic role as supporters of the political authorities in the nations in which their local churches are located, they have been struggling to respond to the nuclear era by developing a needed independent voice on deterrence policy, specifically nuclear deterrence. In Europe and the Americas, church leaders from both Catholic and Protestant bodies have evolved significant doctrinal statements. In Japan, Buddhist groups have given leadership on this concern, and the Soka Gakkai INGO has mounted a particularly strong peace education program reaching from Japan to all continents. Lay members of churches have provided the backbone of local community-based peace movements.

The profession of medicine, similarly ancient, has also studied the effects of nuclear war. The physician's perspective has been the problem of providing medical care in the aftermath of nuclear war. This has involved such an impressive international mobilization of physicians for research and public education that it resulted in the awarding of the 1985 Nobel Peace Prize to the INGO, International Physicians for the Prevention of Nuclear War.

The field of law, another ancient profession, is now forming new INGOs to develop the doctrines of international law that could outlaw nuclear war. Other law professionals are developing a new professional field of conflict resolution and mediation and experimenting with diplomatic innovations like "second track diplomacy" (a back-up diplomacy to intergovernmental diplomacy) to reduce nuclear threat. Several new INGOs have been formed in this field, including the International Peace Academy, which holds international training seminars in conflict resolution for citizens, government diplomats, and military officers as well as college students.

A number of nonprofessional INGOs build on the work of the above-mentioned groups in their own bridge-building activities,

---

[1]The "Bellagio Statement on Nuclear War: Consequences and Prevention" was issued jointly December 1, 1984 by the International Council of Scientific Unions and the Interfaith Peace Academy. It can be obtained from the Center for Theology and Public Policy, 4500 Massachusetts Avenue NW, Washington, DC 20016.

citizen to citizen. Sister Cities International, People to People, Peace Links, the World Peace Brigade, and many other groups send a steady stream of people across boundaries of political hostility, furthering a new kind of citizen's policy making.

For every INGO working to reduce international conflict, there are dozens of national organizations with similar goals. These national organizations are a vital part of the basic infrastructure of civic peace. Some of them may become international organizations in the future. Others will always stay national or local. Most of them contribute in some way to the larger web of civic relations.

INGO OUTREACH AND HOW IT MAY BE EXTENDED

The important thing to remember about INGOs is that they are organized by national sections, and national sections are organized by local branches. The networks of international people's associations thus reach directly from individual households to world forums. No other type of diplomatic activity has this capability. Also, within households, each member of an international people's association may have parents, children, siblings, and a spouse, all of whom are in some way affected by the INGO member's activity. It must also be recognized however, that most people who belong to INGOs are not aware of the transnational identity their membership gives them. If they are Girl or Boy Scouts or Rotarians they may think of themselves as belonging to a local group with a distant national headquarters. They may not even know they are part of an international network, coordinated from an international headquarters. Activating that transnational identity and making it real for local members has become an important project for many national sections of INGOs. Some have been more successful than others in developing transnational awareness. The potential, however, exists for all INGOs in their local manifestations. This is something we will explore further in Chapter 7.

One important new tool for INGO local-to-global linkage is the new UN service called DEIN, or DESI Electronic Information Network (a project of the UN Division for Economic and Social Information). For a fee, DEIN will allow access to substantial parts of the UN information system by any local branch of an INGO that qualifies under UN rules and has access to a personal computer.

An example of the readiness of some INGOs to heighten their international role is the proposal to establish a Second Assembly at

the UN, to be composed of INGOs.[2] Such an assembly would introduce the vitality and inventiveness of INGOs more directly into the
UN system. Many INGOs already have accredited status at the UN
and may make interventions, on an individual basis, during the de-
liberations of certain UN bodies. The Second Assembly as proposed
would be a subsidiary organ of the General Assembly. It would sit
as a deliberative body concerned with issues including disarmament measures, development, the environment, human rights, and
the prevention of war. Seeking to foster international understanding, it would not take sides in international disputes or in ideological differences between UN member states.

Devising a workable formula for the UN Second Assembly will
take time. Which INGOs should be represented? How? It is particularly important that such an assembly not consist of nongovernmental representatives nominated by national governments, since
then the representatives may feel a responsibility to represent government interests rather than the world public interest. It is also important that the bureaucracies of larger, wealthier, bureaucratized
organizations not curb the creativity of the people's assembly input.
Since the basic concern is increasing the flow of ideas, information,
and skills of INGOs into the UN itself, there is need to consider a
wide array of mechanisms to achieve this.

Marc Nerfin's proposal for three UN houses, for "the Prince, the
Merchant, and the Citizen" (Nerfin, 1985), provides another approach to the problem. Whatever formula is used to involve direct
INGO participation at the UN, the goal is to release more of the civic
and problem-solving capacity of INGOs into the international system. This will at the same time strengthen those capabilities in
member states, through the participation of their national and local
INGO sections. Since countries vary in the extent to which their citizenry participate in INGOs, some countries have more of this type
of resource than others.

How well distributed are the national sections of international
nongovernmental organizations around the world? Using the
1983–1984 edition of the *Yearbook of International Organizations*, we
rank-order the countries according to the number of INGO sections
they have. We find that the top 18 countries are all from Western
Europe and North America, except Japan and Israel, which rank
fourteenth and eighteenth respectively. If we go to the next 18, we

---

[2]This proposal comes from the International Network for a UN Second Assembly, 308
Cricklewood Lane, London NW 2, 2PX, UK.

find 6 Latin American countries, 6 Eastern European countries, 3 industrialized countries of Asia and the Pacific, and 3 less industrialized countries of Africa and Asia (India, Egypt, and Turkey). Based on 1982 data, the range of INGO representation in the top 36 countries (taking the more limited category of intercontinental INGOs) went from 2,132 INGOs for France to 631 for the Soviet Union. (The US ranked ninth, with 1,505 INGOs). As has already been said, the INGO process started in Europe, and it will take longer for countries of Africa and Asia to become closely integrated into the INGO system. Latin America's closer ties to Europe and its earlier decolonization have made it easier for its countries to enter the INGO system.

If we look at the countries that fall below the top 36, we find that Asia is the leading continent. The Philippines, South Korea, Indonesia, Thailand, and Malaysia all have between 500 and 600 INGOs. In the Middle East, Iran and Iraq have the highest number of INGOs, 456 and 308 respectively, although the war between these two countries has probably weakened INGO networks there. In North and Central Africa, Tunisia and Morocco lead with 450 each, and Ghana is close behind with 429. All countries have some INGOs. There is no country completely outside of these networks, but it is easy to see that some countries are much more accessible than others. One of the tasks of the coming decades is to bring the countries with fewer INGOs into more international involvement at the people's organization level.

TRANSNATIONAL CORPORATIONS

Transnational corporations (TCs), more commonly called multinational enterprises, stand as separate and distinct entities in the international system, independent of national governments and sharply differentiated from people's associations. Barnet and Muller's (1974) groundbreaking study of transnational corporations compared the annual sales of these corporations with the gross national product (GNP) of nation-states and found that General Motors's sales for 1973 exceeded the GNPs of Switzerland, Pakistan, and South Africa. Royal Dutch Shell's surpassed those of Iran, Venezuela, and Turkey; and Goodyear Tire's sales exceeded the GNP of Saudi Arabia. As entities with vast resources at their disposal and existing outside the control of any regulatory system, TCs have received uneasy attention from both First and Third World governments and from the UN itself. Finally in 1976 the United Nations Economic and Social Council established an Intergovernmental Commission and a UN Centre on Transnational Corporations. The latter publishes regular reports on TC activities; for example, its report on transnational banks covers operators, strategies, and their effects in developing countries (Perez & Kinnock, 1986) and is currently receiving special attention.

While TCs are like INGOs in being nongovernmental, they are very different in their focus, since their purpose is to make money. Their profit-making activity and their size are their most distinctive characteristics. There are roughly 10,000 transnational corporations with 90,000 affiliates. They tend to be Eurocentric, for the same reason that people's associations are Eurocentric. They are products of the cult of bigness and the science of centralization developed in the industrial West. As Barnet and Muller (1974) point out, their financial, technological, and advanced marketing skills enable them to integrate production on a worldwide scale. For transnational corporations, the world is one big market. Their operational strategy is based on the three principals of global mobility, division of labor, and hierarchical organization.

The transnationals themselves promote an image of furthering worldwide economic development, and some respond to fears of their ruthless exploitative practices in the Third World by claiming a sense of global responsibility and a capacity for self-regulation in the public interest. Among the top 500 TCs, 60% of the affiliates are in OECD countries (primarily Western Europe) while only 20% are in the less industrialized countries. The poorer the country, the less likely it is to have affiliates of transnational corporations. Nevertheless, such subsidiaries are spread over 45 African countries, 24 Latin American countries, 16 Middle Eastern countries, and 22 countries in East and South Asia (Stopford & Dunney, 1984).

While they trade everywhere, they do not invest everywhere. When they do invest, it is mostly for resource extraction and the building of low-cost, low-wage factories. The working conditions in these factories are often poor, taking a heavy toll in health and life expectancy of the women and men who work in them.

Much of the power of TCs, from the Third World's perspective, lies in their ability to push undesirable exports and to influence trading conditions to the disadvantage of Third World countries. The dumping in the countries of the South of pharmaceuticals that are considered unsafe for home consumption in the North (Dag Hammarskjold Foundation, 1985), or the promotion in the South of infant feeding formulas that interfere with sound traditional nutritional practices, particularly breast-feeding, are well-known examples of product diffusion that harms the Third World. The sheer size of TCs stands in the way of equitable negotiations between them and most Third World countries. Already in 1963 fully half of the world's 100 most powerful entities in terms of annual production of wealth were transnational corporations (K. Boulding, 1964); given the recent trend of expansion among TCs, this sector of the international system has become an even more potent force that needs to be reckoned with by many different constituencies. While the richest industrial nations of the North share a common culture with the TCs, they do not have very much more control over them than the poorer countries of the South.

The future role of TCs in the international system is hard to predict at this point. Will the data on their operations being regularly collected by the UN Center on Transnationals provide the basis in coming decades for a more effective regulation of exploitative practices? Or will self-interest on the part of TCs lead them to more self-regulation? Or—a third possibility—will the current wave of takeovers and the creation of ever-larger corporate agglomerates gradually peter out, to be succeeded by a wave of divestments that will result in smaller and more regionally oriented economic enterprises in the decades ahead? The future of this particular sector of the nongovernmental structures of the planet may be more in question than its present power seems to indicate.

This very brief discussion of transnational corporations does not do justice to the importance of this phenomenon. Readers who would like to explore the subject further may refer to the articles on multinationals in Keohane and Nye (1970), to Barnet and Muller (1974) and to Sampson (1975), and to the periodical, *Multinational Monitor*.

SUMMARY

We have looked at INGOs from the perspective of their functioning in relation to nation-state actors. Because of their transnational identities, they are able to hold the world public interest above national interest in ways that neither the nation-states nor even the UN itself can do. We have noted that they operate with longer-term time horizons than nation-states, have a better historical memory for issues, are free to lobby nation-states for constructive foreign policies, provide an education in world citizenship for their own members and frequently for the general public, provide opportunities to reverse the North-South teaching-learning roles, serve as information channels, hold much of the world's substantive expertise on pressing global problems, and provide opportunities for action as an antidote to despair. We have looked at many specific activities of INGOs and seen the challenges they face in having their national sections very imperfectly distributed among the world's countries. It seems inevitable that INGOs will continue to grow, develop, and change in ways that will make them more adequate representatives of the world's peoples. That they will also be represented in some more formal way in the UN also seems inevitable. Whatever changes come, the local-to-global nature of INGOs gives us hope that there can be widespread participation in those change processes. What the future direction of development for transnational corporations will be is less clear. Will they also, like INGOs, become more responsive to world needs and more fully representative of world interests? It seems safe to predict that their character will be somewhat different in the twenty-first century than it is in the twentieth.

A Note on the Noosphere. Let us briefly try to hold the many-layered map of the world in our minds that we have been describing in these last two chapters. The stony geosphere; the verdant life-nurturing biosphere; human families and neighborhoods and socioeconomic and political institutions organized into nation-states; the administrative networks of the state-serving UN system; and finally the peoples' layer—the transnational network of international voluntary organizations. If we think about it, we realize that there are continual interactions among the levels in this multilayered system. The biosphere, or the natural environment, sets the limits for what humans can do on the planet, and therefore interpenetrates all other spheres. Governments interact with the UN and with private citizens' groups, INGOs. Transnational corporations interpenetrate all the other structures in the course of their economic activity.

Initiatives can start at any level and travel on through the system. The sum total of all the thoughts generated in the sociosphere, the totality of all social, cultural, economic, and political structures and processes, can be imaged as another sphere enveloping the planet. This envelope has already been imaged by Teilhard de Chardin (1959), and he has christened it the *noosphere.* Most of us are consciously in touch with only isolated segments of the noosphere, yet the larger realm of human thought ebbs and flows around us like an airstream with many currents, while we are all unknow-ing. In that envelope of thought lie the seeds of the new planetary civic culture. The more we involve ourselves in the networks that give us access to that envelope, the more we can contribute to the emergence of that culture. All the information channels that con-temporary media provide can help us, as can seeking out through travel the company of strangers with whom we share the planet.

Experiencing the noosphere doesn't only mean reaching out-ward to others and to elsewhere. It also means turning inward, cul-tivating the reflective life and tapping the creative sources of the noosphere at the heart of the created order. We will turn again to the theme of the reflective life at the end of the book.

SUGGESTED FURTHER READING

Angell, R. (1969). *Peace on the march: Transnational participation*. New York: Van Nostrand Reinhold.

Bernstein, E., Elias, R., Forsberg, R., Goodman, M., Mapes, D., & Steven, P. (1986). *Peace resource book: A comprehensive guide to issues, groups and literature*. (From the Institute for Defense and Disarmament Studies.) Cambridge, MA: Ballinger.

IFDA Dossier. Nyon, Switzerland: International Foundation for Develop-ment Alternatives. (Any issue; a bimonthly publication.)

International Peace Research Newsletter. Available c/o IUPERJ, Rua Paulino Fernandes 32, CEP 22270, Rio de Janeiro, RJ Brazil.

Keohane, R., & Nye, J. (1970). Transnational relations and world politics. Cambridge, MA: Harvard University Press.

Macy, J. (1983). *Dharma and development*. West Hartford, CT: Kumarian Press.

Multinational Monitor. Ralph Nader's Corporate Accountability Research Group, Box 19405, Washington, DC.

White, L. (1968). *International nongovernmental organizations*. New York: Greenwood Press.

CHAPTER 4

Conflict, Diversity, and Species Identity

In the last three chapters we have been looking at the various kinds of bonds and structures that facilitate civic discourse and enable people to work together—intergovernmentally, in the United Nations, and in people's associations. There have been frequent references to conflicts, but always in the context of structures and patterns for dealing with conflict. Now we will shift to a focus on diversity and conflict itself. What divides people, and what can be done about the divisions? Is it possible for human beings to develop a species identity that will not override, but rather crown, their other identities? The concept of a global civic culture requires the acceptance at some level of a shared identity with other human beings.

To explore this problem we will look at some of the major categories of issues that have been the basis for divisions among humans: ethnic and racial identity, religious identity, and—of another dimension but relevant to our problem—gender identity. Then we will consider the bases for developing a shared civic identity across differences on a global scale in various civilizational traditions, and reflect on what a species identity might look like.

ETHNIC AND RACIAL DIVERSITY

The very concept of civic culture comes out of the experience of conflict and diversity. *Civic* and *citizen* both derive from the Latin *civitas*, or city. The inhabitants of cities were historically strangers to one another, strangers resettled at the convenience of kings as the temple-palace cultures of early civilizations developed. To the city came traders and craftspeople from faraway places, as well as slaves.

This company of strangers had to learn to communicate across the barriers of language and custom. They had to develop a set of understandings on how to accomplish the business of life, within the constraints imposed by king, priest, and army.

Through the centuries great empires appeared, creating and extending their own civic cultures as far as soldiers and diplomats could reach. When neighboring empires clashed, new civic cultures gradually emerged from the contact, both through war and through diplomacy. We have tended to read history in terms of a progressive concentration and integration of ethnic and racial populations through organizational technologies evolved in cities. Whether the historical process is seen as dialectical or nondialectical, it is perceived as consisting of increasing integration of local and tribal groups into national societies, and the integration of national societies into some kind of larger equilibrium. The same economies of scale that spurred the development of ever-larger political units spurred interstate cooperation and the development of transnational corporations. So successful have these administrative developments been that the achievement of the integration of diverse units into larger wholes has been seen as a key aspect of economic and political modernity.

If modernity has been associated with integration, ethnic and racial particularism have been considered tribal and backward—something that existed primarily in Africa and Asia. Yet today we find a vigorous revival of ethnic, cultural, and racial particularism in the "advanced" societies of the West. Whether in the form of a peaceful cultural revival or as a violent demand for political autonomy, such movements are now under way everywhere. In the North there is a nostalgia for the old days when people shared common values, when immigrants could be counted on to disappear into the melting pot and become assimilated. There is a fear of social fractionation.

Another way of looking at this phenomenon is to see the underlying process of dealing with diversity as the same in countries of the North as in the South; to consider present unrest in the North as an indication that the former civic culture now being pined for had in fact been so imperfectly developed that it is now going through a necessary redevelopment period.

What communities of ethnic minorities everywhere, on whatever continent, all have in common, whatever their phase of historical development, is that they have been excluded to varying degrees from participation in national development processes on their terms.

They are all economically disadvantaged in relation to the mainstream population of their respective countries.

Spain has two separatist movements, the Basque and the Catalonian. In France the four traditional regional languages have successfully won the struggle for reinstatement in public schools: Breton, Basque, Catalan, and Occitan. In Britain the Welsh, Cornish, Scottish, and Irish peoples all have separatist movements, with Northern Ireland representing one of the most violent and difficult struggles. Yugoslavia is an uneasy federation of ethnic groups, some of which seek separation as autonomous states. Even small countries like Belgium have precarious bi-ethnic governments—a recent uproar in Belgium over a language controversy led the prime minister to resign. Tiny, apparently homogeneous Norway has a separatist movement among its nomadic Same (Lapp) population.

In Canada the separatist movement in Quebec remains alive, though temporarily quiescent. There are separatist indigenous peoples' movements in the Arctic Circle and even in a number of locations in the temperate zone of North America. The Palestinian Arabs have become almost legendary in this century in their struggle for autonomy and statehood in the land traditionally called Palestine. In Africa, tribal groups divided by political boundaries, such as the Somali, are trying to regroup and redraw boundaries to reflect tribal location; unfortunately this leads to war with neighboring states. The redrawing of boundaries continues to embroil India and Pakistan in disputes, although Bangladesh has now become an independent country. Russia and China have a centuries-old border dispute involving indigenous peoples.

The truth is that modern nation-states are not homogeneous at all, and have no prospects of becoming so in the near future. Only tiny countries like Monaco have no ethnic or language minorities. Most countries have between two and seven language groups and ethnic minorities. Among those with the greatest number, Indonesia has 3,000 separate ethnic and linguistic communities.

How can we speak of an emergent civic culture for the planet as a whole if there are so many separatist struggles and border disputes going on in the world? Since the need for common understanding and agreed-on ways of working together is more necessary now than it has ever been, the challenge is to find ways of working with the ethnic diversity problem rather than pretending it doesn't exist except among "backward" peoples.

First we have to reconsider what ethnic and racial separatist movements actually mean. It is possible that they are not tribal throwbacks at all, but foreshadowings of emergent structures. Each group just mentioned is responding to contemporary economic and social needs, using contemporary communication and mobilization techniques. Their strength lies in the traditional familistic and community-oriented infrastructure that all nonassimilated ethnic, racial, and cultural groups have retained.

These people belong to the periphery and not to the center of their respective societies. This has left them free to keep intact mutual-aid structures that industrial urbanism—with its emphasis on the nuclear family, individual achievement, and universalistic values—tends to weaken. This is the meaning and value of ethnic and racially homogeneous neighborhoods in cities. Social theorists expected ethnic groups to disappear in industrial society. In the face of the incapacity of urban welfare systems to deliver all the services needed by the poor, however, the mutual-aid skills of the ethnic community leave ethnic families less helpless when confronted with unemployment and family trouble than many middle-class, highly educated nuclear families. They may also have more self-help skills for economic survival, including "illegal" skills of growing, processing, and selling food and animal products in the very heart of the world's capital cities.

Since ethnic groups are solving social and economic problems that central governments have been unable to deal with, the next developmental stage would appear to be a devolution of governmental power, passing it on to groups that are competent at the local level, with an accompanying willingness on the part of local groups to cooperate within an administrative system that gives them more recognition. This process has already begun, assisted by IN-GOs that are focused on grassroots development. The Sarvodaya INGO mentioned in the last chapter is one example of a Third World initiative in this direction. In the United States there are now a number of national neighborhood-based associations and newsletters that share know-how about local self-help and appropriate linkages with local and state government. The process is slow, but it is going on in all regions. The importance of people's association involvement cannot be overestimated, because, through association newsletters, journals, and computer networks, information about these local ventures travels around the world.

RELIGIOUS DIVERSITY

In addition to ethnic diversity, we have religious diversity. While ethnic groups are separatist, they are less often expansionist, preferring instead to look after their own. Religious groups, on the other hand, have highly complex sets of attitudes to and relations with people of other religions.

All the major world religions—Buddhism, Hinduism, Judaism, Christianity, Islam, and others—contain two sets of teachings: the teachings about violence and holy war, and the teachings about living in peace. The holy-war teachings are about the conquest of the others, those who are different. The peace teachings are about the oneness of humankind. The holy-war teachings are more visible in history, but the peace teachings never disappear from the record. Peace-teaching saints appear just often enough to ensure the survival of those teachings.

> The holy war culture is a male warrior culture headed by a patriarchal warrior god. It demands the subjection of women and other aliens to men, the proto-patriarchs, and to God (or the gods). We see it in the ancient Babylonian epics, in the Iliad, in the Bhagavad Gita, in the Hebrew Bible used by Jews and Christians, and we see it in the Koran. There are many who argue that while battle-scene scriptures were taken literally at the time they entered the written record, literal meanings have been gradually replaced by metaphoric meanings. The only holy war going on, according to this view, is the holy war in the soul. Gandhi notably reinterpreted the warfare depicted in the Gita as a parable of the spiritual struggle between light and darkness. Many Jews and Christians do the same with the "Old" Testament. Yet the template of patriarchy as a social institution continues to mold generation after generation in each tradition, continuing the practise of warfare and the subjection of women. (Boulding, 1986, p. 503)

Each of these religious traditions provides role models for men and women. The role model in the holy-war culture of Israel is the warrior with sword ever at hand to defend city or kibbutz from enemies. The role of women is to produce the next generation of warriors (women in today's Israeli army are not allowed in combat). The role model in the Muslim Jihad or holy-war culture is the warrior with sword ever at hand to defend hearth, village, or pastureland from enemies. The role of women is to produce the next generation of warriors. The role model in the Christian crusader culture is once again the warrior with sword ever at hand to defend home and homeland from the enemy, and the role of women is to produce the next generation of warriors. In the Middle Ages, Christian knights fought not only under the banner of a warrior god, but under a warrior king, Jesus.

The more colorful holy-war stories tend to come from Antiquity and the Middle Ages, but the tradition remains unbroken down to the present, even though more progressive systems of governance have evolved in the intervening centuries. Each of the three previously mentioned religious traditions—Judaism, Christianity, and Islam—is now experiencing fundamentalist revivals that are promoting a return to a more overt reliance on the holy-war culture. These revivalist movements have history to help them. Even in the more secular and "modernized" wings of these religions, the tradition of supporting one's country in time of war is strong, even when the enemy is of the same faith.

The holy-war culture does not tell the whole story of these religions, however. Teachings about how to live in peace are also present in all three, bearing many of the characteristics of the utopian imagery discussed in Chapter 1. Interestingly, the role models for peace makers tend to be the same for both women and men and include young and old as well. They are all nurturers and reconcilers, seeking justice and equality for all. Victory is not in their vocabulary. This is equally true for Judaism, Christianity, and Islam. The peace cultures tend to divide in all three traditions between the mystics who emphasize mystical oneness with creation, and the practical peace makers who nurture the social order. The mystics do through prayer what their nonmystical brothers and sisters do through social action. Hasidism in Judaism and its present-day incarnation in the teachings of Martin Buber; Sufism in Islam; the historic peace churches in Christianity (Quakers, Mennonites, Brethren), and the many peace saints in Catholicism and Protestantism—all represent the "peace face" of the church.

Each religious tradition is badly handicapped by the polarization between the holy-war culture and the peace culture within it. It is hard to find a middle ground. However, as John Bowker (1986) puts it, the anthropologies of each religion are so different, and the feelings about these anthropologies run so deep, that pragmatic conflict resolution which leaves belief systems intact is the only alternative to Armageddon. Such pragmatic conflict resolution was precisely what was achieved between Catholics and Protestants in the Treaty of Westphalia in 1648. Pragmatic conflict resolution is what the international nongovernmental organization, the World Conference on Religion and Peace, works at in its biennial world congresses and in its interim commissions.

The image of the reconciler is always a hidden presence in the background of church teachings. Practical politics now require that the world's major religious traditions to some degree work together to activate that reconciler image. Whether out of idealism or survival instincts, then, the churches of the world have a special contribution to make to the task of turning enemies into a "company of strangers." Once they are defined as strangers, we are in the familiar domain of shared public space, and civic dialogue can begin.

FEMINISM AND THE TWO CULTURES OF WOMEN AND MEN

We have followed the theme of two cultures in looking at ethnic diversity, seeing ethnic cultures in contrast to the mainstream culture of the society of which they are a part, and in looking at the war and peace cultures in the major religions. The concept of two *gender* cultures, one for women and one for men, is a more recent concept. Gender-based divisions represent a different dimension than other types of categorizations, because gender cuts across all other divisions of ethnicity, race, religion, and class. In earlier times, the concept of a woman's culture was unthinkable. There was thought to be one culture—the male culture—and then there were women, quiet creatures who inhabited the spaces protected by men and who reproduced the species. What feminism has done is to identify the male culture as being the patriarchal order and to show that the rule of men over women, children, and other weaker men is a social artifact, not a biological necessity. The patriarchal order has been identified by many feminist writers with dominance, the use of force, and with war (Brock-Utne, 1985; Lerner, 1986; Reardon, 1985). Patriarchy has also historically been wrongly identified as the sole source of social order, the rise of civilization as we know it, and with science, philosophy, the arts—in fact, with all human creativity except the physical act of childbearing.

The concept of a women's culture has been one of the great discoveries of feminist historians, anthropologists, sociologists, and psychologists. It has been a culture nurtured for the most part in the private spaces of society (what I have elsewhere called the "underside"; Boulding, 1976), since public spaces have been for the most part denied to women. Women have not been part of the "company of strangers." Yet much of the strength of public life and civic culture in any society has come from the women's culture. Three particular spheres of women's work as traditionally defined have to do with the civic culture. One is the teaching of children. If the world view of a child is set by the age of seven, as doctrine has it in many traditions, then women have set that world view because they are in full charge of male as well as female children up to the age of seven in most societies. If they reproduce the warrior mentality in little boys, they also teach them whatever they know about listening and caring.

The second is the productive labor of women that keeps the economy going. This part of women's work is widely ignored by economic planners, a fact that contributes to the continuing failures of development planning in both the more and the less industrialized societies. That special set of spaces in every society where women carry out their productive roles I have called the Fifth World:[1]

> The fifth world exists invisibly, uncounted and unassisted, on every continent, in the family farms and kitchen gardens, in the nurseries and kitchens of the planet. The fifth world also sends its fingers out to the most poorly paid work spaces of business, industry, and the service sector. Within the rural and nonindustrialized parts of that fifth world, women give birth to babies, produce milk to feed them, grow food and process it, provide water and fuel, make other goods, build houses, make and repair roads, serve as the beasts of burden that walk the roads, and sit in the markets to sell what their hands have made. (Boulding, 1980, p. 5)

The third traditional activity of women is as peace makers, though this is never formally labeled. Women are the social cement of every society. Through marriage alliances that are mostly planned by men, intravillage and neighboring-village amity is ensured; and at the international level, daughters of royalty cement inter-state alliance systems. Women are trained from early childhood by their mothers for the peace-making roles they will have to perform after marriage, within the family, with neighbors, with neighboring villages, and (for the upper classes), with neighboring states.

When women are playing their peace-making roles, they are often not even noticed because this is so much a part of what is expected of them as women. But women have played nontraditional roles as guerillas, freedom fighters, and revolutionaries, just as they have also been scientists, artists, and philosophers. Again, this is not noticed. In short, whether they are carrying out traditional or nontraditional roles, women tend to be made invisible.

The social order has suffered through the centuries from this

---

[1] The term *Fifth World* has to be understood in context with the usage of the term *Fourth World*, which encompasses the poorest of the Third World countries.

invisibility of women, because it has meant that all their nurturance, all their productive labor, all their peace making, has been put to one side as secondary activity, not the main business of public life. In a world so badly divided, do women and men have to be divided too? Just as we have pointed to the possibilities of linkages between ethnic minorities and mainstream societies, and of negotiation between differing religious systems, so we can point to the possibilities of partnership between women and men that remove the old distinction of male=public, women=private. Even more important, removing the designations, male=warrior and woman=peace maker will give both women and men the opportunity to develop peaceable civic skills and bring them into the public sphere, *together*.

BEYOND DIVERSITY: THE DEVELOPMENT OF SPECIES IDENTITY

Is it possible to conceptualize a common identity while acknowledging differences? Of course. We do it all the time. I have a common identity with anyone from the town I live in, which is Boulder, Colorado. Regardless of how different the life ways and values of its roughly 80,000 residents may be, we are all Boulderites. I certainly have a common identity with all my fellow citizens in the United States, which includes people of different races and ethnic groups, who speak different languages, and who are of very diverse religious beliefs and employments. I myself was born in Norway and am a naturalized citizen, but that does not affect my commitment to acknowledging certain common obligations to anyone who is a fellow citizen of the United States, including the obligation to pay taxes to support the services from which we all benefit.

One of the extraordinary realities of living in the modern world is that we all have multiple identities. Some of these identities take up only a small part of our lives, such as the associations we belong to. Others are part of our core identity, such as our family identity. The INGOs we belong to give us transnational identities. Sometimes our different identities come in conflict with one another, and then we have role conflicts. How much time should we give to our family identity, our career identity, our organizational identities? And what might a species identity mean?

In looking for answers to some of these questions, we can search for sources of species identity in some traditional conceptions of the international order. We will turn to this shortly, but first we must have an understanding of the concept of *species*, which denotes a category of biological classification. Its simplest meaning is "a class of individuals having common attributes and designated by a common name" (Webster, 1979). The species designation for humans is *homo* (add *mulier*, for women) *sapiens*. Because of our special mental capacities, humans have a more highly evolved concept of *kind* than any other species. Yet our common humanness is rarely thought of as a key part of our individual identities. Once we have moved past our own core identity in family and community, most of us let our national identity absorb the residuals of our sense of self. Therein lies the problem of the human species itself. Nations become empires and evolve identities that come to be seen as univeral/species identities, which the nations then feel called to impose on others who have not experienced that particular historical evolution. Competing empires offer competing "species identities," legitimated by cultural/religious traditions that also are experienced by their adherents as universal. Since every religious and cultural tradition has some component of authentic (civilization-transcending) universalism, this sets the stage for the struggle in every society between those who have an intuitive experience of authentic universalism, and those who equate species identity with their own historical sense of mission. Out of those struggles the world civic culture is emerging. Let us see how the claims of the nation-state conflict with the claims of species identity.

As the core political unit in the modern world, the nation-state is able to make demands that are normally considered to override all other demands. This is particularly the case in wartime; our identities as United States citizens then become overriding. However, if a person's religious beliefs include the teaching that all human life is sacred, thus forbidding the taking of lives in war, then the state may acknowledge the religious identity as an overriding one and allow conscientious objectors to fulfill their obligations to their country by giving alternative service of a nonmilitary kind. This does not involve a denial of obligations to the state; rather, it is their fulfillment in the broader context of obedience to what is sometimes called a "higher law." This higher law is thought of by religious conscientious objectors as the law of God. However, there are also secular conscientious objectors who base their beliefs in the inviolability of human life on ethical teachings in a humanist tradition.

Whether based on religious or secular-humanist beliefs, there are people in all countries who feel allegiance to a community that in one sense does not exist—the community of humankind. It is this allegiance that we are calling species identity. The community of humankind is a country without borders, with no capital city and with only one law—to avoid doing harm to any fellow human being. However, one cannot feel allegiance to an abstraction. That is where the concept of civic culture comes in. This allegiance can only become operational through a set of common understandings developed on the basis of interaction in all the ways we have been describing in these chapters: between governments, in the United Nations, and between people across national borders. We have to enter into more social interaction and become more consciously linked across national borders, to give substance to that civic culture.

Each cultural tradition has ways of thinking about this hoped-for community of humankind. The shared civic culture has to be built up out of each of those traditions, with no one predominating. The World Order Models Project of the World Policy Institute is one very important effort in building up that shared civic culture. Mendlovitz (1975) gives an overview of the efforts of a transnational group of scholars to visualize preferred future worlds that allow for diversity.

Let us examine the concepts of the international order that have emerged in the West, in India, in China, and in Islam, to see what materials we have to work with in the forming of a species identity.

A View from the West

The concept of the social order in Roman law was of an ideal universal state that would administer a rule of law for the world. This concept of a universal state survived in the ideology of the Holy Roman Empire and was conceived of as a universal Christian state in the Middle Ages. Divisions in Christendom after the Reformation brought that idea to an end, so the ideal shifted to a "concert of states."

Since the Treaty of Westphalia in 1648, the development of a plurality of democratic nation-states has been seen as the endpoint of a process of freeing human beings from the tyranny of despotism. In the United States, sometimes called the "first new nation," the ideal was that each individual was free to seek "life, liberty, and the pursuit of happiness," so long as that pursuit did not injure others. The nation-state was thus seen as the ideal vehicle for creating and safeguarding the liberties of each citizen. The French Declaration of the Rights of Man (1780) defined these liberties as basic human rights.

Since separate nation-states might discover conflicting interests in the course of protecting their citizenry, it therefore became necessary to accept a common constraint of international law which all states would acknowledge. Originally, that law was conceived as based on Roman law; however, by the late nineteenth century it came to be seen that international law, to be acceptable, could not be based on the laws of any one national or civilizational tradition. It must therefore be a synthesis of the legal traditions of all civilizations. This would provide "the broader intellectual foundations necessary to give it worldwide authority in an age which is no longer prepared to accept the leadership of any one nation, culture, ideology or legal system" (Larson & Jenks, 1965, p. 3). The process by which this synthesis was to take place began at the Hague Peace Conferences, which included China, Japan, Ethiopia, Turkey, and Mexico, as well as the nations of Europe and North America. It continued with the formation of the League of Nations and its successor, the United Nations. From the perspective of the West, the Roman law tradition is seen as dominant, but other traditions are to be taken account of. The system of sovereign nation-states guaranteeing the liberty of their citizens, living at peace with one another, and abiding by international law is seen as both generating and maintaining that minimal degree of world civic culture required to assure a stable future order. World government—the ceding of sovereignty to a central power—is not seen as desirable but rather as a regression to tyranny and despotism.

A View from India

India has never had a tradition of a universal state. Experiencing successive invasions over the centuries from the North and the West, India has historically conceived of itself rather as a society of many races in continual adjustment. Tagore (1924), who wrote about the dangers of the incursion of Western ideas concerning the nation-state long before India's independence from England, maintained that kings and emperors were never important in India until the West arrived. Tagore saw India's genius as precisely in *not* being a nation, and in being a society focused on the social regulation of differences and the spiritual recognition of unity. In the Hindu tradition, rulers are subject to the law, the Dharma; the law is not subject to the will of rulers. There is divine authority first, and state authority is strictly secondary. Tagore saw the Western nation-state as being a political and economic mechanism for competition, conquest, and acquisition—in short, essentially anti-people.

As a leading internationalist in the 1920s, Tagore valued the spirit of the West but not its mechanisms. The ideal he held forth, also upheld by Gandhi and by the leaders of India today, is of the world as an assembly of societies, not nations. India's own 1,652 racial groups, and its border problems with other ethnic groups, assure a focus on finding ways of living together across deep and often bitter differences. As Tagore (1924) said, what India has been, the world is now. The world must find a basis of unity that is not political. The world civic culture must be rooted in an acceptance of a great diversity of life ways. The multicultural society, rather than the nation-state, is the ideal. This is also an attractive ideal for many African and some Asian countries that face similar problems.

A View from China

China, like the West, held an ideal of a universal state with one ruler. The Chinese, however, arrived at the concept of the universal state in a very different way from the West. Western political development, from the Greek city-state to the modern military-industrial security state, is seen from the Chinese perspective as one that has weakened interpersonal bonds and made people individualistically competitive rather than mutually cooperative.

Facing the dilemma of a fractionated world community, some Chinese thinkers feel that their own historical traditions offer an alternative and more peaceful developmental path toward a modernized international system (Xiaotaong, 1987). While the endpoint is not unlike that visualized by many Westerners, the path is different, and therefore some characteristics of the resulting order would also be different. The Chinese path builds on ever-widening circles of familial relationships, from clan to society. In the clan-based patterns of the East, it is suggested, we may find some clues for overcoming the blocks to creating a mature civic culture which have emerged in the West.

In Confucian thought the universal state is called the "land under heaven." A core saying is, "Everybody in the land under heaven serves the public interest." There are three important concepts in this saying. One is the concept of the land under heaven, which implies that land is a whole, an indivisible entity, without boundaries, belonging to everyone. The second is that dwellers in this boundaryless land all share a common public interest. The third, which provides the integrative dynamic for the other two, is the kinship principle. The folk who live in the land under heaven belong to extended families organized as clans interlinked in one macrofamily.

The kinship principle provides the basis for the precept that the love, respect, and obligations one exercises toward one's own family are also to be exercised toward all other families within the total social order. One respects not only one's own parents, but all parents. One cares not only for one's own children, but all children.

In one sense traditional Chinese society was very hierarchical, operating on an explicit center-to-periphery model. The ruler, who was responsible for the good order of society, lived at the center. Clans built up relationships in ever-widening circles from the en-lightened moral center where the *huaxia* or the *han* people lived, outward to the peoples of the border, the *manyi*. What is different from the center-to-periphery models of the West, however, is that exactly the same obligations and rules of behavior applied to the re-lationships between center and periphery peoples as applied among center people. One did not have different sets of obligations to dif-ferent classes of people.

It might be said that there is no public/private interface in such a social order because carrying out family duties according to the highest standards of morality provides the model for carrying out civic duties; the obligations are the same. One puts the state in or-der by beginning with the family and expanding outward.

This approach turns on its head the Western concept of "devel-opment" as a movement away from kinship-based and toward con-tract-shaped relationships. The Chinese political tradition would leave family and clan intact as building blocks of the larger society. While the clan formula may appear regressive to Westerners, it fa-cilitates the coexistence of many nationalities within the larger so-ciety without breaking the moral bonds of interclan responsibility. Chinese tradition uses the family in an instrumental way as a means to a world bond, a world civic culture. Today the universal-state idea has been abandoned, as in the West, but the coexistence of nations is cemented by an interclan bond and a sense of world public inter-est ("the land under heaven") that is unlike the concept of a loose association of autonomous states in the West. While West and East both use the concept of family, China uses it instrumentally and the West metaphorically.

A View from Islam

The original Muslim concept of gradual movement toward a universal Islamic state, *dar al-Islam*, has been replaced by the con-cept of the coexistence of *dar al-Islam* and *dar al-harb*—the peoples that remain outside Islam. The treaty between Francis I of France and

Sulayman the Magnificent in 1535, providing for the coexistence of Christianity and Islam, marked the end of the earlier universalist idea. In this respect Islam, China, and the West have all followed the same path. At the same time, the state does not have the central importance in Islamic tradition that it has in China and the West because the rule of Allah takes preeminence and the state is subservient to divine law. This is more like Hindu doctrine. Islamic society tends to be very localist, organized around local mosques and their resident teachers. Scholar-teachers have a central importance in Islamic society. The authority of the *ulama,* a central core of scholars, is as significant as that of the ruling *caliph* (Rahman, 1966).

Islam is in many ways an unusually egalitarian society, a legacy of its nomadic origins. This egalitarianism is translated into a strong feeling of responsibility on the part of every Muslim for the welfare of the *umma,* the total community of the faithful, and a keen sense of social justice. Muslims are said to do better at tithing than any other religion. One interesting application of this egalitarianism is the unusual extent of the provisions for the freedom of non-Muslims living in a Muslim land. Devices such as the *aman* and the *millet* system gave legal protection in premodern times for non-Muslim residents and made provision for them to live under their own laws. There was no comparable system at the time for non-Christians living in Christian lands. However, the egalitarianism is very unevenly applied to women. In some countries, strict *purdah* (seclusion) of women is practiced, while in others there is no seclusion at all. Generally, upper-middle-class Muslim women have good opportunities for professional training (as doctors and teachers, for example), sometimes because of, sometimes in spite of *purdah* traditions.

The Muslim religious obligation to extend principles of social justice to non-Muslims provides a strong basis for the development of a peaceful society of nations. The lack of emphasis on the state itself, and the great importance given to the quality of life as lived in the local mosque-centered community, provide a basis for an international community of peoples, somewhat along the lines of the Hindu concept of a multicultural international order. The system of dialogue at the local level, linked to a national dialogue process, would have to be more fully extended beyond the *umma,* to make its full contribution to a world civic culture. While this is already happening in the Non-Aligned Movement, the present high levels of conflict within Islam make further developments along these lines seem highly unlikely at the moment. In the longer term, the social inventiveness of Islam will be very important to the emerging civic culture of the future. For examples of this promise, see Khan (1985).

How these Four Views Contribute to Species Identity

We have looked at the facts of diversity in the social order in terms of ethnicity, religion, and gender differences. These diversities have caused deep conflicts, but in each case we have also found approaches to managing that diversity that reduce conflict and enhance the common interests of adversary groups.

Moving on to the more difficult question of species identity, we first looked at ideas about world order in four major civilizational traditions. The assumption behind that examination was that community in the sense of common fate and shared expectations on a world scale is an important basis for the development of both civic culture and species identity.

Earlier concepts of a universal state have been rejected by the West and also by China and Islam, as the impossibility of imposing one cultural pattern on the world as a whole has become clear. India, more aware of diversity from its inception, never even developed such a concept. Each tradition has subsequently sought to define a common bond based on common survival needs, through structuring the recognition of diversity and accepting common rules about protecting that diversity. In the West the tradition of international law has developed out of common self-interest, with an underpinning of Judeo-Christian ethics. For China, India, and Islam, the recognition of humans as spiritual beings "under heaven," under the Dharma, or under Allah, has been primary. This recognition has been accompanied by practical recognition of the need for local community. China uses the family/clan nexus as the model for community at every level, from local to planetary. Hinduism and Islam focus on the protection of diverse local ethnic groups and communities and the fostering of mutual recognition and respect. The interesting thing is that none of these traditions depend primarily on spiritual transformation to achieve a peaceful world order and a common species identity. Each is operating in terms of the everyday realities of diversity and conflict, to achieve awareness of a common interest, a common bond in the diversity itself, that will make gradually increasing levels of cooperation possible across the diversity.

EMPATHY, ALTRUISM, AND SPECIES IDENTITY

Empathy, the ability to feel what another is feeling, can be thought of as the basis of all social interaction. This was the conclusion reached by Adam Smith in *The Theory of Moral Sentiments* (1759/1976), where he set out to develop a basic theory about how human beings could transact business with one another in an orderly and predictable fashion. The proposition set forth in *Moral Sentiments*—that we know what gives others joy and pain because we know what gives ourselves joy and pain—became the unstated basis for his economic theory in *The Wealth of Nations* (1776/1939). While the failure of empathy, as in rape and violence of all kinds, is another issue that requires separate explanation, the capacity for empathy, when not pathologically distorted or otherwise impaired, continues to be accepted as a basis for social intercourse three centuries after Adam Smith.

Within cultures the development of empathy is easier than across cultures, because the forms in which we experience pleasure and pain are in large part culturally determined. However, all human beings operate with certain predispositions for social bonding, rooted in the experience of being nurtured in infancy. All spontaneous adult gestures of greeting, reaching out with the hands to help another, comforting another, and fleeing to another for protection derive from the infant's clutching and the adult's nurturant response. Photographic research comparing different cultures has convincingly demonstrated that spontaneous gestures of nurturing and seeking nurture are startlingly similar in all cultures (see Eibl-Eibesfeldt, 1972; and the photo-essays of Hans Hass, 1970).

This capacity to recognize nurturant and welcoming behavior has stood human beings in good stead over the millennia. The capacity to recognize threatening behavior is similarly useful and can become the basis for wary negotiation when there are common interests to be served. It must be remembered that threat, from the standpoint of the threatener, is protective behavior—protective of the interests of the threatener. Social bonds with others are possible because we learn to read and respond appropriately to these behaviors.

Being able to see other individuals as human beings like oneself is a necessary but not sufficient basis for species identity in the planetary sense. Even the simplest behavioral signals may be misinterpreted, and communication difficulties lie at the root of many though by no means all conflicts. We may at times purposely give confusing or false messages. Even chimpanzees can deliberately set out to deceive one another, as Goodall's (1986) remarkable studies of chimpanzee communities have shown.

Another step beyond the capacity for empathy is the capacity for altruism. Altruism involves wanting something good for another and helping to bring it about, at some cost to the self. The altruist cares. Parenting is the prototype of altruistic behavior (Ruddick, 1985). Altruism and caring outside the family circle, extended to other members of a society, are more developed as cultural themes in some societies than others, but in no society is such altruism absent. Beyond its simplest form, it is learned behavior. Experimental studies have shown that children who witness altruistic behavior in others, and are themselves the recipients of such behavior, are likely to exhibit altruism toward others (E. Boulding, 1978a; MacAuley & Berkowitz, 1970; Midlarksy, 1968; Sorokin, 1950).

The cultivation of an international environment where members of one society can care about those of another and want good things for them is not a mysterious or mystical process. At the interpersonal level, competence and skill are important ingredients in altruism. People have to know how to go about getting things done. They have to have confidence in their skills and be able to cope well with stress. Imagination and the willingness to take risks are also important. People with these kinds of abilities are valued in every society.

What is needed for these caring, altruistic people to exercise their skills at the international level is for them to know the channels we have been discussing in this book, to know the roles open to them. There is already a community of such altruistic internationalists among those who carry out intergovernmental, UN, and INGO activities. They already have a strong sense of species identity, and their numbers are growing, thanks to the ease of travel and communication in our times.

However much we might to wish to celebrate these citizens of the planet, their numbers seem small in the face of the enormous threat apparatus present in the world. But they do not act alone. They act in structures built up out of the growing understanding documented earlier in each civilizational tradition that no one society can impose a universal order. Our technology is at the moment being misapplied. If we can learn fast enough, we can shift that technology to the service of a highly diversified world community bonded together by common interests in peace and the further development of humankind's potentials. Species identity in that future community will not be a concept that rides roughshod over other identities. It will threaten no one. It will rather be a crowning awareness of how all social identities crafted throughout a lifetime by each of us come together in our common humanity.

SUGGESTED FURTHER READING

Boulding, E. (1979). Ethnic separatism and world development. In L. Kriesberg (Ed.), *Social movements, conflict and change* (Vol. 2, pp. 259–281). Greenwich, CT: JAI Press.

Hass, H. (1970). *The human animal: The mystery of men's behavior.* New York: Putnam.

Kropotkin, P. (1956). *Mutual aid: A factor in evolution.* Boston: Porter Sargeant. (Original published 1902)

Larson, A., & Jenks, W. (1965). *Sovereignty within the law.* Dobbs Ferry, NY: Oceana Publications.

Lerner, G. (1986). *The creation of patriarchy.* New York: Oxford University Press.

Mendlovitz, S. (1975). *On the creation of a just world order.* New York: Free Press.

Sorokin, P. (1950). *Explorations in altruistic love.* Millwood, NY: Krauss Reprint.

PART II

Using the Mind in New Ways: New Perspectives on Education Not Found in Schooling

In Part I we traced the emergence in our time of the ideas, social processes, tools, and institutional mechanisms that have brought the twentieth-century world to a critical transition point. We saw how nations are trying to solve national and international problems via their various intergovernmental associations, how the UN with its sharply limited resources is trying to move beyond exclusively state-oriented concepts of internationalism, and how people's associations of every kind are trying to create a new kind of transnational order. We saw that the capacity for empathy, altruism, and caring, which exists in every society, may be expanded as intergovernmental and nongovernmental structures continue to develop.

A basic principle, underscored in Part I, is that no one society can create or impose *the* universal social order; therefore, it is incumbent on societies to find creative ways of working together which acknowledge our human diversity and can maintain an overall level of peaceableness, avoiding destructive strategies that deny our differences.

We haven't yet realized the relevance of what we already know, and the possibility of applying it to the international order. All the traits that make our local and national communities work well—problem-solving competence, skills of coping with stress, confidence in our own integrity, respect for others, and the use of our imagination—are also traits that need to be developed and nurtured in our transborder interactions. These are *craft* skills. The future social order will require the best of human crafts and skill and will draw on everything we know in every sector of society, every profession, every specialization. We ourselves must bring the new forms into being. There is no one specialty responsible for producing a world civic culture; no traditional academic discipline can claim it.

Having identified the transitional, change-ready state of the world in Part I, we will now explore in Part II how we can utilize that information to further the world civic culture by exercising the mind in new ways. Chapter 5 looks at the problems of knowing in a complex high-technology culture and considers the relative contributions of cognitive-analytic and intuitive modes in addressing social problems. Chapter 6 deals with the skills of the imagination, providing a number of examples of how the imagination can be used to deepen our understanding of complex social phenomena commonly studied only in the analytic mode. A section on imaging the future is included in this chapter.

Chapter 7 provides a do-it-yourself guide to personal involvement with the intergovernmental and nongovernmental networks described in Chapters 2 and 3, from the base of one's own local community. Personal involvement at the community level both anchors international civic activity in the reader's own life experience and provides the all-important empirical base for such activity. Chapter 8 is devoted to the civic skills of the peace maker, with suggestions for how to begin to develop those skills, again based on one's own life experience. The Epilogue reconsiders the possibility of the construction of civic culture on the global level and links its emergence to the cultivation of the reflective life in all of us.

CHAPTER 5

Growing Up in a High-Technology Culture: Problems of Knowing

How do we know about the world? How do we find out what it is like? In the urban and suburban settings of the countries of the North, and for some elites of the South, children grow into adulthood without ever discovering anything about the physical and social environment beyond their own personal daily path, except through programmed secondary sources such as television, radio, the telephone, the computer, and of course books. They live in technologically shielded settings that cut them off from feedback about the larger environment in which they live. In fact, it is considered progress not to have to bother with getting or dealing with that feedback.

A classic illustration of that mentality is found as early as the nineteenth century, in Edward Bellamy's utopian novel, *Looking Backward* (1888/1969). In this utopia cities are built under huge umbrellas so that the inhabitants will never have to know when it rains. Some of today's larger covered shopping malls provide the same effect.

The fascination of Americans with technological umbrellas, as well as their ambivalence about them, are well documented (Marx, 1964; Segal, 1985). That this fascination has captured the entire Western world is seen in a thoughtful series of essays from an international symposium on science and utopianism, edited by Mendelsohn and Nowotny (1984). From one perspective, children growing up under these shielded conditions might be said to experience sensory deprivation, if we take *sensory* to mean using all five senses to experience the environment.

In terms of the larger world, these sensorially deprived children of urbia/suburbia are in a minority. Most children, even in North America, live outside the technological shield and deal daily with environmental challenges. To understand the contrast in the world of experience between the children inside and outside the shield, I will first describe the world outside the shield as experienced by rural American youth and then by Third World youth.

TWO VIEWS OF THE WORLD

Lyme, New Hampshire

Lyme is a small rural community in the Upper Connecticut Valley of New Hampshire, north of the college town of Hanover.[1] Most of the 18 young people in its eighth-grade class are the children of farmers, although a few have parents who commute to Hanover and work for Dartmouth College. They are the "seniors" of the Lyme School System, for the town has no high school. These 12-to-14-year-olds face a major shift in their lives next year, as they enter one of the three high schools available to them in nearby communities, including Hanover. They already carry a heavy load of responsibility at home and face with mingled self-assurance and anxiety the prospect of traveling to school in another town and dealing with the more complex culture of the high school world. When asked what they thought of Hanover High after a recent visit, the answer was a one-word chorus: BIG!

Although they have gone to a small school in a small town, they already know something of the complexities of the world that faces them. They feel "old"—old in experience—in relation to their parents and teachers, realizing how little those adults, however sympathetic and well-meaning, know of what they face every day. The Lyme eighth graders are Americans and know well that they belong to one of the great industrial nations of the world. Yet they share with rural children everywhere a workload and a degree of responsibility not known to the more urban children of the Western world.

---

[1]The material on Lyme, New Hampshire comes from working for several years on a community-based learning experiment with Terry Viens, a Lyme eighth-grade teacher, and her students, while I was teaching at Dartmouth College. A manuscript entitled *Children's Perceptions of the Changing Social Order and the Future of Culture* was originally prepared for the World Order Models Task Force on Culture in the World System (Boulding, 1979a).

In the United States they represent a small minority—farm families are less than 5 percent of the population—but in the world they are a majority. The majority of the world's children—between 75 and 80% in Third World countries—live in rural areas.

In Lyme they straddle two worlds, however, for they read urban newspapers, watch television, and go to the movies, as well as milk cows and drive tractors. That some of them have never been out of their hometown world of Lyme is irrelevant. Their two-world experience gives a striking quality to their hopes and fears for the future. Themes appear in their conversation and in their writing that can also be found in accounts of conversations with both urban and rural children in Europe, Africa, Asia, and Latin America, as reported by those who traveled around the world interviewing children during 1979, the International Year of the Child (UN International Year of the Child Secretariat, 1978). The Lyme eighth graders are in a unique way a microcosm of tomorrow's society.

I had the opportunity to hear this class reflect aloud with me about their responsibilities. The following quotes come from my notes:

—"Our parents had to work harder than we do when they were our age, because there were fewer machines, but they led more protected lives. Everything was familiar and safe. We have to make choices continually—where we will go, with whom we will go, and what we will do and whether it is the right thing to do. We have to handle ourselves under a heavy peer pressure our parents never had. We are more independent, we are home less, have more other activities to choose from. Our friends drive, and we have highways to deal with. Sometimes we make mistakes. Our parents think we know more than we really do know, and expect us always to make the right decision."

—"We work hard, but we don't mind work. We do farm chores, take care of the house, and raise our younger brothers and sisters. When things go wrong, we wish our parents would take more time to explain how it went wrong, and not just get mad. We know our parents have too much to do—are too busy. We would like to have more free time than they do when we grow up. Would we want easier work? No! We don't mind hard work."

One eighth grader milks 35 cows regularly, six drive tractors and backhoe cultivators on the farm. Most have driven cars, trucks, snowmobiles, and motorbikes since they were seven or eight. Fifteen out of 18 shoot regularly (girls as well as boys go deer hunting with their fathers), eight own their own guns, and three boys own three guns apiece. One did his first unaided shooting at the age of three. Few of them are old enough to take the National Rifle Association Safety Test, for which the minimum age is 14. Seven use chainsaws alone, one owns his own chainsaw. They all know that the equipment they use daily is expensive and dangerous and can easily go wrong. They have learned to be careful and are intensely interested in learning more skills of machinery repair. Girls are left in complete charge of the farm sometimes on weekends, as are boys. Girls are frequently in complete charge of the house and younger siblings for several days at a time.[2]

A similar conversation with their younger brothers and sisters in the third grade reveals that the eighth graders are not exaggerating in referring to the early age at which they started their activities. Third graders, like their older siblings, drive snowmobiles (a necessity for getting farm chores done in the winter), use power mowers, hunt, babysit, cook, care for farm animals, and split firewood.

Many of the eighth graders work for other farmers or for stores in town, winter and summer. They are used to shaping their own world by now. They are looking for new worlds to conquer after having constructed as seventh graders a new, corrected, and updated map of the town to replace the existing outdated maps. The new map came out of a still earlier project of interviewing old-timers about the last bad flood. This year they undertook another interviewing project, asking long-time residents for stories of what schooling was like when they were young, and finding out what craft skills residents had that they would be willing to teach school children in out-of-school apprenticeships. By their own activities, these young people are building a foundation for community-based education for the children who follow them.

The Third World

Twelve- to fourteen-year-olds in the Third World are far less likely to be in school, particularly farm youth, and are generally working a 10-to-14-hour day, depending on the season of the year.

---

[2]The mothers of these families all work, either on the farm or in town, and rely heavily on both daughters and sons for help with household maintenance.

By the age of eight or earlier, rural children have generally entered the labor force in terms of sustained productive work for four or more hours a day. Urban street children work at least as many hours as their rural counterparts. School is a less important part of the day, if there is schooling at all. However, the fact of responsibility looms large in the lives of youth both in the First and Third World. Consider the following three cases, adapted from the UN International Year of the Child Secretariat reports (1978):

—A fourteen-year-old Columbian girl, like her Lyme counterparts, both farms and goes to school. She gets up at 5:30 each morning and finds the double load tiring but worth it. "You feel more part of the family, working. It is better to both work and study than just to study." She wishes they would learn new things about farming at school, which they don't. Fifteen-year-old Indira in India has never been to school. She works as a hired hand on a neighboring farm, but notices that she can do some things better than the children who go to school. She has been taught by older women of her family, and concludes she doesn't need schooling. "I can count" she says proudly.

—A twelve-year-old Jamaican farms his own land; he decides when to plant and when to sell with his grandfather as teacher and guide. He has been farming since he was seven. There is no school in his life. A wistful fellow-Jamaican, age 11, says "If you don't go to school it kind of mash up your life." A fourteen-year-old Colombian boy left school at age eight. "The studies just would not go in." A confident fifteen-year-old Peruvian girl who has stayed in school says "We should work together with the teachers. We are the ones who are at school, we know the problems so we can help solve them."

—Third World street children do not get to school at all—neither do they have land to work. But like their counterparts elsewhere they are resourceful. They work garbage heaps and do street jobs. A nine-year-old girl working garbage heaps in Nagpur, India, for salable scrap says, "I would like to go to school. I like to see small girls going to school with books and slates. I don't know why I want to go with them. . . . Life will be better when I am older. I will work on building sites and earn money."

While there is no comparison between the hardness of life of an Indian street child and a First World rural school-goer, they have in common a down-to-earth knowledge of their environment and its physical and social complexities. In fact, in a two-year study of children and adults in a small Vermont town (Hart, 1979), it was found that children had a competence in mapping and knowledge of local land use that considerably exceeded adult knowledge of the same terrain. They not only have knowledge, they know how to manage knowledge in relation to their own needs and the needs of adults around them. When children like this have opportunities for schooling, their world expands rapidly. They quickly discover how to link what they know from firsthand experience with the secondary data they acquire in the classroom and from books.

EXPERIENCE WORLDS AND LEARNING

John Dewey would say that the Lyme eighth graders and the Third World children were learning under conditions that would maximize their capacity for making judgments and for choosing when choice was possible, in spite of the limitations of their lives. This is because they all understand the reality constraints on what they can do. They recognize a crunch when they see one. Young people who live technologically shielded lives cannot make such distinctions easily.

Talking about farm and street knowledge may seem a long way from the problem of learning to grasp the complexities of the world as a whole. The challenge that educational systems in any society face, however, is discovering how to insure an adequate firsthand experience on which to build a knowledge structure that corresponds to the real world. Hart (1979), drawing on his two-year Vermont experience, states,

> A radical reorientation of the schools is required. They should recognize children's competent engagements with the environment as central to the definition of, and development of, intelligence. A future-oriented philosophy would see education as the process by which children learn to interact with and, intelligently transform, the environment and themselves. "Environmental competence" in such an educational system would involve more than the effective construction and modification of environments. Children would learn to see a range of outcomes from their environmental manipulations. They would have to learn to make trade-offs within the framework of a developing sense of social and environmental responsibility. Children would not only learn to see themselves as potentially capable builders or modifiers of

their built environment but they would also come to fully comprehend their total resource dependency, involving, for example, learning to provide food through foraging and cultivation. As long as we fail to teach these things, we are enforcing a dependence upon others. Education should be a liberating force. Conscious interdependency (co-operation) should be encouraged; unwitting dependency upon a technocratic society is dangerous for all concerned. (p. 348)

Knowledge built up from abstractions alone has different characteristics than knowledge gained empirically. Both are important. Neither is adequate alone. Also there are many ways of knowing, and each adds to our understanding in different ways. The problem with technologically shielded education is that it has overvalued one way of gaining information and one way of using the mind. Western-style training in deductive, axiomatic, and sequential reasoning, and the learned preference for mechanistic modes of one-way causality to explain physical and social processes, has created certain rigidities of thought and closed off certain types of mental play. Maruyamah (1979, p. 14) describes the elements of this rigid set of philosophical rules: "The parts are subordinated to the whole. There is one best way for all individuals. Universal principles apply to all. Society consists of categories, supercategories and subcategories, structures, superstructures and infrastructures." Such beliefs leave us with only one way of thinking. An alternative philosophical construct might assume that, since all human beings are different from each other, they will be continually evolving diverse life ways. Continuous interaction among heterogeneous individuals and groups, with no one dominant over the others, would then generate a variety of patterns for solving social problems and a variety of social structures, which will be of mutual benefit to various parties.

One Right Path? One Kind of Literacy?

We saw in Chapter 4 how one civilization after another abandoned the idea of a universal law for humankind based on their own tradition. Yet intellectual training in the West is still rooted in the conviction that there is one developmental path to take, and that we are on it. This leads to a certain authoritarianism, both in teaching and in setting the boundaries for research. It also introduces hesitation and fear in the learner. This constricts openness, limits exploratory behavior, and closes the door on free flights of the imagination. To the extent that authoritarianism prevails in the classrooms of the industrial world, schools have thus narrowed, not expanded, the social repertoires of the adults who have passed through them.

Our technological skills in the West are so great that we keep thinking that all problems can be solved through technology. In fact, we have used technological design to limit human choice in the name of eliminating errors—a worthy goal in designing automobiles but not in designing communities. The result is automated security systems that could destroy life without human intentionality ever having been activated.

How did we in the West come to be seduced by the illusory effortlessness of technological solutions to social problems? Part of the answer lies in the particular set of literacies around which social and economic development have taken place over the past six centuries, culminating in the present computer-dependent organization of human work. The keeping of records (accounts, state archives, and laboratory data), the making of maps, and the construction and reproduction of working models of machinery of all kinds, including social machinery, have been the primary skills underlying the activities of the Industrial Revolution. The stimulating experience of playing with ideas and materials to create new tools and new environments released higher levels of social energy into the Industrial Revolution itself. New skills were taught to the peasant populations that moved from rural fiefdoms to the new cities of Europe to become the workers in this revolution. Gradually this experimentation receded in importance. It was the production skills that mattered, not the social vision, not the mental play. The old Greek *paedia*, referring to an ideal of well-rounded education, was reduced to competency-based learning, with the competencies spanning a narrow range indeed.

The result is comments such as, "Jonathan is already four, and he can't do the computer," made by a five-year-old in a private U.S. elementary school, who is quoted in a *New York Times* article that tells us that 15,000 of the nation's 100,000 elementary schools are using microcomputers as teaching tools "to teach ideas and skills that had previously been presented in books and on blackboards (Fiske, 1982). The same article quotes Seymour Papert of the Massachusetts Institute of Technology as saying that the goal is to teach children to manipulate their environment through the use of the computer, in much the same way that popular electronic games already teach people of all ages to manipulate imaginary environments. Papert claims, "The computer can make the most abstract things concrete." The belief is that knowledge about the environment will no longer need to be carried around in people's heads, because it can all be stored and accessed in the computer. Computer enthusiasts say that, because of the precise step-by-step instructions computers need, computer-assisted learning will increase people's rationality. It also redirects social attention to those kinds of social problems that are quantifiable, thus heightening the aura of rationality surrounding the computer.

Computer literacy is the most discussed literacy in the world. Unquestionably it has opened up the world of the infinitely small and the world of the infinitely large in ways that are transforming our understanding of the nature of the universe. Microscopes and telescopes would be useless without computers, at the rate that new data about the matter of the universe are pouring in. Computers help us regulate complex movements of people and goods over the planet. They monitor the environment and provide early warning systems for natural and humanmade catastrophes. When properly used, they extend the reach of the human mind in breathtaking ways and enable even the most hopelessly crippled human beings to communicate with others and manage their personal environments. They will become increasingly important as the carriers of direct interpersonal network communication for members of the 18,000 INGOs described in Chapter 3, and for the countless informed transnational networks that are springing up every day among people with shared interests of every kind. There is no gainsaying the importance of computers to the human species. But how are we using these new tools? Socrates in the *Phaedrus* warned that writing would undermine the oral tradition and destroy memory. What might the computer undermine?

THE NEED TO KEEP OLD TOOLS ALONG WITH THE NEW

Socrates was right about the effects of writing, although it took centuries to have its full effect. Few schoolchildren today have prose and poetry of any kind stored in their heads, although their grandparents still do. The record on the social effects of the literacy of letters is incomplete because few researchers think it worth comparing the creative problem-solving capacities of nonliterate and literate people. It has been simply assumed that the latter are superior. Now even that is being questioned.

Margaret Spufford (1981) suggests that ordinary people lost the ability of dramatic storytelling with the rise of chapbooks—cheap, popular books—in England in the 1600s. Schuman, Inkeles, and Smith (1967) found in comparative studies of the problem-solving skills of literate and nonliterate African workers in the early 1960s that nonliterates were more apt to arrive at creative solutions to technical problems than their schooled fellow workers. Harvey Graff (1981) has assembled a series of studies on the relationship between literacy and social development in the West which suggest that literacy had little to do with economic development and more with gaining social control over workers. African women political leaders have more than once pointed out that it is the nonliterate women who seem to have the most time, energy, and enthusiasm for political activity. "Too much" civic education is seen as easily turning into indoctrination and producing relative political passivity. This is, of course, quite the contrary effect to the one intended by the developers of the concept of civic literacy and indeed indicates serious misuse of the tools of literacy.

Finally, Jack Goody (1968) points out that the homeostatic, or equilibrating effect on social organization of a shared oral tradition in nonliterate societies is unavailable to literate societies. It has often been noted that modern industrial societies find themselves with fewer and fewer shared traditions. Goody sees "literate society as inevitably committed to an ever increasing series of cultural lags" because of the lack of face-to-face settings for the sharing of experience. Whereas enthusiastic modernizers see the homeostatic effect of shared tradition as an obstacle to development, the lack of a shared tradition may have the same effect.

The examples of a shrinking social imagination just given indicate misuse of literacy skills and should not, of course, be taken as a critique of the monumental achievements of letter and number literacy. How should those literacy skills be approached? Howard Gardner (1985) and Benjamin Bloom (1985) work with concepts of multiple intelligences. They point to the crippling educational effect of the emphasis in Western culture on linguistic and logical intelligences. Gowin has shown how schooling has missed its core function by failing to teach children *how to learn* (Gowin, 1981; Novak & Gowin, 1984). Certainly public school education in countries like the United States focuses rather narrowly on certain kinds of reasoning, a trend which the use of the computer only accentuates.

Image literacy is what has been lost in the development of these other literacies. Image literacy involves the individual's ability to combine the materials of inner and outer experience worlds, drawn from all the senses, to shape new patterns of "reality." Children do it all the time, but it is called daydreaming, and they are punished for it.

In the United States, as in other countries, children sit from the age of 5 to the age of 16 in sealed boxes called classrooms, cut off from the experience worlds with which their multiple intelligences could play. Their attention is directed to a certain distillation of those worlds, presented to them in letters, numbers, and television images. They are frequently tested on their mastery of these prepared distillations. There is a reason for the importance placed on such testing: Society is getting more unmanageable, and the felt need for skilled social engineering is great.

The dilemmas of scale and complexity in modern life are overloading institutions of governance designed for simpler societies. It is logical to encourage students to use the computer to learn to handle ever larger numbers in even more complex systems. It is logical, but it doesn't necessarily increase social adaptability. What the young need is the chance to give free play to their own imaginations in making other social designs. In fact, if instructed to "play with their imaginations," students often don't know what to do because there is little in their minds to play with. Little is stored in the memory because they have been taught to rely on looking things up. A trained memory and the art of recall have not been valued by their teachers.

One source of our youth's knowledge of alternative possibilities is the predigested imagery placed on the television screen. Television preprograms reality. One aspect of that preprogramming is the fact that most children see much more violence on the screen than most of them could possibly experience in their own real world, and so come to think of the world as a more scary place than it really is. Another aspect is that young people experience an artificial and mechanical exposure to carefully balanced sets of opinions, instead of the melange of views found in the real world. The education of the general public in political decision making operates within the same type of preprogrammed frame. The constant monitoring of public opinion through the technology of polling increases the tendency of decision makers to depend on composite prepared views. Images of alternative possibilities then become disturbing because they require a reexamination of basic data that decision makers are unprepared to undertake.

The primary reassurance for people who inhabit this alarming world comes from believing that every problem has a technological solution. National security, for example, can be handled by military programming and the continual replacement of "obsolete" weapons systems by more modern ones. In this view, it is perfectly logical that half of the research capabilities of the world scientific community should go to further weapons development, because the greatest threats on the planet are the weapons systems of other nations. Each must have the best.

The relationships among image illiteracy, technological dependence, and feelings of collective and personal helplessness need exploring. The relationship is very probably a circular one. Because people do not know how to image alternative solutions to problems, whether personal ones of health and social relationships or collective problems of social unrest and war, they rely on specialists who utilize physical technologies the layperson does not understand. This causes feelings of dependence, which are exacerbated by the fact that individuals must work through layers of bureaucratic structures in the local community to accomplish many of the most ordinary tasks beyond the level of the household. The trick is to find "someone" to "help" them.

The focus on finding a someone, a specialist in physical or social technology, prevents the development of feelings of collective efficacy in social organizations, much as it prevents the development of feelings of individual efficacy. Albert Bandura (1982) has studied personal and collective self-efficacy for some years. He describes the social despondency and apathy that arise from perception of low efficacy. This indeed corresponds with the situation in which the so-called advanced industrial world finds itself. Low feelings of self-efficacy in Western nations are also reflected in the UNESCO study of images of the year 2000 carried out in the late 1960s by an international team of socialist, capitalist, and Third World scholars (Ornauer, Wiberg, Sicinski, & Galtung, 1976). Countries of the old industrial West were pessimistic about what the world would be like in the year 2000, primarily because they were pessimistic about what they themselves could do. Nonindustrialized socialist and Third World countries were on the whole optimistic, about themselves and their societies. It is not a happy thought that further industrialization has led these countries also to lose their feelings of individual and social efficacy.

THE RECOVERY OF ALL OUR WAYS OF KNOWING

The secret of the recovery of efficacy lies in the recovery of confidence in our ability to learn from and respond to challenge—in the recovery of knowing itself. This involves recovery of oral tradition and of imagination or imaging, as well as the continual development of our skills of number and letter literacy. It also involves attention to different ways of using the mind in knowing.

If we want to describe what is involved in coming to know, we need to distinguish among the actual learning process, learning settings, and agents of learning. This will give us a clearer sense of what needs to be done about learning. One way to talk about the whole learning system is to talk about socialization, which involves all the influences that come to bear on the individual in the process of becoming the kind of person "society" wants. Society, of course, consists of all the individuals and groups and institutions that are involved in that becoming. The process is lifelong, and the influences can be conflicting and sometimes mutually incompatible.

We cannot, however, talk about socialization as if it were a process that simply shaped persons from the outside. Each of us has an inward referee, a choosing self, that makes something of all the socializing influences from outside. The choosing self rejects some influences and accepts others, but mostly it synthesizes influences in a way unique to each choosing person. That is why when we talk about learning we have to emphasize the active, constructive role of the learner. All the outside world can provide is the raw materials, the elements for learning. The putting together into meaningful constructs of the out-there reality is our original, creative work, even if it is an apparently routine activity such as developing an inward representation of the multiplication table.

Studies of categories of people who have been ignored as "thinkers"—minority groups, the handicapped, and particularly that 51% minority, women—give us new insights into the role of the learner in organizing her learning. These insights apply to learning generally and have profound implications both for education and for schooling. Evans (1982) shows us the intentness, the seriousness of purpose, the disciplined quality of the efforts made by those who have mental retardation to come to "know" what is learned so effortlessly by normals, thereby giving us a new respect for the intentionality of the learner.

In a related vein, Belenky, Blythe, Goldberger, & Tarule (1986), by studying women from all walks of life who have elected to return to some form of schooling, have shown how hard it is to become a "knower." The concept of *connected knowing*, knowing-in-relationship (as distinct from separate knowing) has emerged from their work. This type of knowing evolves over time, as Belenky et al. see it. Because they have been oppressed as thinkers, it is a struggle for many women to conceive of themselves as knowers. They begin with a silent, nonverbal experience of reality; move on to receiving knowledge from an authoritative source; and then learn to listen to their own subjective, intuitive inner voice. Analytic reasoning comes after women learn to trust their own gut feelings. The conscious process of integrating information and constructing knowledge can then take place in a connected way, based on empathic understanding of the world of others. Many people never become connected knowers. Women, because they are required to identify connections in order to carry out their role of making community facilities fit household needs, often have a better experiential base for connected knowing than men. It is clear from the new research on knowing that much more goes on in knowing than we realized and that there has been a vast underestimation of the role of the learner in learning.

For our purposes we will draw from this rich array of insight into ways of knowing by concentrating on the growth of three mental faculties which we, the creative learners-coming-to-know, can use in our thinking: the emotional/affective or feeling faculty, the intuitive faculty, and the cognitive/analytic faculty. We will concentrate on these three, as being of central importance in the development of the complex kinds of knowing that will enable individuals to function in the planetary community and contribute creatively to a planetary civic culture. Before we discuss these, however, we will take some time to consider the different settings or social spaces we occupy while we are learning.

Settings for Learning

Knowledge does not develop in the abstract, but rather through direct experience in social settings.[3] It is important that social spaces for learning allow for maximum exercise of the faculties involved in the process and maximum experimentation with and practice of what is offered for learning. What are the settings for learning? First of all, of course, is the family, where we begin to learn who we are and how to cope with other human beings. Here the primary eagerness for or fear of experimenting with the new information is developed, and the primary feelings of efficacy or inefficacy, depending on the openness of the family to the child's growth experience. Next is the neighborhood, where once again the adventure of meeting new

---

[3]The material that follows on socialization as learning is more fully developed in E. Boulding (1978a).

people and discovering new terrain can be either joyful or fearful, depending on the receptivity of the neighborhood to the adventures of childhood.

Then comes the school, which offers teachers and their world views, a collection of books, and other children. Again, either the school encourages creative mental constructs in children or it insists on formalistic learning of prepared patterns. Here is where the cognitive mapping of the world begins, and much depends on the cognitive maps of the teachers who impart data to pupils. But the freedom to play mentally with the information that comes in books is a freedom that children appropriate, even under conditions of very little encouragement.

Finally there are all the other social spaces available to the growing child: informal play groups; churches; scouting groups; after-school opportunities in arts, crafts, theater, and music; and the ubiquitous world of television and other mass media. In all these settings there is information, and there are role models. Both are very important in young people's task of creating their own perceptions of how the world is, how it works.

One of the most important factors in the development of mature adult personalities who can respond creatively to the unexpected, to rapidly changing conditions, and to acute stress, without resort to violence, is the experience of having been free to experiment while growing up, in their various life settings, with their own interpretations of reality, their own roles, their own problem-solving responses to the unexpected. Competence, initiative, and feelings of self-worth arise from such freedom to try out behaviors. More important, the capacity to generate imaginative solutions to new problems comes from such freedom.

Other adults present in these settings are of course important. Prescriptive role modeling (a parent says, "Why can't you be like _____?") is useless. But the evidence presents itself over and over again that children and young people, like adults, choose persons whose ways of doing things they admire, and they teach themselves things from their observations of the admired persons, things no one could put in a textbook. The process of modeling oneself on another person is one of the most complex forms of learning we know.

Maturation of Learning Capacities

The social spaces in which learning and socialization take place change over a lifetime. The family becomes less important and school may disappear, while workplace, neighborhood, and special chosen social settings become more important. The maturation of the learning capacities per se, like physical maturation, continues over the lifetime, through all changes in setting. The fact that our learning capacities never stop developing, even in old age (unless a debilitating illness causes deterioration) is not generally realized.

We spoke previously of the growth of three kinds of learning faculties: the emotional/affective, the cognitive/analytic and the intuitive. *Emotional/affective maturation* means a continuing development of the capacities for learning through negotiating personal wants, for expanding empathic identification with the other, and for the capacity for disciplined, intentional behavior in the face of diversity of choices. *Cognitive maturation* means a continuing development of the capacities to construct complex mental structures out of the confusing and often contradictory data about what is going on in the world; it means particularly the ability to utilize rather than reject new information, no matter how painful the process of mental reconstruction may be. It also means the development of criteria for evaluating new information. *Intuitive maturation* means learning to tune into signals from the natural and social environment that do not lend themselves to verification by ordinary empirical procedures, and to process these signals by creating a correspondence between inner and outer states such that understanding and insight are achieved. It is a capacity that grows by a combination of reflection and inward centering and keen observation of and listening to the outer world.

The recovery of image literacy or the imagination, which we spoke of earlier, depends very much on the balanced maturation of all three of these faculties. Neither reason, emotion, nor intuition alone can generate full fantasy processes; only all three together. We will discuss this more fully in Chapter 6.

The balanced maturation of all three of these faculties means moving outside the technological shield for one's learning experiences, and it means living outside the shield as a fully participating citizen of the planet. That does not mean the removal of technology, but it means using it differently, as an enhancer of the ability to perceive rather than as a barrier to perception of the created order. This nurtures the conditions necessary for creation of a larger civic culture as the world becomes a plurality of learning societies in dialogue with one another. With these three faculties operating in tandem, no culture can be completely opaque to another, no matter how different their customs and institutions. What the cognitive/analytic faculty cannot grasp, the emotional/affective faculty may reach through empathy; what empathy cannot penetrate, the intuitive signaling process may communicate.

The obstacles to knowing lie not in our minds but in the structuring of our institutions, the roles we pattern for each succeeding generation, and the way we use tools. The children of Lyme, New Hampshire and the street children of India have equally good chances of participating in the creation of a world civic culture, provided that enough information about the larger world filters into their social spaces. Their chances are also as good as any college graduate's from the major metropolitan centers of each continent.

The barriers to the development of Third World youth are lack of sufficient secondary data about the world beyond their personal social space. The barriers to the development of the urban college graduate are lack of sufficient primary data about the world *inside or outside* their personal social space. The technological shield itself is the problem. It keeps primary, firsthand experience from the media-raised young, as there is no room for that experience world inside the shield. If swords can be turned into plowshares, can shields be turned into tools?

SUMMARY

We began this chapter by contrasting what it means to live inside or outside the technological shield provided by electronic media and a highly programmed daily existence. We compared farm and urban street experience with middle-class urban experience for youth and found that the classroom world left out many significant learning opportunities. Considering that there might be many ways for society to develop in the future, and not just one right way, we looked at the different kinds of literacy needed for that development, including image literacy, which involves mental play and fantasy.

The recovery of all our ways of knowing involves understanding the socialization situation within which learning takes place. This means attending to settings, agents of socialization, and the kinds of faculties involved in the more complete knowing in which we are interested. The balanced development of cognitive/analytic, emotional/affective, and intuitive ways of knowing depends on stepping outside the technological shield for primary data about the empirical world, as well as for the utilization of secondary data. That balanced development can bring about the recovery of image literacy, or imagination, and lead to a wider range of solutions to the problems society faces.

In the next chapter, we will explore the specifics of the balanced use of the three capacities, as well as the meaning of image literacy.

SUGGESTED FURTHER READING

Bellamy, E. (1960). *Looking backward.* New York: New American Library. (Original published 1888)

Boulding, E. (1978). The child and nonviolent social change. In I. Charny (Ed.), *Strategies against violence.* Boulder, CO: Westview Press.

Hart, R. (1979). *Children's experience of place.* New York: Irvington Books.

Maruyamah, M. (1979, September–October). Mindscapes: The limits to thought. *World Future Society Bulletin.* 13–23.

Marx, L. (1964). *The machine in the garden.* New York: Oxford University Press.

Mendelsohn, E., & Nowotny, H. (1984). *Nineteen eighty-four: Science between utopia and dystopia.* Boston: D. Reidel.

Segal, H. (1985). *Technological utopianism in American culture.* Chicago: University of Chicago Press.

CHAPTER 6

Uses of the Imagination

We have examined at length the obstacles to experiencing the primary realities of life on the planet, obstacles that are created by the phenomenon of the technological shield—Edward Bellamy's umbrella—which keeps us from knowing when it is raining. The technological shield operates in two ways, however. It not only puts up an umbrella, it constrains the mind to keep inventing more umbrellas and limits the imagination to tinkering with the shield instead of exploring new ways of living on the planet. Of the three modes of knowing we discussed in Chapter 5, technology requires primarily the cognitive/analytic; the emotional/affective and intuitive modes have fallen into relative disuse.

In this chapter we will look at ways of freeing the other modes for action by developing the skills of the imagination. The intention is not to belittle the cognitive/analytic mode but to enhance it, and to free us to use more of our potential in social action. We will begin with an exercise in comprehending the complexity of the planet, then move to the use of metaphor in analyzing problems. The importance of mental play will be considered next, followed by the role of imagination in imaging, and then a look at how imaging can affect social imagination. Finally, we will explain a technique for imaging alternative futures for the world.

UNDERSTANDING COMPLEXITY

Complexity is the heritage of every twentieth-century human being. Whether we live in city, mountain, desert, or fertile agricultural valley, we cannot get away from the interrelatedness of all that is on the planet. Nor do we want to. That sense of interrelatedness is what makes us feel whole, feel good about being alive. It is also what cramps and oppresses us, because we can't grasp it all. Too much information comes too fast, and most of it is inevitably secondary data, about phenomena we will never personally experience: the details of the maintenance infrastructure of the world's cities; the state of soil, forests, air, water, from region to region; data on raw materials flows, production flows, regulation of transport systems; reports on health maintenance around the world, employment, working conditions, welfare needs; statistics—birth and death rates; the status of families and children, of women and minorities; progress in literacy programs; the condition of cultural monuments, the state of the arts; new developments in science and technology; the state of internal politics and the alliance structures of nation-states.

We can either retreat behind the technological shield and only accept packaged knowledge, or we can try to "know" the world we live in by exercising our minds in several different ways to compensate for the fact that we cannot know everything experientially. If we really want to "know" in a fresh, unprogrammed way, we will need a template for ordering information so we aren't overwhelmed by it, a system for mentally filing data so it adds to our knowledge without cluttering our minds.

In a sense we are all in the plight of a Chicano student of mine who was faced with the challenge of mastering vocabularies and concepts in the sciences and the arts in a language that was not his native tongue, in a setting—the college campus—that was worlds away from the slow-paced Southwest Colorado town in which he had lived his childhood. Contrary to expectations, he was doing outstandingly well; he was on the dean's list academically and had been elected vice-president of his class. One day he explained to me how he managed his studies. He needed something familiar to hold onto, he said, so he used as his "learning base" the old car he had acquired and lovingly worked over in his spare time in high school. Every new word, every new concept, every new formula that appeared in the course of his studies, he would mentally place somewhere on that car. Once so placed, he "knew" the new bit of information. He could relate it to everything else he knew, and it stayed with him. The car was a device not only for remembering but for integrating knowledge.

We all have the analogue of that car, something we know as well as or better than one can know a car—our own bodies. Our bodies are as complex as anything in the universe. The brain alone has somewhere over 10 billion neurons, about as many as there are stars in the galaxy. Every neuron has two functions: It can be either on or off. The complexity of a system depends on how many states it can be in; in the case of the brain, the number of possible states is 2 to the 10 billionth power. At the rate of one digit per second, it would take an individual 90 years to write out the number that represents. How unimaginably more complex, then, is the total set of systems of the body—the skeletal system, the systems for intake and circulation of food and oxygen through the bloodstream, the neural networks that fire information from cell to cell from the moment of conception until the moment of death, the hormone systems that maintain the chemical balance of the whole. All these systems enable us to eat, breathe, engage in physical and mental activity, and sleep in a remarkable synchronization of rhythms. There are thousands of different rhythmic cycles going on simultaneously in our bodies: the neural oscillations measurable in milliseconds, the rhythms of breathing, the familiar diurnal rhythms of sleeping and waking, the rhythms set by the solar year, and the last rhythm of conception-life-death.

We live daily with the complexity that is our body, and we get a continuous stream of signals from the body that tells us "how we are doing" at any particular moment. Fortunately we don't have to organize our bodily functions. We couldn't. The complexities of interrelationship within the body are beyond human mastery. They are beyond the capacities of computer modeling. Yet we "know" our body. We can therefore use our body as a familiar base from which to understand other complex systems outside us in a way similar to, but different from, the way the Chicano student used his car. We would be totally bogged down if we tried to pin parts of society to our body parts. But we can imagine social systems as if they were parts of our body, and let the complexity of the one be a guide to the complexity of the other.

To illustrate these points, let's try the following exercise. Close your eyes and experience, as much as you can in your conscious mind, the functioning of your body. Feel your lungs drawing in air, your heart pumping blood, your cells processing nourishment from the bloodstream, your brain generating images of your body, your neurons firing messages from cell to cell. Feel your body as pulsing, effortless complexity. Give yourself several minutes for this experience.

Now this familiar body of yours is going to serve as an envelope for a succession of mental experiments in observing societal complexity. First, place the family in which you grew up inside your body. You will see your parents, your siblings, and yourself, as you all move about in the rooms of your house, in your yard. Watch what you are doing, how you look, how you behave with each other. This family of yours is a very complex system of interrelationships. There is a household economy, household decision making, a household culture. Who produces what? Who gives directions, and who accepts them? Who quarrels, who makes peace? What are you telling each other? What do you want from each other? You can see the whole because it is inside you. You are the envelope for your family. Allow yourself to savor all the alliances and cleavages, the work and play, the hopes and fears that are part of your family's continually changing systemic patterns. Give yourself time to sense your family as a whole.

Now your body is to be the envelope for the town you grew up in. You are the boundary of this town, this complex economic, political, and sociocultural entity. Look inside. Find the street you grew up on, the special places you used to play. Find the schools you went to, the parks and playgrounds. Explore the main street, the shopping mall, the town hall, the fire station, the stores you shopped in, the hospital. Look at the churches, the movie theaters, the special landmarks of your town. Everywhere there will be people, working, playing, talking. See how differently activities are patterned for adults, for teenagers, for children. You are the envelope for this busy town, and you can watch all the action simultaneously, see how it all makes one large, complex, "busy-town" pattern, with continuously changing systems. Give yourself time to feel the hum of activity and its interconnectedness.

Now your body is to be the envelope for a whole country, the United States, with its awesomely intricate economy and polity. You will see the great cities from coast to coast, strung together by ribbons of highways and railroad tracks. You will see the gleaming federal buildings of the capital, Washington, D.C. In other cities there will be factories, skyscrapers, department stores, libraries, museums. Between cities lie thousands of acres of fertile farms, open ranch land, and small towns and villages. Planes fly overhead, trains roar on tracks, cars roll on highways, boats sail the bordering oceans. Don't forget Alaska up near the Arctic Circle, and Hawaii over there in the blue Pacific. Don't forget the army, the navy, the air force, and the marines, stationed at home and overseas. This whole great nation, with its population of 225 million, is in you. All its institutions, activities, and projects, at home and abroad, have their existence at this moment in you. They are all interconnected in the continually changing systemic patterns that comprise the United States of America. Take time to feel the connectedness.

Now comes the last part of this exercise. Your body is at this moment the envelope for the planet itself. Look in at the magnificent blue-green sphere. The Himalayas rise in you. The great rivers flow from mountain to sea—all in you. The arctic snows gleam, the desert sands blow. Prairies ripple with waves of corn and wheat. Forests stand tall, oceans heave. And the cities! Here are a thousand jewels, each different, each teaming with people. The planet is crisscrossed with pathways, visible and invisible, the travelways of humankind as it goes about its business of production, consumption, reproduction, and governance. This is Gaia herself,[1] the complexity of the human body magnified beyond all comprehension. Take time to dwell on what you see.

When you have finished this exercise, try to identify what you know that you didn't know before. Consider this in terms of the ways of knowing discussed in the last chapter. In the cognitive/analytic sense there is probably nothing new. No new data have been offered for your inspection. In the emotional/affective sense, you probably have a different sense of identification with the complex systems, at each level from family to planet, than you had before. If your body could successively house family, town, country, and planet, you have felt personal connections you hadn't felt before. In the intuitive area, there probably are some new awarenesses. You can't explain why all the phenomena you have inwardly observed are related, but you "know" that they are. You have a sense of at-homeness with that interrelatedness.

What we have been doing is using the body as a metaphor for complex systems. According to Webster (1979), "a metaphor is a figure of speech in which a word or phrase literally denoting one kind of object or idea is used in place of another to suggest a likeness or analogy between them." In fact, a metaphor is much more powerful than a simile or analogy. It is, rather, a conceptual archetype, a way of seeing that relates apparently very different kinds of phenomena. A metaphor does not provide new data, but it gives insight into relationships. If we stayed at the metaphoric level, just enjoying the metaphor, we could rightly be accused of substituting feeling for

---

[1]The Gaia Hypothesis refers to the theory that the entire earth is one living organism; the name comes from Gaia, the Greek earth goddess (Lovelock, 1979).

thought. If, however, we use the insight of relatedness as a basis for analytic examination of empirical data about the connections, then we are making advances in knowledge.

This is how the Chicano student we spoke of earlier used his metaphor of the car—as a basis for further analytic work on connections. This is also the basic approach we shall take in exploring the skills of the imagination. Metaphor and the feelings and intuitions it provides will serve as the motor for further empirical investigation. We will be in good company with the great scientists, who generally have had intuitive insights first and developed their scientific models later.

The process of creating civic culture involves all of the three modes of knowing we have discussed. It begins with a feeling of potential relatedness to others, to the company of strangers on the planet. It continues with an intuition of how that relatedness works, and it culminates in the construction of working models of relationship which become the basis for new institutional patterns.

THE ANALYTIC USE OF METAPHOR

When we are trying to understand a particular social phenomenon involving complex processes, it is useful to construct a model of what is happening. While a metaphor is much more than a model, for the purposes of this discussion we will stay with the model aspect of metaphors. Our model will reflect our assumptions about what we think is going on in the phenomenon. We may think of the phenomenon as (1) a set of equilibriating or homeostatic processes that serve to maintain an existing state of affairs, (2) as a set of change processes that are modifying the existing situation, or (3) as a set of transformation processes that will provide a completely new social configuration.

Since all three processes are usually at work in any situation of social change, we broaden our understanding of what is happening if we try out all three sets of assumptions in model building. The dynamics of the strategic planning for the "Star Wars" defense system, for example, may be modeled as an effort to maintain the status quo, as an effort to adapt to changing military technologies, or as an effort to alter completely the nature of defense systems. Similarly, the plan brought forward by the Group of 77 for a New International Economic Order may be modeled as an effort to involve the Third World more fully in the existing international economic system, as an effort to adapt to changing economic conditions, or as an effort to alter completely the nature of the economic order. Each assumption provides a metaphor for the phenomenon itself.

Another way of broadening our understanding of social phenomena is to try to describe them in a number of different modes of perception and knowing. Each mode offers a metaphor for the phenomenon in question. The result may be a richer phenomenological understanding than is available by picking one set of descriptors, and engaging in the full process may clarify the extent to which change or equilibrium forces are at work.

For example, take the phenomenon of a boundary conflict between two neighboring countries. We can translate that conflict into a number of different modes, each of which will tell us something about the conflict. To begin this exercise, a careful verbal-analytic description of all the factors in the conflict is required, including the primary parties and their interests, the secondary parties and their interests, resources available to each, outside forces at work, and the past history of the conflict. When the maximum amount of available information has been laid out in analytic terms, additional modes of representation can be used.

First might be the mathematical mode. The conflict can be given a mathematical expression, such as an equation showing that the total area of the two nations involved in the boundary conflict is constant; as A increases, B diminishes, and vice versa. The equation can be written showing the different values each nation gives to different parcels of land on each side of the boundary, making it possible to show a boundary line that would give equal satisfaction to both parties. The mathematical equation thus gives insight into quantifiable dimensions of the conflict.

Next the conflict could be diagrammed, so that all the actors and forces at work can be visually perceived in relation to one another in a "social force-field."[2] Another mode would be to represent the conflict in terms of patterns of colors, with all the emotional overtones that color-coding brings. Another is to choreograph the conflict as a ballet; as the leaders and the publics of each nation posture and move, new insights emerge as to how each perceives self and other. The conflict can also be orchestrated as a symphony, evoking the aspirations of each people, written as an epic poem recalling the heritage of two histories, two traditions. It can be painted or

---

[2]This terminology is used in group dynamics; see Kurt Lewin (1948).

sculpted. Each representation brings to light new dimensions of the situation, and each becomes a metaphor for the conflict.

Therapists will recognize these devices as among their familiar tools for working with disturbed individuals, or in family therapy. The new view of the situation that comes from moving away from words and toward expression through the creative arts has over and over again liberated people trapped in rigidly repetitive pathologies so they are able to invent new ways of behaving. These devices need to be made equally respectable as tools for approaching serious social problems.

Each representation can of course be carried out in a multitude of ways. There are many possible equations, diagrams, color patterns, ballets, symphonies, poems, paintings, and sculptures. The point is not to explore all possible ramifications, but to think about the conflict in enough different modes so that understanding of the meaning of the conflict is deepened. This is not specifically recommended as a way of dealing with conflict alone, but as a way of deepening the understanding of all social phenomena and of insuring that they are approached in holistic, not piecemeal, ways.

The phenomenon of a boundary conflict was deliberately chosen for this exercise in clarification by metaphor, because boundary conflicts (read jurisdictional disputes, turf struggles) are among the most persistent and bloody of human problems. A holistic approach to such problems might suggest new, more peaceful strategies that leave human values intact.

In this metaphoric exercise, the initial cognitive/analytic state of gathering all available evidence is critical. It is also true, however, that other kinds of "evidence" will accrue while going through the additional modes of representation. Therefore a final stage in the exercise is to return to the initial analytic description and modify or add to it according to whatever new elements or factors have appeared during the exercise. While it is not practical to turn every problem situation into an orgy of artistic creativity, some experience with this kind of activity alters basic mindsets and humanizes problem solving. When a generation trained to think in these ways enters the world's foreign offices and multinational corporate headquarters, we may find the world's business conducted differently.

It is strongly recommended that you try this as an exercise for yourself. Choose a problem situation that you already have some information about. Write down what you know, looking up more information if your knowledge is too scanty. Then go through a series of alternative representations of the situation. Finally, go back to your initial description, and see what new insights the other modes of expression have given you.

MENTAL PLAY

When we are using metaphors we are engaging in mental play. Playing is perhaps the most important thing we ever do in our lives. Play is an absolutely primary activity, not reducible to any other activity. It is fun, and we do it for its own sake. It is complete in itself. As Huizinga (1955) says, play lets us know that we are more than rational beings, because we play and also know that we play— and choose to play, knowing that it is irrational.

Huizinga (1955) has provided the best formal definition of play. It is "a free activity standing quite consciously outside 'ordinary' life as being 'not serious,' but at the same time absorbing the player intensely and utterly. It is an activity connected with no material interest, and no profit can be gained by it. It proceeds within its own proper boundaries of time and space, according to fixed rules and in an orderly manner" (p. 13). Play is a stepping out of real life into a temporary sphere of activity with a disposition all its own, but that temporary sphere has its own seriousness. Huizinga's story of the father who found his four-year-old son sitting in front of a row of chairs playing "trains" exemplifies this. As the father hugged his child, the boy protested, saying, "Don't kiss the engine, Daddy, or the carriages won't think it's real" (Huizinga, 1955, p. 8).

One of the extraordinary things about play, in all its spontaneity and fun, is that it creates order. Do you remember inventing secret clubs, secret languages, and secret hiding places as a child? You may have forgotten, but every space you ever played in was an invented space. (You were playing when you were doing the previous exercise on imaging.) It is not overstating the matter to say that new patterns of reality emerge out of play. Most such patterns, like your own forgotten play as a child, are evanescent. Huizinga (1955) argues, however, that the whole phenomenon of culture and civilization originates in the initially spontaneous patternings of play.

The creation of language is play. Certainly dance, drama, song, poetry, and painting are play by Huizinga's definition. So is the creation of rules, and rules eventually make up the political and judicial order of each society. Ritual is the bridge between spontaneous play and the emergence of formal social institutions. Ritual itself is play. How we love the familiar rituals of family celebrations! The few public ritual celebrations we have, like Thanksgiving, Independence Day, and Memorial Day, are very important to local communities as rare opportunities for public play. Many people travel to New Orleans at Mardi Gras time to enjoy the wonderful spontaneity of the ancient Feast of Fools, a European ritual tradition that has been carried down to modern times.

In societies like our own, which largely limit play for adults to contests that have become spectator sports, have we lost our spontaneity? How shall we evaluate the depth and variety of new cultural patterns as they appear? Do life ways tend to become lifestyles as stylistic innovation replaces cultural inventiveness?

We would argue here that the recovery of play and playfulness for adults is an important part of the recovery of the social imagination. Playfulness will enable us to live more of our lives outside the technological shield. In a study of household time budgets (Boulding, 1977a), I discovered that the only families that listed "play" as a daily activity were families with children. Since each family member recorded his or her own activities in 15-minute intervals for a week, an inspection of the records made it clear that the children were the ones who played. The adults sometimes recorded "watching children play" as an activity, but never their own primary play. When there were no children in the house, there was no one to "perform play" for the family. The best route to the recovery of adult play, therefore, is to watch children play in order to discover what is "at play" in the activity.

The following exercise, which I propose you try, involves watching both child's play and adult play and then comparing the two. First locate a spot where children congregate regularly to play in your community. This may be a school or preschool playground, where children appear at scheduled times. It may be a favorite after-school playspot, such as an empty field or someone's backyard. For the purposes of the exercise, it does not matter whether this is a school space, empty field space, or back-yard space. The spontaneity of the play will be the same. To enter school or backyard space, however, you will need permission. So when you have chosen the time of day and the space in which you want to observe children at play, by all means obtain permission from gate-keeping adults if necessary.

You will want to keep sufficient distance from the children you are watching, so you are not intruding on their play. If they notice you and seem to want to interact with you, respond to their advances in a friendly way but make clear that you prefer to watch, not play. Children are used to "watchers," including other children. Watch for at least 30 minutes, if possible. During this time, play activity may change character, theme, and players several times. Record all changes. Watch carefully what goes on. Details are important. Where are the boundaries of the play space? What roles are children playing? How is "role assignment" handled? What are the rules of the play? What kinds of object transformations are going on in order to make the setting appropriate for their play? (Remember that in "let's pretend" nothing is as it appears to be.) What happens if someone breaks the rules, violates the "pretend"? Have pad and pencil handy and write down what individual children are actually doing. (Try to be close enough so you can hear what they are saying as well.) You will be observing a miniature social order created by children.

As soon as you leave the play area, sit down and write the most complete description you can of everything that you have seen. Try to write it in such a way that other adults not present could visualize the same scene by reading your description. As you reflect on what you have observed, consider how the three modes of knowing enter into play. The cognitive/analytic mode is important for creating the rules of play. The emotional/affective mode enables children to identify with their roles, their "parts." The intuitive mode enables them to make the play action move forward with "let's pretend" consistency without bothering with details of how this world holds together. Note that the world will have its own kind of completeness.

Next, take the opportunity to observe a structured adult play group, such as a team sport, played either in an arena or in a more informal setting. There are likely to be two categories of "people at play": the actual participants and the spectators. Both are "playing." Giving the same attention to detail that you gave to children's play, describe exactly what you see the two groups (participant-players and spectator-players) doing. Note boundaries, roles, rules, the nature of the "let's pretend," and what happens when rules are broken. Again you will want to write down what you have seen so that others can visualize it.

Then study your two sets of descriptions and compare them. To what extent were new patterns invented for the play situation, and to what extent were they ritualized formats? Compare the spontaneity of the two play groups. Compare the operation of the three modes of knowing in the two groups. Finally, reflect on the comparative opportunities for inventiveness of children and adults at play.

Of course, we are comparing two very different types of activities here. We know that most adult play is ritualized, so we don't expect to find the spontaneity and inventiveness of child's play in it. It would be no different if we watched both child and adult play in tribal societies. The change in play behavior is not a phenomenon of industrialization, it is a phenomenon of maturation plus habituation and the defining of social patterns that comes with them. The reason for the exercise is to recapture what play initially was about and to consider under what conditions play might retain more of its inventiveness for adults. Dare we play at the reconstruction of the social order? Dare we play at the development of civic culture, at communication across language and custom barriers? These are questions not to answer, but to explore.

THE PLAY OF THE IMAGINATION IN IMAGING

We have explored several nonconventional ways of using the mind to understand the changing social order. The adding of the emotional/affective and intuitive mental modes to the cognitive/analytic was not in order to insert something into reality that wasn't there, but in order more fully to comprehend the empirical reality itself. This was the goal in the use of metaphor, and it was the goal in the observation of play. We were discovering how empirical realities of the social world are created and maintained. Now we are ready to do something different. We are ready to enter into the active imagining of something that does not yet exist, the dreaming of a world as we would like it to be.

This is a very different kind of activity from that of understanding what already exists. It involves reaching out into that second half of the 200-year present discussed in Chapter 1. Yet it also involves the same three modes of knowing we have been referring to. In this activity the emotional/affective mode becomes primary in enabling us to say what kind of world our deepest feelings about humanity lead us to want. The intuitive also takes over, allowing us to fantasize how such a world might actually look. The cognitive/analytic completes the imaging act by helping us figure out how such a world could work in terms of sustainable institutions.

There are many different kinds of future worlds that could be imagined. We are focusing here on one particular feature of such a future world, primarily because that feature may be crucial to the survival of the human race. We will focus on imagining a world without weapons, a world in which other conflict-management arrangements are functioning and military defense systems are no longer necessary. This kind of imaging is utopian in the fullest sense of the word: picturing the very best we can imagine, even though that best seems totally improbable in an operational sense. Exploring how to delineate the barely imaginable seems an appropriate conclusion to this chapter on the skills of the imagination.[3]

In Chapter 5 we spoke of different kinds of literacies, and particularly referred to the lack of "image literacy" or familiarity with imaging, as a characteristic of industrial societies. Nurturing the capacity to image was suggested as a way out of the trap of apathetic technological dependency. Imaging is not, however, a panacea. Like other human activities, it can generate both goods and bads. Because our biological makeup includes the equipment for imagery, the activity goes on all the time in the human subconscious and sometimes erupts during sleep in terrifying nightmares. We have all imagined disaster and scenes of horror from time to time. There are certainly images of the future that are to be feared, the image of a nuclear holocaust being the most fearful of all. In literature, both utopias and counter-utopias suggest ugly possibilities of reduced individuality and forced conformity "for the public good." Huxley's *Brave New World* (1968) and Orwell's *Nineteen Eighty-Four* (1949) are only too vivid in our imaginations. Neither free-floating, unfocused imaging nor the obedient visualization of the directed imagery of others will help society out of its trap. It is important to understand the distinction between fantasy as pure play, escapist daydreaming, conscious reworking of sleeping dreams, and focused imaging.

Free-Floating Fantasy. Like physical frolic, this is pure play, complete in and of itself. It has no other purpose. While many of our more purposive social constructions derive from it, as Huizinga (1955) has shown, it cannot be deliberately harnessed. It must be let be, encouraged as an end in itself, making us more fully human and better able to do the other things that humans do.

Escapist Daydreaming. This form of fantasy is not pure play because it is used to remove the individual from immediate realities. It creates alternative realities of highly personal nature. These realities may range from the creative to the destructive and may or may not have beneficial effects on the dreamer. This depends on the feedback system that develops between the dream world and the real world.

---

[3]The following material is based on a paper prepared for a United Nations University Symposium on Crisis and Innovation in the Western World (Boulding, 1982a).

Conscious Reworking of Sleeping Dreams.   Our dreams while sleeping are as much our creation as our waking thoughts, but they come from another level of consciousness. Many different therapies make use of the fact that dreams recalled during waking hours give insight into complex interactions of our cognitive, emotional, and intuitive faculties, as they deal with inner conflicts not fully accessible to conscious thoughts. One approach to dream therapy developed by La Berge (1985) and Watkins (1976), among others, involves training people in "lucid dreaming." This develops the awareness of dreaming while dreaming and allows one to intervene in one's own dreams, either in the original moment or immediately after waking, to produce an outcome that leaves the dreamer in control instead of helpless. One important rule in lucid dreaming is that ordinary rules of waking life do not have to be followed. The conscious dreamer may create her own reality. Therapists working with this method hope that lucid dreaming might be extended to help people take charge of their waking social imagery and begin altering outcomes of perceived fearful social futures.

Focused Imaging of Personal/Social Futures.   Focused imaging draws on all the previous types of imaging. The capacity for free-floating fantasy is essential; this as well as practice in daydreaming and acknowledgment of the reality-constructing process at work in night dreaming all help to facilitate focused imaging in the social dimension.

Focused imaging can also be used for personal healing. Readers familiar with such healing therapies will recognize the similarities; focused social imaging can be thought of as a healing therapy for society. A critical feature of both personal and social therapeutic imaging is that the imager must be able to picture some significant details of the well person or the healthy society. The language of therapy, however, is too limiting for the much broader functions of social imaging. The significant aspect of imaging for present considerations is that human beings construct social reality in their minds before they act on external reality. They can do this casually and unconsciously, without ever being fully aware of what they are doing; or they can realize, take responsibility for, and fully participate in what takes shape in their minds.

IMAGING AND THE SOCIAL IMAGINATION

The social imagination can be thought of in many ways. One way to think of it is as a problem-solving faculty. It continually reworks human experience by means of image formation. The more problematic the experience, the more critical the reworking process. Clearly, as Hilgard (1981, p. 10) states, the social imagination involves "futures of richness beyond the mechanics of image formation and memory retrieval." All of the sensory experience of one's lifetime provides the raw materials for the imaging process. This includes not just visual imagery; remembered sound, touch, taste, and smell are all *materia prima* for the imagination.

To get the imaging process going, it helps to ask people to recall childhood scenes or events. There is something about remembering that helps evoke vivid detail. Toffler (1970) confirms that experimental subjects asked to tell stories taking place in the future give less rich and imaginative detail than subjects asked to use the past tense. Yet the future is no more a mental construction than the past. Historians are well aware that when they write of the past they are in fact reconstructing a time that has been described in other ways by other historians. The chief difference between exploring the unknowns of the future and the unknowns of the past is that we feel more insecurity in the face of the unknowns of the future.

People have to be encouraged to image, taught to exercise a capacity that they indeed have but are unaccustomed to using in a disciplined way. The obstacles to imaging lie partly in our social institutions, including schools, which discourage imaging because it leads to visualizing alternatives which challenge existing social arrangements. Other obstacles lie in the minds of a generation grown rusty in the use of capacities that society has not encouraged.

Those capacities can be reengaged. The widespread current interest in meditation techniques in the West offers a starting point. Imaging, like meditation, requires an emptying of the mind, but it also "works in the middle of all senses and puts experience together in a living and breathing object-structure" (Ahsen, 1981, p. 24). Neurophysiological study gives evidence that "imagery unfolds over the same neural substrate as perception and that images represent stages in object formation" (Brown, 1981, p. 26). Images are also sensory experiences, occurring in the mind's eye and ear and on the mind's skin. They are not mental photographs of anything else; they are constructions *sui generis*. Imaging also has the quality of storytelling, of constructing a scenario. What comes through in various attempts to describe imaging is that it has an experiential quality and that the mind is actively engaged in the work of processing experience during imaging. It is indeed work, although work of a very special kind.

In focused social imaging, a person is being asked to engage with a group of colleagues in work on behalf of normatively defined social goals. They begin with agreement on shared social concerns—in this case a shared social concern over the dangers of nuclear war. Each person is then asked to step into a future time, say, 30 years from the present, in which the problem in question has been successfully dealt with.

There is a powerful contradiction between the invitation to enter into the free-flowing inner world of mental imagery, with its evanescent material that defies conventional treatment, and the instruction to see a community in which previously stated goals have been realized. Yet it can be done. The interaction between individual imaging and small-group discussion in which each person describes her own imagery and addresses questions to others about their images gradually brings out more and more details about what this future world is like. Further details emerge from the same inner sensory world from which the original image came. Certain features of this reality begin to take on a compelling character as the imager examines them further. Eventually, a working group develops shared imagery and more and more details are built up. The future has not in any way been determined by this activity. Rather, participants have discovered that they can visualize an alternative possibility for the future.

IMAGING A WORLD WITHOUT WEAPONS

The imaging techniques used in the workshop format to be described here were developed originally by Warren Ziegler, founder of Futures Invention Associates (Ziegler 1982, 1987a, 1987b). They were designed to help organizations and community groups, trapped in apparently unsolvable conflicts, to break out of their deadlocks. Ziegler was strongly influenced by the work of the Dutch sociologist Fred Polak (1955/1972) on the role of societal images of the future in motivating social action toward the realization of envisioned possibilities. Drawing on Polak's work, Ziegler concluded that, if parties in conflict could visualize a future situation in which their conflict had been successfully managed, they would be able to deal with their differences in the present in the light of that perceived future. Ziegler added to the imaging of a desired future the idea of standing in that imagined future and "remembering" how the parties got there. This technique has been repeatedly demonstrated to be effective. Shifting the emphasis from a deadlocked present to a realized future solution seems to release creative search behavior in participants. Part of the secret of the success of this approach lies in the fact that, while parties in conflict visualize different realized futures, there inevitably are enough commonalities in the images to enable the participants to give each other more space, so to speak, and to be willing to work out joint strategies in the present.

The workshop format to be described here applies the general theory of imaging realized solutions to a far more difficult and complex problem: the achievement of a substantially weapons-free world. Ziegler has developed an excellent workbook, entitled *Mindbook for Imaging/Inventing a World Without Weapons* (1987b), which guides participants through a special workshop format on imaging a world without weapons. The workshop itself is difficult and demanding, preferably taking at least two days of group activity, and requires a skilled and experienced leader.[4]

What is offered here is a description of a somewhat simplified and shortened version of the workshop format that I have developed over the past few years on the basis of work with Ziegler in the development of the original World Without Weapons Project. A summary description is included here, while the simplified workshop format itself will be found in Appendix 2. Both the summary and the expanded protocol are intended as background information on how workshops operate, but not as adequate instruments for a self-organized workshop without leadership.

Introduction to the Workshop: Background Information

If we consider the problem of reducing present arms levels, our first thoughts are that there are so many parties in conflict, at so many systems levels, within and between nations and blocs of nations, that overlap in imaged futures between parties to the conflicts seems unlikely. The development of common strategies for achieving any common goals that might be agreed upon seems even less likely. At the same time, it is also true that one of the major obstacles to achieving substantial weapons reduction is that none of the parties concerned, from individual citizens to heads of states, can really picture a viable, sustainable social order that is not secured by

---

[4]Trained leaders who can provide guidance for a regular workshop can be located by contacting the Imaging a World Without Weapons Project at 4722 Baltimore Ave., Philadelphia, PA 19143.

powerful armed forces. This inability to visualize a believable weapons-free world has characterized much of the nuclear freeze movement and most sectors of the peace movement, as it has characterized those with responsibility for governance and for national security.

Since no one can work seriously for an outcome that seems inherently impossible, the unimaginability of a world secured by other social arrangements than those of military establishments stands in the way of serious political moves toward arms reduction, let alone disarmament. Fear of nuclear holocaust, the primary motivator of arms control efforts to date, is a poor stimulus for creative problem solving because fear rigidifies search behavior. Hope, on the other hand, provides an excellent stimulus for problem solving and extends the capacity for search behavior. What imaging realized futures does is to provide hope to social actors involved. This is one universal outcome of imaging workshops, whether held to solve specific community conflicts or to generate scenarios of a disarmed world. The hope itself, however, is not left to hang free, in a useless euphoria. It is immediately anchored to planning strategies in the present.

Until recently, workshops for imaging a world without weapons have primarily been held for groups already motivated to work in the peace movement, with occasional participation by scientists and administrators. While the quality of initial imagery is often high, the analytic work of world construction which must follow the imaging phase is limited by the experience and knowledge of the participants and the range of strategies generated is similarly limited. Since the fantasy mode and the analytic mode are equally important in imaging the future, it has become clear that it is time to involve participants trained in the natural and social sciences, as well as experienced diplomats and government officials. However, the very training in analytic thinking that makes the work of such participants so valuable in the world-construction stage of the workshop is also a barrier to their full entry into the fantasizing process required in the preliminary imaging stage. They will frequently distrust the fantasizing itself. Learning how to honor one's own capacity for fantasy is an achievement in its own right.

The imagery involved in fantasy accesses the coded lifetime store of human sensory experience in a way that the conscious mind cannot evoke. Since the imaging is directed imaging, directed by the desire to discover how a world without weapons would look, the unconscious does its own editing.

Although I am using the words *imaging*, *visualizing*, and *seeing*, imagery is not visual for everyone. There are other ways of constructing fantasy, and individuals must explore and develop their own fantasy bent. The word *reverie* describes this experience for some people. In any case, the quality of the world construction that follows fantasizing depends on the quality of the image fragments evoked in the fantasy mode. This is the input that gives participants something new to work with, rather than merely rearranging familiar ideas and concepts.

Workshop Procedures

While this process can be gone through by an individual alone, it is best done in groups, so that the challenge of integrating others' images into one's own is present. The ideal workshop size is between 20 and 45 persons, although it has been carried out with both smaller and larger groups. It is helpful to do the imaging with an ongoing group that already shares common concerns, so there is an opportunity to develop both a shared image of the future and common action agendas in the present. It is also a valuable experience, however, to do this in a very diverse group with different cultural backgrounds and experiences. The more different the participants' experiences of the past, the more different the ingredients they will contribute to the images of the future.

The workshop is carried out in seven stages, as described briefly here.

1. *The Goal Statement: Checking Out Your Own Hopes for the World.* Because the individual's hopes, wishes, and intentions for the future are so important in directing the imaging, the first task in the workshop is to write out a goal statement about what you would like to see achieved in the social order three decades from now. These are not goals for your personal life, but for society. The goal statement should, by workshop definition, be compatible with an arms-free world.

Note that the future moment chosen is 30 years into the future. This is far enough away for substantial changes to have taken place. The number of independent nations in the world more than doubled in a three-decade space after World War II. At the same time, it is close enough to the present that many of you will be alive at that time and so can feel a personal stake in that future.

Giving yourself permission to state what you would like to see achieved in the future, rather than what can realistically be expected, is generally very difficult. We have all been taught to set a high premium on being realistic. This exercise requires a deliberate setting aside of ordinary notions of the possible and a focus primarily on hopes and wishes. The effort can be treated as a conscious act of disciplining the mind to ignore what it "knows" about reality constraints in the social order.

2. *Exercising the Imagination: Memories.*   This exercise is intended to free up the imaging capacity by having you step into remembered images of the past, in order to experience the type of imaging you will be doing when you move into the future.

3. *Moving into the Future.*   It is the responsibility of the workshop leader to help participants move through the barrier separating the present-present from the future-present. Some can do it easily; others take longer. An exploratory trip and a brief return to the present-present to discuss how it is working are provided for, followed by a 20- to 30-minute stay in the future, observing and recording.

4. *Clarification.*   The experienced imagery becomes clarified through explaining it to others. At this point more can be added to the imagery as each of you checks forward mentally to the future in response to questions by others in the small group in which the clarification takes place.

5. *Consequence Mapping and World Construction.*   Given what you have seen in your explorations of the future-present moment, what kind of world is this? How is it ordered; what institutions function and how? Particularly, how is conflict managed? What has been seen in the imaged visit to the future must now be treated as a set of indicators of the condition of that world and examined analytically in order to create a construct of the social order they hint at. This is at first an individual exercise, although carried out in two- or three-person groups. Once each individual has a clear image, then larger groups are formed, based on common themes. Contrasting or conflicting imagery among participants is a problem that must be dealt with in the same manner as it is in the real world of conflicting perceptions—by negotiation. These world-construction ideas are transferred to newsprint or other paper, using pictures and/or diagrams and schematic representations to indicate how the social order functions. Since the whole social order can hardly be accounted for in the time available, each group will choose major themes based on its own initial input of image fragments, to be developed more fully on the paper.

6. *The Future's History.*   Standing in the future-present moment and looking into the past, you will individually remember how the world got to where you have imagined it. You will work from the future to the past of 30 years ago, in five-year periods. For some of you, watershed events will appear; others will record a gradual change. This exercise should also be repeated in the world-construction teams, going again through the process of negotiating conflicting historical "memories."

7. *Action Planning in the Present.*   The pictured future and the remembered events leading up to it now become the basis for short-term action planning in the present and long-term strategy planning about the future. The difference between the planning we normally do and the same activities in this context is that we now have in a certain sense experienced the future reality of what is being planned for. This gives the wished-for future a quality of "thereness," of authenticity in relation to the human possibility, that adds new dimensions to practical reality testing in the present.

What kind of imagery comes out of these workshops? This varies from individual to individual and group to group. Some are urban and high-technology focused, others rural and "low-tech." All have managed to reduce violence within and between societies. The most common themes across different specific images are those of localism, egalitarianism, and lack of hierarchy. Most workshop participants see some form of world cooperation that does not erode localism. Some see a gradual development of a new consciousness; sudden transformation themes are rare.

Many imagers visualize some form of catastrophe, big enough to shake people into new learning but not so big as to destroy whole populations. What is most important about the workshop experience is that participants feel empowered by their own imagery. It is a gift they have given themselves, and it generates new energy for action in the present.

Not everyone can enter into imaging a positive future as these workshops require, because they feel too much despair. Joanna Macy has developed a different type of workshop that deals specifically with despair and with releasing the power for positive imaging of the future. Her *Despair and Personal Power in the Nuclear Age* (1983a) is strongly recommended to those who are overwhelmed by fear of the future.

DOES THE SOCIAL IMAGINATION CHANGE THE FUTURE?

In this chapter we have focused on the social imagination—the capacity to visualize the present in fresh ways and to visualize the not-yet in positive ways, in order to release society from the paralysis induced by technological dependency and the fear of nuclear war. Can we change the future by acts of the imagination? History, as Polak (1955/1972) tells us, can be read as just such a succession of acts of the imagination, subsequently inspiring social action in the direction of the imagined.

Just how does this process work? At any moment, there are hundreds of images of possible futures being generated within each society, and thousands for the planet as a whole. In any cultural epoch, only certain images of the future out of that much wider pool develop enough cultural resonance to affect the course of events. There is a selective empowerment of certain images, which "explode" later, like time bombs, into the realized future. The images of ideal island societies providing for the welfare of all their inhabitants, coming out of literature inspired by the fifteenth- and sixteenth-century voyages of discovery, created such a time bomb for modern society, producing the completely new phenomenon of the welfare state in the West.

We can never know which images are going to take hold in the future, but we know something about the conditions that generate creative imagery. Freedom of movement, participation in communication networks that make one aware of the world's diversity, and literacy in several languages all help generate imagery. Free time for daydreaming and reflection is important. Living with manageable rates of social change, instead of being swamped with continual crises, is important. A continual sense of crisis cripples the social imagination. This is supported by Toynbee's (1934/1972) challenge-and response theory of history, which proposes that some experience of change is necessary, while too much is bad.

A pluralistic society generates more imagery than an authoritarian one. A general social environment that encourages broad-ranging exploration of uncharted territory, not merely innovation, is a good environment for generating creative social imagery. Imaging per se is not specifically predictive, nor is it intended to produce immediate blueprints for social planners. Such short-term activities have their own importance, but imaging has to do with the long term. It can, however, provide planners and decision makers in different social sectors with the necessary thought materials for policy development in the present. We have seen how the imaging workshops link fantasizing about the future with action in the present.

All the approaches to the future described in this chapter involve thinking in the cognitive/analytic as well as the emotional/affective and intuitive modes. All involve trying to build linkages between a desired future and the empirical, factual present. Now that we have explored what the imagination can do, it is time to move on to identifiable action skills relevant to working at the transnational level. We will begin with learning how to make specific local-global linkages.

SUGGESTED FURTHER READING

Belenky, M., Blythe, M., Goldberger, N., & Tarule, J. (1986). *Women's ways of knowing: Self, mind and voice*. New York: Basic Books.

Boulding, E. (1978, September–October). The dynamics of imaging futures. *World Future Society Bulletin*, 1–8. Or: (1978). Futuristics and the imaging capacity of the West. In M. Maruyamah & A. Harkins (Eds.), *Cultures of the future*. The Hague: Mouton.

Dewey, J. (1934). *Art as experience*. New York: Minton, Balch and Co.

Gowin, D. B. (1981). *Educating*. Ithaca, NY: Cornell University Press.

Huizinga, J. (1955). *Homo ludens: A study of the play element in culture*. Boston: Beacon Press.

Lovelock, J. E. (1979). *Gaia: A new look at life on Earth*. New York: Oxford University Press.

Macy, J. (1983). *Despair and personal power in the nuclear age*. Philadelphia: New Society Publishers.

Polak, F. (1972). *Image of the future* (abridged ed.) (E. Boulding, Trans. & Abr.). San Francisco: Jossey-Bass/Elsevier.

Toffler, A. (1971). *Future shock*. New York: Bantam Books.

Ziegler, W. (1978). *Mindbook for imaging/inventing a world without weapons* (5th ed.). Denver, CO: Futures Invention Associates, 2260 Fairfax St.

CHAPTER 7

Crafting the Civic Culture Through International Nongovernmental Organizations

In Part I we talked about the different ways the planet can be mapped. Now we want to focus on the development of one particular set of skills related to the mapping of people's associations, or international nongovernmental organizations (INGOs), described in Chapter 3. These are the skills of finding and working with these INGOs, of actually becoming a part of the emergent world civic culture. INGOs, it will be remembered, are transnational voluntary associations covering the whole range of human interests from sports, occupations, civic affairs, science, and commerce, to culture and religion. We have already described what the rise of INGOs has meant in terms of enabling people to pursue common goals across national boundaries. Since this is a continuing process, with new shared interests being discovered and new organizational networks being created every day, it is more important to learn how to find and work with INGOs than to try to count them.

First, we will need to know what the general characteristics of these organizations are, so we will know when we have found one. The following are the criteria used by the Union of International Associations for choosing INGOs to include in the *Yearbook of International Organizations*:

> (a) *Aims*. The aims must be genuinely international in character, with the intention to cover operations in at least three countries. Hence such bodies as the International Action Committee for Safeguarding Nubian Monuments or the Anglo-Swedish Society are excluded. Societies devoted solely to commemorating particular individuals are therefore likewise ineligible.

(*b*) *Members*. There must be individual or collective participation, with full voting rights, from at least three countries. Membership must be open to any appropriately qualified individual or entity in the organization's area of operations. Closed groups are therefore excluded. Voting power must be such that no one national group can control the organization.

(*c*) *Structure*. The Constitution must provide for a formal structure giving members the right periodically to elect governing body and officers. There must be permanent headquarters and provision made for continuity of operation. Hence the exclusion of ad hoc committees or the organizing committee of a single international meeting, though standing committees which link a series of meetings are eligible.

(*d*) *Officers*. The fact that for a given period the officers are all of the same nationality does not necessarily debar the organization, but in this case there should normally be rotation at designated intervals of headquarters and officers among the various member countries.

(*e*) *Finance*. Substantial contributions to the budget must come from at least three countries. Hence the exclusion of the many "international" unions and societies operating in North America on budgets derived almost wholly from the United States members. Foundations are excluded unless their funds derive from three or more countries. There must be no attempt to make profits for distribution to members. This does not exclude organizations which exist in order to help members themselves to make more profits or better their economic situation; but it does exclude international business enterprises, investment houses, cartels.

(*f*) *Relations with other organizations*. Entities organically connected with another organization are not necessarily excluded, but there must be evidence that they lead an independent life and elect their own officers. Internal or subsidiary committees, appointed by and reporting to one of the structural units of a given organization, are excluded.

(*g*) *Activities*. Evidence of current activity must be available; organizations which have given no sign of life during the previous couple of years are treated as dead.

—Institutions primarily concerned to provide education, instruction or training are excluded. [Author's note: Religious missions have been included under a special heading, beginning in the 1980s.]

—Social clubs or forums existing solely to provide entertainment for members are also excluded.

—It will be readily inferred from the foregoing that secret societies and organizations which are not prepared to reveal their aims, membership, structures, etc. cannot qualify for inclusion.

—On the other hand no stipulations are made as to size, whether in terms of number of members or financial strength. No organizations are excluded on political or ideological grounds, nor are fields of interest or activity taken into consideration. The geographical location of headquarters or the terminology used in an organization's name have been likewise held to be irrelevant in the determination of eligibility.

—There are many shades of "internationality." Where, despite the above criteria, borderline cases give evidence of being internationally active then a few exceptions are made. (Union of International Associations, 1972–1973, pp. 15–16.)

While the yearbook gives 21 subject-matter categories for organizations, they can be grouped under six aggregate headings (Feld & Coate, 1976, p. 3): (1) education/communication, (2) religion, (3) social/health, (4) scientific/technical, (5) political, and (6) economic. INGOs can have many different organizational formats, including the "conventional" ones that are universal, as well as those that are intercontinental and regional. There are also confederations of INGOs, and INGOs spun from other INGOs. Special forms like foundations and religious orders have recently been included in special classifications. Whatever their subject-matter orientation or organizational form, there is a strong commonality of overall objectives. Skjelsback (1974), of the Peace Research Institute of Oslo (PRIO), did a study of the objectives of about 2,200 INGOs in 1967. Table 1 summarizes the findings.

Improving communications, promoting cooperation, helping members make contact, working for social and economic development and peace—these are all objectives that further the development of an international civic culture. According to the PRIO study (1967), 70% of the respondents saw their task as extending beyond the confines of their own membership. Information on the growth of various categories of INGOs since 1900 (Feld & Coate, 1976) indicates that the scientific/technical INGOs have grown the most rapidly. The social/health, political, and education/communication categories, in that order, have been the next most rapid expanders. Again, these are areas in which the growth of common civic understanding is very important.

It is important not to overestimate what people's associations can do. Few are rich. Some make excellent use of very limited resources, while others make poor use of rather extensive resources. In examining any particular organization it is useful to look at its structural features: size of paid staff, budget, frequency of membership meetings, number and frequency of publications, interactive links with other organizations, extent of consultative status with UN bodies (there are 16 UN bodies that give consultative status to qualified INGOs), and type and extent of special projects and programs. Per-

TABLE 1:   General INGO Objectives and Methods

Goals	Percent This Goal
To improve communications between members in the specific field of the organization so that they can do a better job	87
To promote general cooperation and friendship between the members .	79
To let members know each other so that they have contacts in other countries for travel, correspondence, etc.	56
To work for social and economic development in the world	51
To improve general cooperation and friendship among all human beings	48
To work for peace among all nations and peoples in the world	45

Source: Werner Feld and Roger Coate (1976). The Role of International Nongovernmental Organizations in World Politics. Learning Resources in International Studies, Learning Package No. 17:5, Table 2.

formance standards have yet to be set for this category of organization, and they are accountable only to their own members. Yet in the emerging world civic culture a framework of accountability may develop that can raise performance standards for weak organizations. In our further examination of INGOs we want to be both critical and constructive, looking to the day when INGOs can fulfill the high ideals associated with their founding. We will begin our exploration of international nongovernmental organizations by looking at personal family and community involvement in them, and then move to an examination of several general categories of INGOs.

STARTING POINT: START WHERE YOU ARE,
WITH WHAT YOU KNOW

Your Family in the World and the World in Your Family

The best way to begin to explore the international nongovernmental civic culture is by finding out your own family involvement in it. Check with family members easily available to you in your own home or by phone, and ask about the international organizations to which they belong. Since they may not be familiar with the INGO concept, you may need to explain to them the type of organizational memberships you are asking about.

Church membership will certainly belong in the INGO category, as will service clubs, the Chamber of Commerce, business and professional organizations, sports associations, the YWCA and YMCA, scouting groups, and so on. Make as complete a list as you can, not forgetting to list your own memberships. Include any that are doubtful; you can always check later on whether or not it is an INGO. Make notes about the level and type of participation experience involved in each membership.

The next step is a trip to the library to look up the organizations on your list in the most recent available volume of the *Yearbook of International Organizations*. (An updated volume appears every two years.) Each organization is listed in two ways in the main index of volume 1 of the yearbook: under the international name of the organization (which will not be the same as the U.S. name) and under key word(s) in the title. Therefore, if you do not find the organization under the name you expect, look it up under one or more key words.

For example, there is the organization you know as the Girl Scouts. The international name is World Association of Girl Guides and Girl Scouts. It is found in the main index under w, for world. It will also be found under the key words *girl guides, girl scouts,* and *scouts*. Each entry gives the same organizational reference number, which is B3469. Open the yearbook to section B (it is divided into sections A through N, according to type of organization) and turn to organization number 3469. There you will find all the information that this organization has reported to the Union of International Associations, including the countries in which it has sections.

You may have difficulty in finding some organizations. Be creative in thinking about key words, read the yearbook supplementary instructions if necessary, and be patient in looking up organizations. The information is there for 20,000 organizations, including intergovernmental organizations and treaty organizations. However, the book has to be used according to its own complex coding system to find the information you want. If some organizations for which you have established family linkage do not provide a listing of their country membership, that is the fault of the reporting organization and you will only be able to find out about national sections by writing to the international headquarters.

Now that you have your list and know how to use the yearbook, you can go as far as you want in your research on your family's INGOs. At the least, you will want to look up the entry for each organization on your list and read its purposes, ways of working, where the international headquarters are, and which countries have sections. If you are interested in a visual representation of your family's international networks you can take a world map outline, color code each organization, and place dots of the appropriate color in each country having a section. This will give you a sense of the extent of the international contacts available to you personally if you wished to ask family members to activate one of their networks to assist you in a project relevant to that organization. If family members have not had occasion to explore the international dimension of their own memberships, this becomes an opportunity to do so. Nearly all INGOs issue an international newsletter from their headquarters, so it is not hard to explore any particular organization's activities. You can get the address of the international headquarters from the yearbook. (Since many INGOs are hard up financially, such inquiries should be accompanied by a return addressed envelope and a universal postal union coupon obtainable from your local post office and exchangeable for stamps in any country.)

The range of subject matters and interests around which INGOs form is very wide. Just reading through a few pages of the yearbook gives you a sense of some of the things your fellow human beings are involved in. If you want to know whether there is a people's association on a certain topic, you can look up the topic in the key-word index. Try to get a sense of the organizations you might personally wish to become involved with, in pursuit of your own international interests. The international headquarters can tell you where the U.S. section office is, if you have no other way of finding out.

The distribution of national sections of an INGO is important in determining the scope of activity available to you as a member. If you are particularly interested in East-West contacts, then you will want to choose organizations that have sections in both the United States and the Soviet Union, as well as in other Eastern European countries. If you are particularly interested in North-South contacts, then you will want to choose organizations that have a substantial membership in countries of the South. If you have strong regional interests, then look for regional INGOs. Later in this chapter suggestions will be made on using the yearbook for networking with people in particular countries.

If you are interested in finding out all the organizations that work on a particular kind of problem (it could be anything—pollution of marine environments, working conditions for journalists in the Third World, help for handicapped persons, or whatever), another book you can turn to is the *Yearbook of World Problems and Human Potential*, also published by the Union of International Associations (1986). It provides cross-referencing on several thousand social problems by type of international agencies and associations involved with each problem, relevant occupations and periodicals, and relevant intellectual disciplines and sciences. It is a new and fascinating kind of handbook for the internationally oriented problem solver.

Your Community in the World and the World in Your Community

This project—your community in the world and the world in your community—originated in Columbus, Ohio (Alger & Hoovler, 1978) and is currently being carried out in a number of American cities. The basic premise behind the project is that individuals and community organizations in local communities are making and carrying out foreign policy every day in the course of their normal transactions. This is because these transactions have international dimensions not always fully recognized or articulated. These dimensions may contribute to the enhancement (or diminution) of social welfare at home and abroad, without ever touching directly on governmental foreign policy transactions. The export and import policies of the businesses in your town may be an important source of international goodwill. The activities of local leadership training programs channeled, for example, through International Rotary, may enhance leadership potentials in Third World countries. The activities of local churches—helping to fund scholarships, leadership training, and development aid programs—are channeled through international church bodies and may directly affect levels of living among Third World poor.

Programs for children and youth, through the local Girl Scouts, Boy Scouts, YWCA, YMCA, and other local organizations with international links, can strongly affect present and future world attitudes and related career choices of young people at home and abroad, through both direct and indirect contact. Similarly, the scientists, students, businesspeople, and public figures from abroad who choose to visit or work in your town for longer or shorter periods of time affect the perceptions and choices made by local residents in relation to their countries or the action arenas they represent.

While sister-city projects and international visitor/host programs carry out their activities with a high level of awareness of their potential for increasing international goodwill, most local activities with international implications are not necessarily perceived as such. However, all of these types of contacts and transactions contribute to the development of alternative ways for human beings as individuals and in groups to help one another across national boundaries. These activities are supplementary to inter-state interactions and may indeed create a stronger climate of cooperation than formal intergovernmental activity is able to do. They are therefore significant to national and international well-being, as well as to the welfare of the local community.

Just as you have explored your family INGO involvement, now you are encouraged to explore your town's involvement. In this case, you may not wish to confine yourself to people's associations, since transactions of the business community are an important part of your town's international relations. However, most of the contacts you discover probably have a people's association involved somewhere. In undertaking this investigation, focus if you wish on special interests—your own, or those of a group you are working with. Special studies can be done of local businesses engaged in international trade, the international contacts of local churches, the international networks of universities, international contacts in sports, and so on.

The purpose of such a project is not only to find out how your community is linked to the larger world but to help increase the awareness of local groups that they are part of such linkage systems and could use them more actively than they do. My own experience of doing such projects in Boulder, Colorado and Hanover, New Hampshire is that community organizations themselves enjoy the new perspectives they get on their activities as a result of interacting with students and/or community investigators in a your-community-in-the-world study. An internship system whereby high-school and college students become international interns in a local organization and help it activate its links with the international structures of which it is a part is one rewarding activity that can be included in such a project.

Most important of all in INGO networking is for individuals to develop a sense of how they can reach out from their local community to participate in matters of global importance. Sometimes that participation operates hierarchically. For example, a local branch of the Womens International League for Peace and Freedom (WILPF) might generate a project for giving teenage girls leadership training that involves conflict-resolution skills. The project could begin at the local level. But suppose the local branch feels this would be a good project to build into WILPF national and international programs, helping WILPF relate more actively to younger women just entering adulthood. After local testing the proposal would travel from the local to the state branch and then to the national section. If approved nationally, it can be forwarded for consideration as a new WILPF international program at its next international congress. The process may take a couple of years, but the result could be a new type of international leadership and conflict-resolution training seminar for young women, carried out by WILPF in a number of locations on different continents.

The participation does not have to travel the hierarchical route, however. The sister-city organizational model now operates in a number of international associations, so that local groups from different countries work together directly. Working with counterpart units, such as between towns, cities, states/provinces, or national capitals, or across continents, is becoming increasingly feasible with ease of travel, telecommunications, and, most recently, computer networking. In this century, a person with an important idea can act directly in the international community, given sufficient energy and knowledge of the communication networks. It can be done through one's nongovernmental association membership by taking an idea to its international level and then being authorized to present it to the appropriate bodies in the UN system. This is done through the device of using the consultative status that many INGOs have with UN bodies.

A nongovernmental organization with consultative status to any UN organ (e.g., UNESCO or UNICEF) may send a representative to attend that body's meetings as an observer. The observer may make interventions, including proposals, by permission of the presiding officer of the body. This is how the UN designed its implementation of the "we, the peoples of the United Nations" theme; hence, people's ideas may come directly to it through people's associations.

Sometimes the ideas of individuals enter the world arena even more directly, although the identity of the individual is usually lost in the process. I have often told the story of how one day in the early 1960s a Kansas housewife had the idea while she was folding laundry that there must be millions of women around the world doing exactly what she was doing. Wouldn't it be fine if all these women could know about each other? And then her thoughts went on to all the other daily maintenance activities of the world that are carried out locally by men and women who are never aware of each other. Her reflections led her to imagine a whole year set aside to celebrate all the cooperative and peace-building things human beings do locally around the world—a year in which international teams of ordinary people would travel from continent to continent, visiting local communities.

On impulse, she picked up the phone to tell her idea to a family friend who was an East Coast international lawyer serving as consultant to several UN delegations. The lawyer was intrigued with the idea and passed it on to a Third World ambassador interested in promoting more programs at the UN involving peaceful cooperation internationally. The upshot of this was a resolution naming 1965 as the International Cooperation Year, which was introduced and passed at the UN General Assembly. Records at the UN and in the annals of many nongovernmental organizations will show that many such teams did travel around the world that year and that many organizations took on new cooperative projects as a result of the naming of the year. Perhaps the most striking thing that happened was a new level of networking among women's organizations. The Kansas housewife and I were active in a women's committee to plan International Cooperation Year activities. It is no accident that 10 years later the International Women's Year and the International Women's Decade came into being, with the first serious international mandate to improve the conditions of life and level of participation of women in public affairs.

There is a similar story behind the founding of the Oxford Committee for Famine Relief (OXFAM), and of a number of other international activities that now provide important services in different parts of the world. We all know small-scale innovators in our own neighborhoods and in fact in our own families. The creative impulse can now travel over many channels and be felt far away. This impulse is neither mysterious nor magical; it is made of the same stuff as our own daily lives. These are the sources of our global civic culture.

A LOOK AT INGO CAPABILITIES

We have already discussed in Chapter 3 some of the things that scientific INGOs have done in relation to the threat of nuclear war. Here we will look at two categories of nongovernmental organizations—religious and women's associations—to get some idea of their aggregate capabilities on the world scene.

Religious INGOs

Generally, when transnational people's networks are considered, it is in terms of the secular networks that provide human services of various kinds, or deal with economic and social development. Transnational religious networks do not receive much public attention, except when they make pronouncements on nuclear war or family planning, partly because they are seen as vestigial institutions from a former era, not relevant in the late twentieth century. Yet if we think in terms of communication channels, religious associations provide the most far-reaching networks available in the modern world. They touch individual hearths in every village of every continent, as well as in every major population center. No other associations have the grassroots capabilities of the local congregations of religious bodies. The fact that the network infrastructures of religious bodies are largely devoted to the maintenance and service of local congregations does not prevent these same infrastructures from carrying some vital parts of the human knowledge stock and of human aspirations for the planet as a whole. Further, the human-development and social-change missions of these congregational structures, historically always present in communities of faith, is translating into social action at an increasing rate. Fundamentalist movements, in the broadest sense, must be seen as part of this increased activity addressed to social issues.

How are communities of faith organized transnationally? The 1972–1973 *Yearbook of International Organizations* listed 232 organizations under the heading "Religion and Ethics." Table 2 shows the distribution of religious faiths in the world population, and the percentage of transnational organizational structures for each faith. It can be seen from the table that, while the Christian denominations have only 26% of the world's population, they have 69% of the religious INGO networks. Islam and Hinduism, each with 13% of the world's population, have only 1% each of the INGO networks. Buddhism, with 8% of the world's population, has also only 1% of the INGO networks. While the number of INGO networks associated with religion has increased dramatically over the past fifteen years, so that the 232 INGOs from the 1972–1973 yearbook have in the 1985–1986 edition become 1,266, the proportion of Christian to non-Christian INGOs has remained the same.

There are discrepancies here that need to be paid attention to, however. Part of the large increase in religious associations stems from a difference in reporting. Instead of the general heading "Re-

TABLE 2: Distribution of Religious Faiths in World Population
and in Transnational Networks*

	Percent World Population	Percent of Transnational Networks
Christian	28.0	69
Protestant	9.0	39
Catholic and Eastern Orthodox	19.0	30
Jewish	0.4	9
Muslim	13.0	1
Zoroastrian	.003	0
Shinto	1.0	0
Taoist	1.0	0
Confucian	9.0	0
Buddhist	8.0	1
Hindu	13.0	1
Other (animist, atheist, humanist, no religion)	25.0	19
Totals	98.5	100

*Data taken from Yearbook of International Organizations, 1972-1973, and Britannica Book of the Year (Encyclopaedia Britannica, 1972).

ligion and Ethics" of 15 years ago, there are now many headings: "General"; "Prayer and Meditation"; "Divination"; "Rites, Rituals and Ceremonies"; "Scriptures"; "Priesthood"; "Pontifical Bodies"; "Orthodox and Patriarchate"; "Churches"; "Monasteries"; "Missions"; "Evangelism"; "Ecumenism"; "Orders"; and "Laity." This means that many of the older Christian networks that predate INGO development are now being recognized as INGOs, and also that much of the new organizational energy of the past two decades has gone into new special-purpose religious associations.

What is missing in this picture is that new organizational energy has also gone into religious associations in Islam, Buddhism, and Hinduism, but because of the differences in traditional organizational practice in the countries of the South, these are not showing up as INGOs. The fact that there are now growing numbers of people in Europe and the Americas who identify themselves as Moslems, Buddhists, or as practitioners of yoga and meditation in one of the Hindu traditions, is not revealed in the INGO statistics. There are six major interfaith nongovernmental organizations.

Are they carrying the whole burden of interfaith dialogue for the 5 billion inhabitants of the planet? No, but there are not enough networks sharing in the task. That leaves a frail infrastructure to communicate diverse and intense convictions about the meanings and purposes ascribed to the created order.

Religious associations highlight all the contradictions of the modern era. Historically, churches have always supported the nation-states in which they have been located in time of war; "holy-war" teachings in all religious traditions help fuel the willingness to go to battle. Yet, side by side with the holy-war tradition is the tradition of the peaceable kingdom, again in all traditions (as we saw in Chapter 1). The peace movement in each community of faith is trying to forge a new praxis appropriate to the nuclear age.

In Judaism, for example, the form of Zionism represented by Martin Buber (1949) involved trying to create a model political community embodying the highest spiritual values of Judaism while practicing a nonviolent, reconciling relationship with Arab brothers as co-tillers of the same soil. The kibbutzim were to be the practical experiments in creating this model society, which was to include a model relationship with Arabs.

In Islam the Sufi way represented an effort to realize more completely the divine origin of humankind through living a life reflective of the creator. Standing against bureaucracy and formalism, Sufism has had a wide appeal in the West as well as within Islam, although it does not lend itself directly to political action. The Baha'i, on the other hand, although treated in Islam as heretics, combine Sufi spirituality with a vigorous practical program of social action to combat injustice and inequality. They have a very strong peace action commitment and have used their Baha'i transnational network vigorously on behalf of the International Year of Peace during 1986. (See Khadduri, 1955, for material on peace and war teachings in Islam.)

Buddhism came into center stage internationally during the Vietnam War, through the courageous public witness of Buddhist nuns and monks (Thich Nat Hanh, 1967). The Buddhist peace witness represents a strong potential for the future, and increasingly Buddhist religious orders have participated in international peace witness events, such as the international nongovernmental contribution to the Second Disarmament Session of the United Nations in 1984. The link between local development and international peace made by social-activist Buddhists will be found reflected in Macy's *Dharma and Development* (1983b).

In Christianity, both a minority wing of Catholicism and the Anabaptist tradition in Protestantism have generated peace activists from the time of the Reformation to the present. (See Bainton, 1960, for a general account of the peace witness in Christianity; and Musto, 1986, for the story of the Catholic peace tradition.) The Catholic Worker Movement has pioneered the combination of serving the poor and witnessing against war. The historic peace churches have consistently opposed wars and war taxes and began the first peace studies programs on college campuses in this century. Every denomination has its peace activist saints—Martin Luther King and Coretta Scott King, Dorothy Day, A. J. Muste, and many others whose names are less well known.

There are some striking examples of mediation by religious bodies in very tense situations. Examples could be given from each denomination. It happens that Quaker mediation has been particularly visible, though not necessarily more important or more successful, than the activities of other churches. Yarrow (1978) has written an important book on Quaker experience with conciliation in post–World War II Europe. The quiet political reconciliation described there continues in an important if undramatic way in the ongoing work of the Quaker Program at the United Nations in New York. These activities can perhaps stand as symbols of what religious networks have to contribute to international civic discourse.

If the peace movement in each community of faith is trying to forge a new praxis appropriate to the nuclear age, common civic discourse between faiths is nevertheless hard to achieve. However, the cooperative activities between communities of faith during the Second Session on Disarmament at the United Nations in New York in 1984 provided an important step in the right direction. The potentials in the infrastructure for developing a common civic discourse would seem to be ideal, given (1) the combination of localist oriented congregations coordinated by authoritative central bodies in most faiths, and (2) the fact that the major faiths are now represented on all continents.

Each faith faces a challenge in this new situation of expanding communities of faith. It will be interesting to see how that necessary common discourse, which respects the diversity of faiths, develops in the coming decades. When Islam, Hinduism, and Buddhism develop their existing networks in more INGO-compatible formats, their presence in the North will seem less exotic and more like a welcome addition to the world community of faith. This can happen without their giving up their highly unique identities.

When the INGO representation of each community of faith more nearly matches the distribution of communities of faith in the world population, the world civic culture will be greatly enriched.

Women's INGOs

Women's international nongovernmental organizations represent a very special category of transnational infrastructure. Women's gradual entry into public life from the middle of the nineteenth century on was not paralleled by an increasing acceptance by men of women in such roles. The momentum of their increasing involvement in public affairs was slowed but not stopped by the unwillingness of men to give up the convenience of always having half the population available for back-up roles, a reserve maintenance force for the species. The concept of women as civic beings, participants in shaping the conditions of their own lives and the life of the body politic, is here to stay.

The world's fairs that played such an important part in the development of INGOs generally, played an equally important part in the development of women's transnational networks. A great International Congress of Women took place at the Chicago World's Fair in 1893. On this occasion women from all continents met for the first time to define publicly the changing nature of social needs in the industrial era and to put to bed the old feudal traditions of women as invisible helpers. A vivid sense of that 1893 congress can be gained by reading Eagle (1895/1974).

Between 1880 and 1900, five international women's organizations were born: the World Young Women's Christian Association, the World Women's Christian Temperance Union, the International Council of Nurses, the General Federation of Women's Clubs, and the International Council of Women. Much of their work, whether from a religious, professional, or humanitarian perspective, was focused on the plight of women and families in rapidly growing urban industrial centers. From 1900 to 1970, most of the growth of women's organizations came in the professional categories, as women set out to use their education and training to "mend the world" in specific ways. By 1970 there were 47 women's INGOs. A parallel development of women's religious orders freed thousands of young women for the reflective life and for social services in nontraditional roles outside the family.

Between 1970 and 1985, women's INGOs have grown from 47 to 189, roughly a fourfold increase. Part of this change comes from a more inclusive listing process, but it chiefly reflects an increasing level of energy being put by women into transnational networking. Unlike the religious INGOs, which continue to reflect the 1970 North-South imbalance today, the women's INGOs are showing more indigenous regional development. Whereas the 47 women's organizations of 1970 were all Eurocentric, the 1985 listing includes 10 all-African women's organizations, 12 Asian, 4 Arab, 1 Buddhist, and 2 that identify themselves as part of the Third World Non-Aligned Movement. One new women's INGO, Sisterhood is Global, has a formula written into its bylaws for insuring that Third World women will have strong proportional representation. The new African, Asian, and Arab organizations represent long-standing traditions of highly effective women's councils in the countries of the South, translated into INGO formats. During this same period women's religious orders (not included under women's organizations) have become increasingly innovative and daring in translating religious teachings into work for social justice and peace in settings where violence and injustice prevail.

It is clear that in the closing decades of this century we are witnessing a very innovative period in the development of participatory mechanisms for women in the public sphere. What have the concerns of women's INGOs been? They can be summarized in three categories:

1. Improving the conditions of women. This involves redistribution of resources toward Third World women and poor women in every society and improvement of education and training, of living and working conditions, of legal status, and of the quality of cultural/spiritual life.
2. Preparation for the participation of women in society. This involves training in leadership, political action and policy skills, peace and justice education, and a general awareness of the nature of public life and the falsity of the boundaries drawn between the domestic and the public arena in civic affairs.
3. The activation of women's perspectives. This includes involving women in creating political, social, and economic change, especially through the creation of international infrastructures enabling women to work collaboratively across national borders on peace and justice issues.

These are not new concerns. They have been the concerns of women's INGOs since the nineteenth century. The United Nations, however, provided a new international public platform for women to pursue these long-standing priorities by declaring the Women's Development Decade from 1975 to 1985. This drew the attention of governments and created the conditions for women's infrastructures to develop with fewer than usual obstacles. We have already mentioned earlier in this chapter the increase of women's involvement in international activity, from the 1960s onward, which culminated in the Women's Development Decade. During the decade itself, 104 out of 137 reporting governments acknowledged authorizing specific bodies to work on the improvement of the status of women. For many countries, this was the first time the status of women had been publicly acknowledged as a civic issue. Of those 104 countries, 71 created special bodies within the government, while the other 33 authorized women's organizations to carry out these duties on behalf of the government. Only 24 countries made no institutional response at all. The 104 countries that made specific provision for women's affairs have made those structures permanent. However weak those channels may be, they are there and available for further development.

The fact is, however, that in spite of the attention focused on women's issues for the decade, only 45 of 167 states and territories have ratified both the United Nations Convention on the Elimination of all Forms of Discrimination Against Women and the International Covenant on Civil and Political Rights. This means that the civic roles of women are still more or less severely restricted in the great majority of countries. The discrepancy between the readiness of women to contribute to the world civic culture and the willingness of society to accept women's participation is great.

Yet change is occurring, and it is occurring from the bottom up. Data from a study conducted for the Women's Development Decade (Boulding, 1982b) indicate that women's political participation is increasing most rapidly at the local level, next at the national level, and most slowly at the international level. This phenomenon is true for the world as a whole. If we imagine political participation of women in the world as a whole as a pyramid, we see women most involved at the base, in local government councils (11%). They are less visible in national parliaments (7.3%) and least visible at the international diplomatic level (4.6%).

When we look at the kinds of INGOs that women have formed in recent decades to deal with their interests, we find the following categories of organizations represented among the 189 women's IN-

GOs listed in the 1985–1986 *Yearbook of International Organizations:*

General civic and public affairs, international understanding	61
Professions and occupations	58
Research, training, and development	35
Religious	28
Sports	7
Total	189

The general civic category includes both the oldest women's organizations, such as the International Federation of Women's Clubs, and the newer Third World women's associations, such as the All Arab Women's Federation and the Pan African Women's Organization. The professional and occupational associations seem to cover almost the whole possible range of occupations, including the Whirly Girls (an association of helicopter pilots) as well as the more staid International Conference of Women Engineers and Scientists. A completely new category compared to 1970 is the large number of women's associations that exist to conduct research and training, usually in a context of concern for an economic and social development that will include women. Examples here are the Association of African Women for Research and Development and the Asian Women's Research and Action Network. Religious associations are still active in significant numbers, but their relative importance in the total spectrum of women's INGOs is declining. Nevertheless, new ones are forming; one is the International Buddhist Women's Center in Sri Lanka. Sports have not disappeared. In addition to the traditional bowling league, there are women's sailing, surfing, and fishing associations, but all with headquarters in the United States.

We need to know more about the functioning of these organizations. A comparative study of women's religious and civic-educational INGOs carried out a decade ago (Boulding, 1976) indicated that only the specifically international relations–oriented INGOs did significant legislative work. With the new theme of legislative equality introduced by the women's decade, probably more organizations carry out legislative activity now. Training and information gathering were surprisingly widespread in 1970, which suggests that the need for the new research and training organizations was already keenly felt at that time.

Comments about network size and program diversity can only be made after a careful inspection of all women's INGO entries in

the most recent yearbooks, a task yet to be undertaken. In 1970 only
a few women's INGOs were large enough to offer substantial program diversity. With the rise of so many more regional INGOs, there
is probably more development of special-purpose programs appropriate to a particular region. The challenge then becomes to have
enough communication between regional networks to keep the sense
of international connectedness alive. Several INGOs that developed
during the Women's Development Decade, such as ISIS International in Rome/Santiago and the International Women's Tribune
Center in New York, are focusing entirely on that interregional networking problem. Considering where women started from at the
beginning of this century, the growth of women's networks, particularly networks that fit the INGO format, is nothing short of phe-
nomenal.

What do women offer to the world's civic culture that women's
INGOs can further strengthen? Based on comparative studies of
men's and women's approaches to problem solving,[1] it can be said
that women offer a nonhierarchical, listening type of culture, and
skills of dialogue and conflict resolution, to replace a culture based
on the ability of the strong to dominate the weak. Generally, women
operate with longer time horizons, are less reactive to crisis situations of the moment, and work harder to maintain relationships over
the longer term, than men. They have more skills of empathy and
therefore can see situations holistically. Because they have lived at
the margins of the public sphere for so long, they are less emotion-
ally invested in existing ways of doing things and can visualize alternative approaches to problems more easily.

Women's skills are social skills, socially acquired, and not genetically based. They are the products of the special environments
in which women have lived for centuries. When brought into the
public sphere, they will interact with men's culture and men's skills
to produce a more listening and peaceable world civic culture. At
least, that is what is to be hoped for.

USING NETWORKS FOR SOCIAL ACTION

Sister-city projects are very popular as transnational networking projects that emphasize local-to-local contact in a global context.

---

[1]The best-known example is Gilligan (1982). Another important book is Belenky et
al. (1986). An early insight into the distinctiveness of women's ways of thinking is
found in Charlotte Perkins Gilman's *Herland* (1916/1979).

It is hard to go from the general idea of contact to meaningful relationships based on common interests, however. Once a sister-city project is in operation, it is relatively easy to mobilize interest on the part of the city council, schools, and churches. Most residents of a community, however, remain uninvolved and do not respond to the opportunity to expand their own transnational identities. One way to increase and enrich the points of contact between sister cities is to consult the Geographic volume (Volume 2) of the current *Yearbook of International Organizations* and photocopy the list of INGOs represented in the country your sister city is in. An inspection of such a list will reveal a whole set of occupational and special-interest INGOs to which many members of your community belong. The next step is to find out which of these INGOs also have a local branch in your sister city. This immediately expands the bases for contact between residents of the two cities.

Let us take the examples of Nicaragua and the Soviet Union. Here are two countries with which we have very tense relationships, but which have also been the foci of efforts to decrease tensions by increasing civic dialogue. Nicaragua happens to have a total of 440 INGOs listed in Volume 2 of the 1985–1986 yearbook. The Soviet Union has a total of 1,098 INGOs in the same volume. INGOs that are easily accessible in the Soviet Union, Nicaragua, and the United States, and widely recognized in all three countries, are the Red Cross, the International Federation of Library Associations, the International Olympic Committee, the International Federation of UN Associations, the World Chess Federation, the International Federation for Game and Wildlife Conservation, and the International Mountain Society (whose international headquarters happen to be in my hometown of Boulder, Colorado). In Nicaragua you will find Amnesty International, the Girl Scouts and Boy Scouts, the JayCees, the Rotary, the Kiwanis, the Lions, and hundreds of professional associations to match those of any American city. In the Soviet Union you will find Amnesty International, the International Red Cross, the International Voluntary Services, the World Student Christian Federation, the Amateur Radio Union, the United Towns Organization, and many more specialized professional associations than a country the size of Nicaragua could support. A wide variety of sports associations will be found in both countries, as well as INGOs related to the artistic and cultural fields. The Soviet Union is very big on Esperanto, and the number of special-focus Esperantist INGOs could have a field day making local contacts.

What is good to remember is that every community with a library can help you get access to the *Yearbook of International Orga-*

nizations, even if only to identify the nearest library that has it. That yearbook is your citizen's guide to the transnational links available to you and your fellow citizens in the world as a whole. It is not just a book for scholars.

SUMMARY

The title of this chapter, "Crafting the Civic Culture," is not meant to imply that INGOs and the world civic culture are one and the same. However, INGOs do represent one of the most accessible parts of the potential domain of a world civic culture, a domain that can be entered and expanded through citizens' participation and where social events can be made to happen. We have defined what INGOs are, structurally and in terms of purposes, given some idea of how they have developed over time, and then provided some suggestions on how to map INGO networks that are relevant to you personally, first through your own family and second through the community in which you live.

Two special categories of INGOs—religious and women's associations—have been discussed, to give an idea of the potential contributions of each to international civic dialogue. Suggestions have been made on how to use INGO networks in sister-city projects with the help of the *Yearbook of International Organizations*. Since INGOs rarely live up to their potentials, an effort has been made not to idealize them, while still leaving a sense of the possibilities for the future inherent in them. Information on inter-INGO liaison groups has only been touched on, although this will become an increasingly important form of activity in the coming decades. The *Yearbook of World Problems and Human Potential* (Union of International Associations, 1986) is an important indicator of collaborative potentials in transnational organizational networks. Starting with any specific problem, it becomes possible to identify any nongovernmental association that has an interest in that problem and thus to establish new interconnecting communication channels between associations.

Already-existing coalitions affect United Nations programs. UNESCO, for example, has 546 people's associations relating to it through some form of consultative status. These organizations meet annually as a liaison body to make program recommendations to UNESCO. Whether or not there is a Second UN Assembly of INGOs, people's associations are bound to affect the future development of the international community profoundly. However, since the strength is in their grass roots, too much emphasis on high-level coordination may detract from what they can do best. In the meantime, local involvement in the nongovernmental organizations that reflect one's own life priorities, and awareness of and participation in the international dimensions of those organizations, is one of the best ways to make concrete events happen, thus contributing to the long-run development of the world civic culture.

SUGGESTED FURTHER READING

Alger, C., & Hoovler, D. (1978). *You and your community in the world.* Columbus, OH: Consortium for International Studies Education, Ohio State University.

Boulding, E. (1977). *Women in the twentieth century world.* New York: John Wiley.

Bussey, G., & Tims, M. (1965). *The Womens International League for Peace and Freedom, 1915–1965: A record of fifty years' work.* London: Allen and Unwin. *Or:* The history of any INGO that interests you. The reference librarian in your local library can help you find the history you want. Most INGOs, once they have reached 25 years of age, prepare histories.

Feld, W., & Coate, R. (1976). *The role of international nongovernmental organizations in world politics.* Learning Package No. 7. New York: Learning Resources in International Studies.

Gilligan, C. (1982). *In a different voice.* Cambridge, MA: Harvard University Press.

Keohane, R., & Nye, J. (1970). *Transnational relations and world politics.* (Part II, pp. 93–168). Cambridge, MA: Harvard University Press.

Union of International Associations. (1986). *Yearbook of World Problems and Human Potential.* London: K. G. Saur.

Yarrow, C. H. (1978). *Quaker Experiences in International Conciliation.* New Haven, CT: Yale University Press.

CHAPTER 8

Peace Praxis:
The Craft and Skills
of Doing Peace

There are several ways to think about the conflicts that sometimes seem to threaten to engulf our world. One is to focus on the integrative achievements of the modern world and to see it as containing islands of stable peace (i.e., not-war) which are spreading out from Euro-North America to the rest of the world. This view has been eloquently stated by Kenneth Boulding (1978). Another, associated with the Marxist perspective, is to focus on the conflicts of interest that arise between the haves and the have-nots. These conflicts will be found on all continents—in the North, in the South, and between North and South. In that view, peace is a condition of distributive justice achieved through a long and painful dialectical process of class struggle.

A third way, which I propose, is to see peace processes—those activities in which conflict is dealt with in an integrative mode—as choices that lie at the heart of all human interaction. Each of us comes into the world as a unique individual with unique perceptions, needs, and interests; yet each of us finds ourself surrounded by others with different perceptions, needs, and interests. In that differentness lies threat to the self. Yet we also come into the world needing the other, dependent on the other for nurturance, feeling a common bond of unity with the other in our humanness, in our need, and even in our isolation from each other. We are social beings and cannot find completeness alone. How we deal with the tensions between the two conflicting needs determines whether we are "peace makers" or "war makers."

"DOING PEACE" IN THE MIDST OF CONFLICT

Gary Cox (1986) has pointed out that, while we use the word "war" in a verb form (to war on evil, for example), "peace" does not have a verb form. We cannot "peace" on an adversary. "We think of war as an activity in which people can purposefully engage. It is something soldiers can learn how to do. In contrast, we think of peace as a kind of condition or state which is achieved or simply occurs. Unlike warring, peace is not thought to be something we can do" (p. 9).

We do have the terms *making peace* and *peace maker*, but these still carry the connotation that, after the making, there is an achieved state of peace. The term *peace activist* also has the connotation of acting on behalf of a desired condition. (*Peace activator* might come closer to what we want to say.) We will use all these terms interchangeably, with the understanding that the meaning we assign has to do with action.

If we accept that there is a potential conflictual element in all human interaction, then doing peace is one of the ways we deal with the ubiquity of conflict. Unfortunately we live in a society that places a high value on dealing with conflict as something that has to be won. The goal is to vanquish the adversary, or at the least successfully to threaten (deter) the adversary. Yet we all know there are other ways of dealing with conflicts. These ways of managing conflict may be thought of as ranging on a conflict continuum, as in Figure 2. At

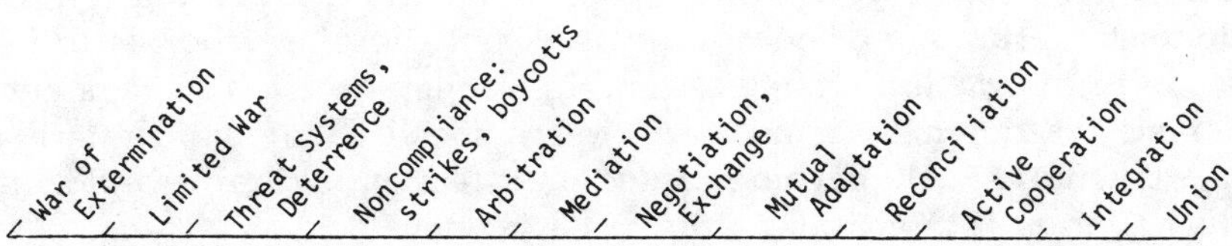

FIGURE 2. The Conflict Management Continuum

one end of the continuum is the war of extermination; at the other is integration/union. The continuum moves from violence to non-violence, from destructive to integrative behavior, from left to right. Limited war, deterrence, and threat are all on the violence side of the continuum. Noncompliance, arbitration, mediation, and negotiation lie in a violence-neutral middle region; and reconciliation, active cooperation, and integration/union lie on the positive, nonviolence side.

There is a paradox in how social behavior ranges itself on this continuum. In international relations we rely heavily on threat and even limited war in dealing with our adversaries, and we quarrel with our allies over how threat is to be applied. To be willing to negotiate with the adversary is to be seen as weak. There is only one acceptable outcome to the conflict: for our side to win. In sports the same is true. A "draw" is not considered a satisfactory outcome of an athletic contest.

Yet, while business firms sometimes try to obliterate each other, on the whole most of our economic affairs are conducted in the violence-neutral zone ranging from noncompliance to negotiation on the continuum. So is much of government activity and politics, and of protest movements. Strikes and compulsory arbitration are the most conflictual of the middle-zone interactions. Third-party mediation and direct negotiation are the most positive. Winning is less important than working out a deal that satisfies both parties.

Once we move to mutual adaptation, reconciliation, and active cooperation/integration we are dealing with the positive "doing-peace" behaviors. Here there is a strong normative commitment to a win/win outcome. Everybody is to be better off. We are in the domain of peace movements and constructive public leadership.

The paradox in our conflict-management behavior is that the same people may be fixated on the threat mode in international relations and yet be very skillful negotiators and even reconcilers in domestic situations. They do not see that there are choices to be made in interaction strategies. Foreign policy decision makers and sometimes business firms, and violent social change and guerilla movements as well, become fixated on threat and winning and conduct all their interactions in the threat mode.

An ideal view of social process over the long term and one that fits Kenneth Boulding's (1978) "spreading islands of stable peace" concept, would be to move more and more of our social behaviors, personally, domestically, and internationally, from the violence side of the continuum to the violence-neutral and the positive nonvio-

lence side. What we have going for us as a species is that most of
our daily behavior is already on the violence-neutral side, and some
of our behavior is even now toward the positive, nonviolence or integrative end of the continuum. We already know a lot about "doing
peace."

If we stop to think about it, we will realize that we negotiate our
way through our daily lives from the moment we wake up in the
morning until the time we go to bed at night. No one ever wants to
do things just the way we do; others' interests rarely coincide exactly with ours. So we begin negotiating in the family: who gets into
the bathroom first in the morning, who gets the hot water (most
families still have to choose between morning laundry and morning
showers), and who gets which section of the morning newspaper.
At breakfast there may be negotiations on the use of cars for the day
and on how to spend the evening. At work we negotiate with our
colleagues on how to organize work schedules, handle difficult cus-
tomers, allocate interdepartmental budgets, and deal with all the
dozens of other problems that come up in a normal working day. In
our civic organizations we negotiate how much time we will give to
volunteer work. In our recreation we negotiate with family and
friends about where to go for dinner, what movies to see, what TV
show to watch, where to go on a vacation. Every event becomes a
subject for negotiation. (For a useful perspective on the centrality of
negotiation to everyday life, see Straus, 1978.)

In a sense, then, we all have negotiation skills—some more than
others. We all know people with whom it is easy to negotiate and
others with whom it is almost impossible. But we do it. These stable islands of peace may of course be jarred by eruptions of violence. Researchers are finding out that more violence takes place
within families than was ever dreamed of (Straus, Gelles, & Steinmetz, 1980). Urban areas, particularly when there are conflictual racial and ethnic relations, and boomtowns, with great influxes of
newcomers who are all strangers to each other, also may experience
fairly visible levels of violence. Nevertheless, violence in family and
community settings is more the exception than the rule. On the other
hand, the fact that we have to continually engage in negotiation to
get through our days reminds us of the ubiquity of the conflict potential in human affairs. If we didn't negotiate, there would be much
more violence than there now is.

Our shock when we hear of terrorist acts is an indicator of how
strong our expectations of peaceful interaction in the public sphere
are. Terrorist activity is a particularly striking example of the con-

flict between human bonding and separation impulses. Terrorists are generally motivated by high ideals, a passionate sense of the wrongs done to their people, and a longing to right those wrongs. They are also motivated by fury against those they see as preventing the righting of wrongs.[1] Palestinians, Irish nationalists, Sikh and Basque separatists, Shiite fundamentalists, and in the 1970s the Weathermen Underground in the United States are all examples. Sometimes terrorism is simply the random pathological cruelty of diseased people, but more generally an ideal or goal can be identified.

To the outside observer, there may seem to be little connection between perceived wrongs and the tactics used to right them, but the terrorist willing to die for her people (and not a few terrorists are women) is certainly expressing an intense bonding impulse. The tragedy here is that the middle ground where negotiation can take place may have been so long left uncultivated that the mutual learning needed to get to the point where the adversaries can shift to nonviolent interaction is difficult to achieve. Everything has to start "from scratch." Yet even in the most apparently bleak situations some common ground of civic discourse remains. It should not be forgotten that low-key negotiations are in fact taking place continually on behalf of the adversaries in each of the cases involving terrorism just mentioned, by neutrals who wish both sides well. To expand this neutral ground and increase the amount of dialogue is one of the greatest challenges to the peace maker today.

A very different type of violence, which has been much analyzed in recent years and does not easily fit the conflict-management continuum, is structural violence. This concept, developed by the Norwegian sociologist Johan Galtung (1969, 1980), addresses the structured maldistribution of resources that causes the infants of the poor to die of malnutrition, that keeps minorities in ghetto areas living in unsafe houses with no access to schools and jobs, and that keeps whole countries in a state of poverty. The fact that most peace movements now think of themselves as peace-and-justice movements indicates how seriously peace movements take this type of violence. Addressing it is a very important part of "doing peace."

The ubiquity of conflict leads us all to experience both an internal and an external struggle over dealing with it. Inwardly we experience conflicting impulses either to express our own individuality

---

[1] Insight into the complex states of mind and social motivations of terrorists can be gained from reading the powerful novels of Herrick (1981, 1983). Also, striking descriptions of terrorism in prerevolutionary Russia can be found in Broido (1977).

and differentness or to identify with others, to bond with them. This internal struggle with conflicting impulses translates to our external behavior with other people. There have been arguments about whether women or men have the stronger bonding impulse (the "male bond" versus "sisterhood"). There have also been arguments about whether women or men have the greater capacity for violence (males fight wars, females will kill to defend their young). While socialization practices in most societies encourage aggression in men and gentleness in women, there doesn't seem to be much doubt that genetically both women and men are capable of both very violent and very gentle behavior.

To what conclusions does this line of argument lead? It leads to the understanding that peace making is learned behavior. Negotiation is a skill. Societies that don't expend attention on teaching the skills of negotiation and peace making are by default vulnerable to outbreaks of violence in their midst. Furthermore, the skills of international negotiation do not exist in a vacuum. They depend on experience built up at other levels of interaction, beginning with the family. But cultural forms of expression differ, so one style of negotiation is not easily transferred to another culture. The American business community has learned this to its cost in trying to negotiate business deals with Japan.

This is why nongovernmental organizations are so important, why the United Nations itself is so important. Both INGOs and the UN provide arenas where a common discourse can evolve that will be understood by individuals coming out of different cultures. Barkun (1968) pointed out some time ago that the behavioral underpinnings for peaceable negotiation with potential adversaries are only developed through repeated interaction which renders each more predictable to the other. Some shared knowledge has to develop between adversaries for negotiation to be possible. Tribal societies achieve a certain level of peaceableness with their neighbors, based on the degree of familiarity that exists between them, even though there are no overarching political structures, no authorities or courts to invoke. We in the United States have only the beginnings of familiarity with most of the world's nations.

Chadwick Alger (1968) observed in the early days of the United Nations how much social learning took place in international committees and working groups at the UN. That process still goes on, except for those who choose to close their eyes and ears and not learn. The same type of learning goes on every time an INGO holds an international congress. Because decisions have to be arrived at and resolutions passed, people learn how to listen to one another, to dialogue, and to achieve some type of mutually acceptable outcomes in the business at hand. I will not soon forget sitting in session with the International Executive Committee of the Womens International League for Peace and Freedom during Israel's Six Days War, with both a Lebanese Palestinian and an Israeli member present. There had to be a dialogue that could insure the continuing existence of WILPF as a peace-making body. We didn't solve the problem of the war, but we kept the channels open. The United Nations is almost perpetually in that situation. It somehow continues to exist, continues to keep channels open.

From the perspective of this book, it is important to acknowledge two universals: the universal of conflict and the universal of the bonding impulse. Even more important is to acknowledge the core fact that peace has continually to be made, moment by moment, in the course of the daily affairs of women, men, and states. Peace never exists as a condition, only as a process. Before we look at some of the processes and settings in which peace making can go on at the international level, we will look at our personal management of conflict. Behavior begins with the behaving individual.

THE INDIVIDUAL AS PEACE MAKER

If conflict potentials characterize our own daily interaction experiences, it is important to examine ourselves as peace doers. If peace making is a skill, there is a craft, a set of disciplines to be learned. Do we have a personal commitment to acquiring those skills? Do we have a personal commitment to multiplying the "goodness" factor in human beings, including ourselves? A sense of the best that is possible for humans, and a willingness to "center down" inwardly and be in touch with that best would seem to be required. A capacity for detachment from the passions of the moment, for putting the bridle on impulsive responses and waiting to get the whole picture, for thinking ahead to what tomorrow might bring of relevance to this situation, is important. Also needed is a special kind of keen observation with eyes and ears so as not to miss any cues, and the ability to use the imagination to "walk in the other's moccasins," as the indigenous peoples of this country say. Mirroring back to others what one understands of a conflict situation— gently, carefully, in a way empowering to a potential adversary—is perhaps the hardest skill of all to learn. Practice is needed, and no potential conflict situation is too trivial for trying out one's skills. Since negotiation situations arise all the time anyway, we can either step into them unthinkingly or we can try to practice the very best we know.

Example teaches more than concepts, and Martin Buber has long represented my own ideal of what a peace maker does. He exemplified in his own life that difficult struggle between withdrawal into separateness and bonding with the other as he moved between mystical experiences and the impossibly demanding task of peace making between his fellow Jews and his fellow Arabs. I think of Buber as a craftsperson-saint, crafting the relationships between person and person, firming up a network of human connectedness in faithfulness to his spiritual calling. His understanding and practice of I-Thou relationships in the human sphere lay at the core of his peace doing.[2]

What is the I-Thou relationship? In the I-Thou relationship we stand in openness before the Other (any other with whom we have to do) and let that Other be in all their wholeness and uniqueness. We may not measure, define, or utilize the other person. We may only relate. We *meet* the other person. The event of meeting lies in the betweenness, in the space that must reverently be left there, between one being and another. The act of meeting also becomes the act of making peace with another.

To see Buber address an audience on a university campus as I did in the 1950s, and to feel that each of us sitting in that audience was a Thou; to see him bring postlecture questioners up to face him on the stage and put their questions to him under that steady, penetrating regard; and to feel answered by the very expectancy of his own expression are unforgettable experiences. That same quality of meeting the Other he brought to even the most tense political discussions and community conflicts. He carried it to Germany when in an ultimate act of meeting God in the Other he accepted a peace prize from the German Association of Book Publishers after World War II, speaking frankly but lovingly of how hard it was to do this, and how necessary.

Buber often spoke of the narrow rocky ridge that humans have to walk in order to balance the I-It, the world of objects to be ana-

---

[2]Buber's teachings on relationship are found in *Between Man and Man* (1947) and *I and Thou* (1958). His applications of those teachings to the conflicts involved in social change are found in *Paths in Utopia* (1949). A biography of Buber that puts his extraordinary life in perspective is Friedman (1960).

lyzed and utilized, and the I-Thou, the world of the creative divine-human potential. His views of peace making were of an evolutionary process of continuous inward spiraling as humankind ascends toward the good; first swerving away in bursts of I-It activities of conquest and exploitation, then returning toward the good in a repentant rediscovery of the meeting with Thou, the Other. The spiral has a direction, the swings are not meaningless, and we come closer to the goal as we learn to be better craftworkers. Developing the tools for redistributive justice, the institutions of conflict resolution, and the skills of mediation will do us no good, however, unless we continually remember to stand back and affirm the Other in that with which we work, in those with whom we work. Buber's teachings about peace doing, which evolved under conditions of violence, hatred, and passion, will stand through the centuries. Buber is indeed an island of stable peace.

And how do we work at our own task of becoming peace doers? For some years now, I have used an assignment devised by Paul Wehr (1979), under the title "Personal Conflict Impact Essay," to help students get a better understanding of the often unconscious processes of conflict and conflict resolution in their own life experience. This understanding is an essential precondition for growth in the craft skills of peace doing. I reproduce it here, in Figure 3, encouraging the reader to reflect on and respond to these questions.

PEACE PRAXIS AS INTEGRATION OF THOUGHT AND ACTION

Peace making is situational. It happens in settings and follows patterns. We will look at peace praxis in three types of settings: at the negotiation table, in swords-into-plowshares demonstrations at symbolic public sites, and in political zones declared as zones of peace.

Records of sitting down at the negotiation table go back as far as the records of states, but state investments in diplomatic capability have varied enormously from era to era. In fact, diplomacy is often seen as part of the military capability. Histories of diplomacy focusing on successful negotiations, agreements pacifically arrived at, and wars not fought are few and far between. With the current threat of nuclear war, however, there has been renewed interest, particularly in the private sector, in strengthening the negotiation skills of governments.

A pioneer in experimenting with facilitated problem solving in

FIGURE 3: Personal Conflict Impact Essay

    Produce a five-page essay in which you discuss the role of con-
flict and conflict regulation in your personal life experience. Some
questions you might respond to are:

1. With whom have you been most in conflict at various points of
   your life?
2. Over what issues?
3. How did conflictual behavior affect you?
4. How do members of your family and your family as a group deal
   with conflict?
5. What devices or skills have you developed to regulate and
   resolve conflict?
6. Have you had direct, personal exposure to violence? If so,
   in what forms?
7. How do you view conflict? As unhealthy? Natural?

Source: Paul Wehr, 1979, Conflict Regulation. Boulder, CO: Westview
Press, p. 184.

international disputes is John Burton, whose own apprenticeship as
a peace maker began in the foreign ministry of Australia. As a minister he was able to facilitate resolution of long-standing conflicts
between Malaysia and Indonesia. He has developed an international facilitation process which brings governmental representatives and private individuals together from each side of a dispute,
in a format that is sometimes referred to as Second Track Diplomacy, since it is parallel to and facilitative of more official negotiations on the same subject (Burton, 1982, 1984). Because the emphasis
in this facilitation process is on having each side give full expression to its perceptions and interests in a supportive, off-the-record
setting, parties with serious objective conflicts have been enabled
to arrive at settlements that give satisfactory allowance for the interests of each side.

    The approach involves rejecting the win/lose or zero-sum game
mentality in which only one party emerges the gainer. Burton (1982)
emphasizes the importance of respecting the adversary and giving a
full measure of that respect in the interaction situation, thus avoiding the status insecurities that so often bedevil negotiations. The
joint public/private and official/unofficial status of the interactions,
with the involvement of concerned and competent citizens groups,
is another special feature of the Burton approach.

    Roger Fisher's technique of principled negotiation (Fisher & Ury,
1981) takes a similar win/win approach with a focus on mutual gain,

but it uses a more strategic technique involving tactical analysis of the moves in the game of negotiation. Using completely different styles, both have a track record of success. The International Peace Academy, drawing on the experience of former commanders in the UN peace-keeping forces and on the research of the scholarly community in training mediators at the professional foreign service level, trains negotiators from various countries in a workshop format that allows for application of several win/win approaches, with an admixture of more traditional diplomacy.

The future of win/win negotiations looks relatively bright, with the amount of attention focused on the new approaches. The Conference on Conflict Resolution and Peacemaking, housed at George Mason University in Fairfax, Virginia, has evolved over the past several years into a federation of groups working at dispute settlement at every level from family to inter-state dispute. It guarantees both a constituency and a growing pool of trained negotiators who can move this important new diplomatic development further along. Furthermore, governments are coming to scholars for help. Gene Sharp, one of the originators along with Adam Roberts (1969) of the concept of alternative defense, developed the term *transarmament* to refer to "the process of changing over from a military system to a civilian-based defense system" (Sharp, 1985, p. 67).[3] He developed the alternative defense concept based on his studies of occupied countries in Europe during World War II and is now under contract to a number of European governments to do feasibility studies on alternative defense systems. The founding by governments of peace institutes and peace chairs at universities[4] gives further legitimacy to this movement. Although the interest in alternative defense and security policies and in civilian-based defense is most pronounced in Europe and the Third World, it is also present in the United States. An excellent overview of the field from the North American perspective is found in Stephenson (1982).

Civilian-based defense at the local level may be thought of as something like a domestic peace corps organized on a community basis but involving all local inhabitants. Training in meeting all the

---

[3]Sharp recently pointed out to Kenneth Boulding that it was Boulding who first used the term *transarmament*, in a pamphlet, *Paths of Glory, A New Way with War*, published in 1938 by the John Horniman Quaker Trust in Scotland. Boulding himself had completely forgotten this.

[4]These include the Stockholm International Peace Research Institute, the Canadian Institute for International Peace and Security, the U.S. National Institute of Peace, the Australian National University Peace Institute, and the Netherlands government-funded peace professorships.

unmet needs of their own community and in developing self-help
networks and local self-sufficiency is provided, in addition to preparation of people for systematic noncompliance with alien authorities. On a larger scale, alternative security initiatives like the
Contadora Group in Latin America and the Five-Continent Initiative, created and carried out by heads of state, are all directed at
ending the arms race and replacing military threat with political negotiation.

The Five-Continent Initiative is an interesting example of a new
fluidity of boundaries between governmental and nongovernmental
initiatives. The six heads of state who began the Five-Continent Initiative—the presidents of Argentina, Mexico, and Tanzania and the
prime ministers of India, Sweden, and Greece—personally visited
other heads of state, including those of the two superpowers. Initially, in 1984, they were calling for a halt to the arms race. More
specifically, in 1985, they carried the message of the Delhi Declaration, calling for an all-embracing halt to the testing, production, and
deployment of nuclear weapons and their delivery systems. In response a new INGO called Parliamentarians for Global Action, with
over 600 members from the parliaments of 36 countries, was formed
to support this initiative. The new INGO was in turn supported by
existing peace organizations in all regions. Peace organizations have
increasingly developed the concept of citizens' diplomatic initiatives, or "citizen summitry" (Carlson & Comstock, 1986; *Nuclear
Times*, 1986). This coalition of governmental and nongovernmental
groups on behalf of an alternative security system is a new phenomenon. (See Vol. 1, No. 1 of the Bulletin of Municipal Foreign
Policy, 1986–1987, published by the Center for Innovative Diplomacy.)

Each of these sectors, and also the new generation of peace researchers and conflict-resolution professionals, will all play an important role in spelling out just what forms alternative defense might
take. It is important to note that many of these governmental figures, scholars, practitioners, and trainers all know one another. There
are alternative security and defense networks spanning all continents now.[5] This, too, is part of the emerging world civic culture.
Let's look at how some of their ideas are being translated into action.

---

[5]The *International Peace Research Newsletter* reports on many current developments.
A specialized international newsletter called *NOD (NonOffensive Defense)* is published at the Center for Peace and Conflict Research at the University of Copen-
hagen. Another newsletter, *Civilian-Based Defense*, is published by the Association for
Transarmament Studies in Omaha, Nebraska.

Nonviolent Public Action for Change

Mohandas Gandhi electrified the world when he led a mass nonviolent public march to the sea on March 12, 1931 in protest against the oppressive British Salt Tax. This was a manifestation of the idea of Satyagraha, the practice of using the force of truth to transform unjust and oppressive laws and institutions, thus replacing violence with an active nonviolence. It had been born, however, in Gandhi's mind in a South African jail three decades before, so the practice had thus already evolved through a series of campaigns in the intervening decades. Because theories of nonviolence have filled many books, it is important to realize that the praxis, the actual experiments with the power of truth, for Gandhi, was what developed the theory. He was a peace-doer.

Mass public demonstrations against injustice were nothing new in history, nor was the practice of noncooperation in the face of unjust authority, as Sharp's monumental historical study (1973) shows. But mass public demonstrations carried out in a disciplined and highly intentional way, on behalf of specific social changes, in the context of a vision of what the future social order might be like, and with a concern for the ultimate well-being of the oppressor as well as the oppressed in the new social order—this was new. This was Gandhi's contribution to the civic culture of the modern world.[6]

Satyagraha is a public art, carried out in public spaces on behalf of the polity as a whole. When Martin Luther King, Jr. adopted Satyagraha in his campaigns of civil disobedience in the South of the United States, rather than a strategy of violent protest, it was because he accepted this new element in the civic culture and accepted responsibility for white oppressors as well as for the black oppressed. Because of the continuing concern for inclusiveness, for bringing the whole society into the process of growth and change, each Satyagraha action lays the foundation for the next, but only when it is done with care both for the spirit of truth and for sound strategy that takes account of the situation and state of mind of the adversary. Continued communication with the adversary is an essential part of nonviolent action. When Satyagraha campaigns disintegrate into chaos or simply peter out, as they sometimes do, it is because these principles have not been observed. Gandhi learned

---

[6]The best source for understanding Gandhi's philosophy and strategy of Satyagraha remains Joan Bondurant's *Conquest of Violence* (1965). Gandhi's autobiography (1948) gives his own perspective on how he worked.

over and over again from his own failures about the importance of the key factors of training and self-discipline, of carefully executed strategy, and of continued communication with the public and the adversary.

The claiming of public space for carrying out nonviolent action against war has been one of the important methods of peace action since the early 1960s. Public nonviolence is always symbolic. One particular place is chosen for action because it symbolizes the evil that is to be done away with. The way of doing the action also symbolizes the character of the hoped-for future social order. This is very important.

Some examples from the peace actions of the past decade include the periodic occupations of the original testing ground for nuclear explosions in Nevada, which take place as a continuing reminder of the genesis of our nuclear war policy. They are carried out in a peaceful and hopeful spirit, always pointing to the positive choices that still lie ahead for the United States in terms of abolition of nuclear weapons. Some people have been doing this regularly ever since the 1950s. In 1978 the Rocky Flats nuclear warhead plant outside Boulder, Colorado was peacefully occupied by a tent city located across the railroad tracks used for bringing weapons materials into the plant and for shipping warheads out. The occupiers called themselves the Truth Force. Alternative plans for plant conversion to peaceful industries were offered to plant and state and local authorities (see Wehr, 1979).

In most cities where there is a defense plant, local peace groups hold weekly, sometimes daily, vigils at the gates of the plant and make themselves available to talk with workers going in and out. They do research, prepare economic conversion plans, and try to help the city see what kind of future it might have without a weapons facility. Similar activities go on as well in all the countries of Europe that have nuclear weapons facilities.

Women's encampments at military bases and at military production facilities have now become a worldwide phenomenon. Unlike temporary tent cities or plant vigils, these are settlements where women stay over a long period of time. Greenham Common in England is the best known and the longest lasting, but there are many: Seneca Falls, United States; Frauenfeld, Switzerland; Comiso, Sicily; Fita Fuji, Japan; Nevi Shalom, Israel, and others. What do women do there? They demonstrate how to live in peace on the very sites where nuclear death is being prepared. Living in tents and small bough-covered shelters, they embody a sharing, caring, dem-

ocratic minisociety. They are trying to live now as they would have
everyone live in the future—the goal of all utopian experiments.
They receive visitors and send out teams of speakers to tell what they
are doing. Most of all, they dialogue with the military personnel
stationed there and with the government authorities who keep
coming out to remove them. They dialogue with words and with
actions, including dancing, singing, and weaving peace symbols into
the high wire fences around the bases. When physically removed,
they return. Frustrations run high sometimes in the encampments,
and certainly internal conflicts arise, but the women don't give up
(Harford and Hopkins, 1984).

Another way that women claim public space for peace is through
symbolic weaving of webs of peace on specific occasions at military
installations. Wrapping the Pentagon in a peace ribbon embroidered in thousands of sections by women all over the United States,
as happened in July of 1985, is one outstanding example. Sewing
together embroidered quilt squares with names of loved ones and
messages of peace to send to congressional representatives, to government officials, to military officers, to the Pentagon, is another
mode of weaving peace webs, The theme is connectedness, interdependence, and an alternative path to security. "Reweaving the
web of life" has been an important theme for women in the peace
movement (McAllister, 1982).

A riskier way to claim public space for peace is to volunteer for
the Peace Brigades International[7] and serve as a nonviolent buffer
between warring parties, perhaps on the border between Costa Rica
and Nicaragua, or in Northern Ireland, or on the Israeli border, or
in other zones of violence. The brigade is modeled on the Shanti
Sena, the nonviolent brigades of India that grew out of the need to
dissipate communal violence between ethnic and religious groups,
particularly in the border tribal lands of India earlier in the century.
The Peace Brigades do without arms what the UN peace-keeping
armies do with arms. Considerable training is required, and loss of
life does occur, but the respites that these brigades provide give an
opportunity for more active peace making to take place.

While all claiming of public space for peace has some risks at-
tached, most of these activities go forward without threat of direct

---

[7]The work of Peace Brigades International is reported in the newsletter *Peace Brigade*,
obtainable from 4722 Baltimore Ave., Suite 2, Philadelphia, PA 19143, or from offices
in Canada, the Netherlands, or Switzerland. A book by Walker (1981) also describes
the brigade's work.

violence to the peace maker. Claiming railroad tracks on which trains with nuclear warheads pass by and seaports where nuclear submarines dock, claiming highways that would be commandeered in wartime by walking across the continent in peace marches—these are important symbolic acts by which peace movements have taken over space to show society how to live in peace. Peace pilgrimages and peace marches have a particular appeal. There is a nomadic quality to the life of the peace activist, even if only in a spiritual sense. Every peace activist is on a journey, a stranger in a strange land. Going on pilgrimages gives physical expression to the feeling of being on a journey.

The great San Francisco to Moscow Peace March took place in the 1960s. The Women's March from Scandinavia to Moscow took place in the 1970s. The Peace March through Central America took place in the winter of 1985–1986. These were all international peace marches. England and many European countries have had their domestic peace marches from the days of the great Aldermaston Peace Marches in the 1960s on. In the United States in 1986 the Great Peace March for Global Nuclear Disarmament walked from California to Washington, D.C., with their ten-point message on the specifics of achieving nuclear disarmament. They held rallies with local supporters at the White House and Lincoln Memorial for legislation to end the arms race. The marchers have since spread out across the country to work locally in peace organizations.

Since some of the claiming of public space for peace involves civil disobedience—being where it is illegal for citizens to be, on territory sacred to the military—it is not unusual for peace activists to experience arrest and jail. When they are in the courtroom, they claim that judicial space for peace as well, giving testimony to the alternative policies they would like to see their country follow. When they are in jail, they claim that space, too, witnessing by the way they relate to their fellow prisoners and their wardens what kind of society they are working for (see Berrigan, 1971; Bonhoeffer, 1967; Deming, 1968, 1971). The peace actions are numerous and diverse. Most of the U.S. groups and projects mentioned here are listed in the *Peace Resource Book* (Bernstein et al., 1986).

What do all these different ways of doing peace have in common? They all involve some degree of noncooperation with the existing military security order; they exhibit an inclusive concern for the society as a whole—indeed, for the world as a whole; they have particular goals in mind for any given action, usually to be found in leaflets and handouts prepared for the action; they have thought out the strategy they will follow in terms of the audiences they want to communicate with; and they give a great deal of attention to the work of communication. Finally, they carry out their action in a spirit that is congruent with the kind of society they want to help bring about, that is, their means and ends match. They may not all know very much about Gandhi, but they are the inheritors of the Satya-graha element of the world civic culture which he helped to create, and they are building up and further enriching that culture.

Zones of Peace

Zones of peace represent a sufficiently specialized way of claiming public space for peace that they will be described separately. The major difference between the zone of peace approach and other public peace action is that it is carried out with the active collaboration of public authorities. Zones of peace are declared by the governmental authorities of towns, states or provinces, countries, and groups of countries (Center for Innovative Diplomacy, 1986). Currently, most zones of peace are declared as nuclear-free zones, meaning that nuclear weapons are specifically outlawed, both in terms of stockpiling and in terms of use.

The movement began in Japan during the U.S. occupation after World War II, when many towns and villages erected markers declaring their town a zone of peace. The concept is much older, going back to antiquity, to concepts of asylum, sanctuary, right of passage through hostile territories, and so forth. At this moment in history, the establishment of nuclear-free zones is intended as a strategy for gradually widening nuclear-free areas to the point where total nuclear disarmament has been reached. (General and complete disarmament for the nuclear-free area would be the next step.) The reasoning behind nuclear-free zones as a defense measure is that such zones are free of threat and would not become bombing targets. They would also become territory in which peaceful negotiations could take place and the normal business of life resumed. They become public spaces in which a more peaceful future can begin to be lived now. Government authorities, peace researchers, and peace activists are cooperating to explore the establishment of nuclear-free zones in a number of places in Europe, including a nuclear-free zone around Austria, one in the Nordic area, and a nuclear-free corridor between Germany and Poland/Czechoslovakia.

Many nuclear-free zones already exist. Table 3 gives information on nuclear-free zone treaties, countries, and communities. New

TABLE 3: Nuclear Free Zones in the World

5 Nuclear Free Zone Treaties

The number of countries that have signed and ratified the treaty is given in parentheses.

Antarctic Treaty, 1959 (26 states, including USA and USSR)
Outer Space Treaty, 1967 (83 states, including USA and USSR)
Latin American Treaty, 1967 (also known as the Treaty of
  Tlatelolco; 24 states, including USA and USSR)
International Seabed, 1971 (73 states, including USA and USSR)
South Pacific, 1985 (10 states with 3 pending; not yet signed
  by USA and USSR)

17 Nuclear Free Zone Countries

Countries that either explicitly or implicitly prohibit nuclear weapons by law, policy, or as part of their constitutions. (? means that NFZ law may not be enforced.)

Austria	Federated States	Spain
Faeroe Islands	of Micronesia	Sri Lanka
Greenland (?)	New Zealand	Sweden
Iceland (?)	Republic of Palau	Vanuatu
Japan (?)	Papua New Guinea	(Wales, by counties)
Malta	The Seychelles	
The Marianas (?)	The Solomons	

3,260 Nuclear Free Zone Communities in 23 Countries

NFZs declared by cities, counties, and provinces. The NFZ movement is spreading quickly thoughout the world, and so many of the figures given below may be out of date. Please inform NFA of any corrections or additions to the list.

```
    1 Argentina
  102 Australia (over 56% of the population)
  281 Belgium (over 45% of the population)
  111 Canada (23% of the population, including all of
       Manitoba and over 50% of British Columbia)
   13 Denmark
    1 Finland
    1 France
  180 Great Britain (includes all of Wales and over 60%
       of the population; 32 communities in Scotland)
    1 Greece
  117 Ireland (over 50% of the population)
  170 Italy
  924 Japan (first NFZ declared in 1958; 322 declared in 1985;
       includes 5 provinces and over 48% of the population)
  400 Netherlands
  101 New Zealand (over 66% of the population)
  107 Norway (including 23 NFZ ports)
   10 Philippines
   86 Portugal
  350 Spain (over 45% of the population)
    6 Sweden
    1 Tahiti
  118 United States of America (46 are legally binding
    1 Vanuatu
  154 West Germany
```

Source: The New Abolitionist, Volume 4, Number 4, September/October, 1986.

zones are being declared every month, so it is impossible to provide an up-to-date list. These declarations and treaties are not easily enforceable at present, given the nuclear defense policies of NATO and the Warsaw Pact, but they represent intentions and may become more enforceable in the future. The fact that the list keeps growing is in itself significant. Civic culture requires institutional mechanisms for its nurture, and the peace zone mechanism is particularly important in supporting common understanding about the nonuse of military force from country to country and continent to continent.

SUMMARY

It may seem strange to include a chapter on doing peace in Part II, which was labeled "Using the Mind in New Ways." However, reflection and action, imagining and doing, are closely connected. We cannot act what we have not in some way thought. We began with thinking about peace not as a state but as a process of dealing with the conflict potentials that inhere in all social interaction. The conflict-management continuum was examined, as was the range of choices open to individuals and societies on how to handle conflicts, destructively or constructively. It was suggested that peace making is learned behavior. We have a good start with our own experience of negotiation in the numerous small conflicts of daily life, but peace making takes skill, and those skills can be continually improved.

We looked at what it takes for an individual to become a doer of peace, a peace maker, in terms of inner development and discipline, and relational skills. Then various modes of peace praxis were examined: around the negotiation table, in public spaces claimed for demonstrations of what peace is, and in the development of the tools of governance to create formal zones of peace. In talking about praxis we have been focusing on a variety of creative public acts that develop the peace-making dimension of the world civic culture. There are many other types of activities that have not been covered here. Action for social justice, for development, and for the environment all contribute to peace praxis. The intention here has not been to be exhaustive, but rather to give a sampling of what goes on in some of the more direct forms of peace praxis. Just as peace is process, so civic culture is process, and the reflective action of each individual peace practitioner contributes to its further growth.

SUGGESTED FURTHER READING

Bernstein, E., Elias, R., Forsberg, R., Goodman, M., Mapes, D., Steven, P. (1986). *Peace resource book: A comprehensive guide to issues, groups and literature.* Cambridge, MA: Ballinger.

Bondurant, J. (1965). *Conquest of violence.* Berkeley: University of California Press.

Boulding, K. (1978). *Stable peace.* Austin, TX: University of Texas Press.

Buber, M. (1949). *Paths in utopia.* (R. F. C. Hull, Trans.). London: Kegan Paul.

Burton, J. (1982). *Dear survivors.* Boulder, CO: Westview Press.

Carlson, D., & Comstock, C. (1986). *Citizen summitry.* Los Angeles: Jeremy P. Tarder (New York: St. Martin's Press).

COPRED Chronicle. Quarterly publication of the Consortium on Peace Research, Education, and Development, George Mason University, Fairfax, VA.

Fisher, R., & Urey, W. (1981). *Getting to yes: How to negotiate without giving in.* Boston: Houghton Mifflin.

Harford, B., & Hopkins, S. (1984). *Greenham Common: Women at the wire.* London: The Womens Press.

McAllister, P. (Ed.). (1982). *Reweaving the web of life: Feminism and nonviolence.* Philadelphia, PA: New Society Publishers.

Sharp, Gene. (1986). *Making Europe unconquerable: The potential of civilian-based deterrence and defense.* Boston: Porter Sargent.

Stephenson, C. (Ed.). (1982). *Alternative methods for international security.* Washington, DC: University Press of America.

Wehr, P. (1979). *Conflict regulation.* Boulder, CO: Westview Press.

Epilogue

In the months during which this book was being planned and written, the world became measurably more dangerous, less secure. The level of terrorist violence has increased as homeland-seeking Palestinians and homeland-defending Israelis have raided each other's territories in a seemingly endless cycle of vengeance and retribution. Holy wars are being fought with increasing intensity between Iran and Iraq, in the Sudan, in Sri Lanka, and in South Africa. The undeclared wars are also increasing in intensity: the U.S. against the people of Nicaragua, the Soviet Union against the people of Afghanistan. We are being treated to the sight of the superpowers breaking treaty agreements, ignoring the UN Security Council, and defying the International Court of Justice at The Hague. The presummit meeting of Premier Gorbachev and President Reagan in Iceland, which was to set the stage for serious arms control agreements, ended in childish diplomatic games of tit for tat. The specter of powerful invisible arms merchants jockeying nations into preparations for war for the merchants' private gain, an "old-fashioned" image from the turn of the century long rejected by sophisticated analysts, has suddenly reappeared as an empirical fact in, for example, the "Irangate" hearings. As heads of state try to explain secret dealings, no nation's word appears credible any longer.

In these same months the North has continued to grow richer, the South poorer. Computer technology applied to the international money market hastens the speed of impoverishment in the South, and national economic policies are mired in uncertainty everywhere. The international drug trade runs like a scarlet thread through economic misery, under no one's control. The powerful cling to whatever power they have and expand it when they can, whether through corporate takeovers, bribery of public officials, or simply by brute force. The number of U.S. citizens who own guns, and the number of deaths they inflict on each other with those guns, continue to rise.

Is this the time to write a book about long, slow processes like the emergence of a world public interest, when self-interest—individual and national—is at a peak? When the capacity for moral judgment has declined to a new low? When cynicism is rampant?

If not now, when? Ever since I was young, people have been saying there is no time for long-range processes, that all energies must be bent to solving today's crises. Yet tomorrow has always brought another crisis. It became clear to me a long time ago that either we have time or we do not. If we don't, that's that. If we do, then *taking time*, using it to ponder and act on the best possibilities for the human race, to develop our own capabilities to work for those possibilities, and finding our own role in the stream of history is the best we can do for our world.

Taking time is the key. The pace at which life is lived in the twentieth century precludes insight, prevents the slow maturing of the human spirit that is necessary to the proper conduct of human affairs. It also keeps us from identifying the whole picture of what is happening in the world. We take our self-image from the television screen, as I pointed out in Chapter 5, and mistakenly accept as a description of the real world the selective offerings of violence presented there. I began this epilogue by listing the disasters of recent months. What else has been happening recently that gives us hope? The Great Peace March, apparently in collapse and jeered at in the California desert last March, made it to Washington, D.C., held meetings and rallies and left its message. Those mobilized by the march continue a new level of peace activism in local communities around the country, and continue national networking. Wave after wave of demonstrations in Washington, D.C., through 1986 and 1987 by a broad coalition of groups concerned with economic justice, nuclear disarmament, and withdrawal from Central America, involving women, labor, and the entire array of national peace and justice organizations, have been bringing together all the issues dealt with in this book in a powerful statement about the failures of existing economic, security, and welfare policies and the need for new ones. The Great Peace Journey has traversed all continents with the same message. Elections and other political processes on several continents have sometimes brought creative new leadership to the fore which may contribute to changing the political and social climate at the level of inter-state interaction. Recent breakthroughs in health technology pioneered by UNICEF mean that children need no longer die of the diseases of malnutrition. Major new reforestation projects in Latin America and elsewhere mean that the world may once more recover its ancient canopy of green. All these developments we will know of only if we take time to discover them.

It takes time to become a person. The civic culture, and the public interest, only develop where there are human beings with a fully developed sense of individual personhood. Self-centeredness, the "Me Generation," the "Me Nation," come not so much from an excess of individualism as from an undeveloped individuality, a failure to experience the depths of the differentness and otherness which surround us, a failure to learn to live with difference creatively.

Learning takes time. Everything we have been talking about which can contribute to the building of a world civic culture involves learned behavior—involves learning *new* behaviors. In the civic sphere we have all been slow learners. While we must be patient with ourselves, we must also be serious about our intention to learn, and take time to make more learning settings available in our communities, to meet our new needs to know.

Paradoxically, by taking time, we can also be more ready to respond to crises. I have said a great deal in this book about how to cultivate the temporal sense as an aid to dealing with change, particularly in Chapters 1 and 6. Let me add here that there is a way of living simultaneously on different time tracks which can keep us unrushed and centered, even in the midst of busyness. I learned it when our five children were small. A parent has to be crisis-sensitive because life is full of small crises in early childhood. So, on one level I was always *there*, in the immediate moment, watching and listening, even while sleeping at night (instantaneous wakefulness out of an apparently deep sleep is a special parental skill). But no one can survive living only moment to moment. There was also the weekly rhythm of community affairs. One had to know just where one was in the week, so to speak, to make sure that all responsibilities for social action projects could be fitted in. Partly this involved planning, but partly it involved an intuitive sense of a second rhythm. Then there was the seasonal rhythm, the span of months in which larger community projects took place; in the household, seasonal wardrobes, furnishings, and diets were shifted.

Beyond that was the sense of even longer, slower rhythms—the time it took to develop and build an urban renewal project, to change community attitudes on nuclear testing, to develop peace education programs in local schools, to develop communication networks across national boundaries. Some of these things might take years, and impatience led to backlash. In the 1950s one worked only with great care at peace education with public school teachers, with the Scouts, and with churches. People were easily frightened in the McCarthy era, and one learned to move very gently with new program ideas. There were successes, as when toy stores agreed not to feature war toys in their display windows during the Christmas shopping season. (There is a project that needs to begin again from scratch, with the new renaissance of the war-toy industry in the mid-1980s.) There were failures, and some of them were very hard to take, particularly regressive international behavior such as the resumption of nuclear testing in the 1960s and the series of escalations in the Vietnam War in the 1960s and 1970s.

But there was a larger rhythm that encompassed all other rhythms—the rhythm of creation itself. It was the sensing of that larger rhythm as the living, moving frame for all the smaller rhythms, right down to the moment-centered rhythm of family life, that gave breathing space no matter what was going on. Awareness of the larger rhythm cannot be taken for granted, however. It has to be cultivated through reflection. The reflective life is a life in which time is taken for full attention to that larger rhythm. The attentive process goes by many names: meditation, contemplation, reverie, "just plain thinking," and prayer. There are many ways to enter into the process. The one thing required is intentionality. One has to *intend* to reflect. In our fast-paced life, reflection does not come of itself. Neither does the ability to sense the many different rhythms nested one within the other, in a larger synchronism, come of itself. It is good to practice, for just a few moments in the midst of a particularly pressing task (organizing a big public event, meeting a report deadline, or chairing a tense committee meeting) the sensing of all your different concurrent life rhythms. I think of it as getting my bearings in eternity.

Reflection in the midst of busyness is one thing. Taking time for solitude, for time apart, is another. Both help us get synchronized. Time alone is the hardest thing to come by for the average person today. (A student of mine, trying to carry out a 20-minutes-a-day-of-solitude assignment for seven consecutive days, found the only way he could get solitude was to sit on the bed in his dormitory room with a sheet draped over him to shut out the world!)

Reflection is a key to the development of personhood. It is a tool in the crafting of a life. The crafting of human beings to become what they already are is fundamental to all other tasks—to education, to peace making, to the creation of civic culture, to being able to love other humans. As already indicated in Chapters 6 and 8, it is a life-long task involving both the discipline of listening and waiting and the exuberant freedom of play. We begin by intending to do it. Everything depends on the quality of our intentionality.

In the company of strangers we can always identify those who are on the path of becoming persons. Unhurried, they are at home in the world in a special way, wherever they are; present to those around them, in a special way. They are already a part of the world civic culture I have been writing about. They have been formed by it and are in turn forming it. Their mental maps of the planet are rich in detail, and they serve as connecting points for many different networks. They understand how difficult a thing it is to grow up human in any society, and how necessary it is for us to help one an-other deal with our differences. They know that good intentions have to be assisted by enabling institutions, customs, some shared cul-ture (however minimal), and some shared ritual (however simple). They know a good deal about the current state of those enabling in-stitutions, customs, shared culture, and shared ritual which already exist. They know that we live in great crisis, and they see how in-adequate our tools and understanding are to dealing with that cri-sis. But they also know something else. They know that human beings are inventive, because they see and participate daily in hu-man inventiveness. They also know that more is at work in the world than human inventiveness. They know what an important role the unexpected plays in human affairs and are ready to be responsive to the unexpected. Most of all, they see the world as it already is.

The world civic culture, however fragmentary, is there ready to be named and worked with. The *materia prima* is at hand. We can join the company of persons-in-becoming who are working to give it shape, or we can stand on the sidelines wailing. The choice is ours.

APPENDIXES
REFERENCES
INDEX

Portfolio of Global Experience

In our study of global systems we want to build on the background of world experience and perceptions of the planet you already have. Preparing this portfolio will make it easier for you to utilize your own experience as you work your way through this book.

I. EXPERIENCE OF RESIDENTIAL MOBILITY

List all the home addresses you have had since you were born, including moves within the same town. These addresses must be for places that were your home for six months.

Town (or farm)	State	Country
1)		
2)		
3)		
4)		
5)		
6)		
7)		
8)		
9)		
10)		

11)_____   _____   _____

12)_____   _____   _____

13)_____   _____   _____

14)_____   _____   _____

15)_____   _____   _____

II. EXPERIENCE WITH SUBCULTURES IN U.S. OR ELSEWHERE

Indicate the subcultures (ethnic, racial, religious, political) you have
been part of or known. Check one of the three columns on the right for
each.

	Type of Subculture	Been Part of	Been in Close Interaction with	Had Some Exposure to
1)				
2)				
3)				
4)				
5)				

III. TRAVEL EXPERIENCES

List all the regions of the U.S. and foreign countries you have been in,
with indication of length of stay.

	Region or Country	Under 7 Days	7-30 Days	1-6 Months	Longer (Specify)
1)					
2)					
3)					

4)_____   _____ _____   _____ _____

5)_____   _____ _____   _____ _____

6)_____   _____ _____   _____ _____

7)_____   _____ _____   _____ _____

8)_____   _____ _____   _____ _____

9)_____   _____ _____   _____ _____

10)_____   _____ _____   _____ _____

11)_____   _____ _____   _____ _____

12)_____   _____ _____   _____ _____

IV. LANGUAGES YOU CAN USE (BESIDES ENGLISH!)

			Read and Speak		
				Moderately	
Language	Read Only	Speak Only	Poorly	Well	Fluently
1)_____	_____	_____	_____	_____	_____
2)_____	_____	_____	_____	_____	_____
3)_____	_____	_____	_____	_____	_____
4)_____	_____	_____	_____	_____	_____

V. MEDIA EXPERIENCES THAT SHAPED YOUR WORLD VIEW IN SOME CRITICAL WAY

1. Books in English:

2. Books in other languages:

3. Radio, TV, theater:

VI. PERSONS IN YOUR LIFE THAT SHAPED YOUR WORLD
VIEW IN SOME CRITICAL WAY

1. Parents, older siblings, or other relatives; mention only if particu-
    larly relevant to your global understanding, and give example of
    type of influence for each:

2. Other persons you have known; again, give typical example of influ-
    ence for each:

3. Public personages you have only known through the media:

4. Radio, TV, theater:

VII. EVENTS IN YOUR LIFE THAT SHAPED YOUR WORLD
VIEW IN SOME CRITICAL WAY

1. Can you remember the very first time you ever had a vivid impression
    of the planet as a <u>whole,</u> as an interdependent community of peoples?
    Describe, and give your age at the time:

2. List the five major events since your childhood that have affected
    your country:

    a)_____

    b)_____

    c)_____

    d)_____

    e)_____

3. List the five major events since your childhood that have affected
    the world:

    a)_____

    b)_____

    c)_____

    d)_____

    e)_____

4. Describe any other world-orienting events that were personally
    significant to you, and your age:

APPENDIX 2

A Workbook for Imaging a World Without Weapons*

I. The Goal Statement: Checking Out Your Own Hopes for the World

State one or more particular sociocultural/institutional achievements in relation to the overall goal of the abolition of the war system that you, bringing your own expertise to bear in the most hopeful and optimistic vein that you can draw on, would like to see realized three decades from now, in 20____.

A. On completion of this exercise, members of the group will briefly share out loud some of their goal statements. If there is time, this can be done in 3-person groups.

B. Now, after this brief discussion, reread your own goal statement and then rewrite, edit, or modify that statement in any way you wish. As the workshop proceeds, you are always free to go back and improve upon your initial goal statement.

II. Exercising the Imagination: Memories

We are going to enter the word of 20____ through the door of our imagination in a few minutes. First we need to get into the imagining mode. To do this each of us will enter our personal memory world and pick one memory to reexperience. It may be from our recent or long-ago past. It should be a "good" memory, one you will

---

*This format, used by Elise Boulding, draws on procedures developed by Warren Ziegler and to be found in his *Mindbook for Imaging a World Without Weapons*, published by Ziegler's Futures Invention Associates, 2260 Fairfax St., Denver, CO 80207. Anyone wishing more information on how to set up a workshop and contact qualified workshop leaders should write to Mary Link, Coordinator, World Without Weapons Project, 4722 Baltimore Ave., Philadelphia, PA 19143. Information about training workshops for leaders can be obtained from the same address.

enjoy reliving. You will be able to describe in detail the setting; the people involved; and the smells, sights, sounds, and feel of the place. The longer you explore the memory, the more you will see. Make some notes about the memory so you do not forget the details. In a few minutes you will divide into pairs and tell each other these memories.

III. Moving into the Future

Now we are almost ready to step into the world of 20____. To do this we will pass through an opening—whatever opening we can find once we have stepped mentally outside this building. We will keep our minds tuned to the remembering mode, only now we are asked to remember the future. How will we do this? Know that everything each of us has ever experienced, seen, heard, tasted, touched, thought, felt, from our time in the womb to the present, is encoded in some manner in our being. This record of our total life experience is not available to our conscious analytical mind except in fragments at certain moments. When we fantasize, however, that whole repository is opened up and contributes, in ways we do not consciously design, to that which we fantasize. What you are now being asked to do is focused fantasizing, or imaging. It is focused because you are bringing intentionality to it. Remember your hopes for the world in 20____. Then allow your fantasizing mind to draw on your own rich storehouse of experience to construct/remember a world in which these hopes have been realized. You are not producing or creating a model world in an analytical sense. In terms of your conscious mind you are stepping into 20____ as an observer, looking to see what you can find there. Your fantasizing/imaging capacity will do the rest. Do not try to analyze what you see. That comes later. Now you are looking, recording.

It's all right to ask questions, however, in order to see more clearly. It's all right to let your imagination move you around in 20____ to get a better view, to see more things. You are watching a movie unreeling in your head, so to speak, only unlike the movie-watching situation you can question the characters.

You want to look for specifics. You have brought your hopes with you. Look to see what is happening in concrete instances in specific arenas of life. Look for demonstrations that this world of 20____ actually represents a way of life that incorporates your goals of 30 years ago. What are people doing—the children, the elderly, the middle-years folk, the men, the women? What kind of household groupings do you find, what kinds of buildings? What is the physical environment like? Can you identify neighborhoods? Are

there cities? What kinds of occupations do you see people following? Can you tell how decisions about the polity are made, or how
people travel and make connections across distances. How do people of different ages learn new things? How are conflicts and differences handled, both the local conflicts and the far-away ones? Do you
see anyone playing? How do they play? Do you see anything that
might correspond to the churches of 30 years ago?

Some people will actually see the equivalent of a movie unreeling in their heads. Others only see disconnected image fragments,
momentary flashes of individual scenes. Still others will not experience the future visually, but through other senses, other modes of
representation. However you arrive at your perceptions, record what
you experience. There is no one "right way" of imaging. Make notes
and sketches about what you see.

(*Note*: Because some people have more difficulty than others in
moving into the future in the imagination, the group will step into
the future for a brief exploratory survey, then come back to 19___ to
discuss what people saw, how difficulties were overcome, and so
forth. With the second return to 20___, you will be left free to explore. *However*, a few may have continuing difficulty with getting
into the future. Please feel free to come to the facilitator and discuss
how to deal with this. A compromise solution for handling this exercise may be to make up a story. Please do not do this, however,
without discussing it with the facilitator first.)

IV. Clarification

What you have seen will become clearer as you tell it to others.
Try mentally to stay in 20___, and describe what is going on to your
partners in the groups of three you will now form. Listen carefully
to each other, and ask questions of each other. The questioning is
for clarification only. What each of you has seen has its own quality
of viridity. It is important to respect each other's images and the
values that lie behind them. Through questioning and clarification,
each of you will understand more fully what you have seen. Just as
in your childhood remembering, a question can send you back to
look again, and you will see more than you saw at first. You will
keep adding to the richness of your seeing; you will continue to
discover new details, new aspects. Make notes about your further
insights into your own imagery of 20___.

V. Consequence Mapping and World Construction

A. Staying in the same group of three, now begin to ask more
analytical questions of your imaging material. What kind of world

is out there? Refer back to your goal statement for a theme to "build" your world around. Draw on each other's future memories to the extent you wish to. For the purposes of this exercise, you are still in 20____. Speak of 20____ as the present. If you wish to refer to 19____, do so in the past tense. Decide what structures must exist in this world you are in to account for what you have seen. How is family life organized? What are the economic and political systems? How is education organized? How does civic and cultural life maintain itself? What makes this society tick? Account for your society locally, and move as far out as you can in terms of regions and the planet as a whole. Are there nation-states?

Time will be a limiting factor here, so begin with those aspects of the society that interest you most. You can add others later (even after this workshop is over). Take turns helping each other analyze the structure of the world you have each seen individually. On the basis of this analysis, each of you will draw a visual or diagrammatic representation of what you know about that world, on the newsprint that will be provided.

B. The next stage is for all participants to hold their newsprint up so others can see it, and to begin moving around to inspect each other's depictions of 20____. Form groups of five on the basis of some degree of theme compatibility. Each team of five will now construct a common world, based on its members' individual depictions. Deal with contradictions and discrepancies between views as best you can, and produce a visual representation of that common world on newsprint. Remember, you are still in 20____. That is your "present" during the whole exercise. Each team of five will then give a brief explanation of its world to the assembled workshop.

VI. The Future's History

You are still in 20____. Working individually again, step back into your fantasizing mode and begin to reminisce about how all this came about. It is important that you do this reminiscing from the future-present moment of 20____. Like historians of the real past, you will work with fragments of "information" and weave them into a plausible story. Your fragments will come to you in the same way that the images of 20____ came to you, culled by your fantasy from your own life-experience repository. Begin with "last year." What happened that year to bring about the world of 20____? Then go back in five-year intervals, ending with the "real" present. While it is important to go back from the future, you will not always be sure in what year something happened (that is true of the real past, too). In that case, jot the happening down in the margins and then insert it when you are clearer about the order in which things happened. Indicate a crucial turning-point year if you can. (When time allows, this future-remembering exercise should be repeated with your world-construction team, to create collective memories.)

VII. Action Planning in the Present

Working individually again, think through what you as an individual might do now, this year, to help bring about this future world you have experienced in imagination. First think about the action settings available to you. List them: your family, neighborhood, community settings, workplace, organizations you are involved in, where you shop, and so forth.

Now, what objectives might you set for yourself—concrete, specific goals that you could achieve in the short term, that is, in the coming months? Who will your allies be? How will you relate to decision makers? Now begin to flesh out one project, based on your answers to these questions. (When time allows, this action exercise should be repeated with your world-construction team to create collective action plans.)

References

Ahsen, A. (1981). Visuality among other senses and the eidetic process. *Journal of Mental Imagery, 5*(1): 19–24.

Alger, C. (1968). Interaction in a committee of the UN General Assembly. In J. D. Singer (Ed.), *Quantitative international politics* (pp. 51–84). New York: Free Press.

Alger, C., & Hoovler, D. (1978). *You and your community in the world.* Columbus, OH: Ohio State University, Consortium of International Studies.

Angell, R. C. (1969). *Peace on the march, transnational participation.* New York: Van Nostrand Reinhold.

Bainton, R. H. (1960). *Christian attitudes towards war and peace: A historical survey and critical re-evaluation.* New York: Abingdon.

Bandura, A. (1982). Self-efficacy mechanisms in human agency. *American Psychologist, 37*(2): 122–147.

Barkun, M. (1968). *Laws without sanctions.* New Haven, CT: Yale University Press.

Barnet, R., & Muller, R. (1974). *Global reach: The power of multinational corporations.* New York: Simon & Schuster.

Belenky, M., Blythe, M., Goldberger, N., & Tarule, J. (1986). *Women's ways of knowing: Self, mind and voice.* New York: Basic Books.

Bellamy, E. (1969). *Looking backward.* New York: New American Library. (Original work published 1888)

Bernstein, E., Elias, R., Forsberg, R., Goodman, M., Mapes, D., & Steven, P. (1986). *Peace resource book.* Cambridge, MA: Ballinger.

Berrigan, D. (1971). *Geography of faith: Conversations between Daniel Berrigan when underground and Robert Coles.* Boston: Beacon.

Bloom, B. (1985). *Developing talent in young people.* New York: Basic Books.

Bondurant, J. (1965). *Conquest of violence.* Berkeley: University of California Press.

Bonhoeffer, D. (1967). *Letters and papers from prison.* New York: Macmillan.

Boulding, E. (1974). Network capabilities of transnational religious associations. *International Associations, 2*: 91–93.

————. (1976). *The underside of history: A view of women through time.* Boulder, CO: Westview.

————. (1977a, January 3–6). *The human services component of nonmarket productivity in ten Colorado households.* Paper presented to the Roundtable on the Economy and Sociology of the Family, in Royaumont, France, sponsored by the Centre National de la Recherche Scientifique and the National Science Foundation.

————. (1977b). NGOs and world problem-solving: A comparison of religious and secular women's NGOs. In E. Boulding, *Women in the twentieth century world* (pp. 185–210). New York: Halsted Press.

————. (1978a). The child and nonviolent social change. In I. Charny (Ed.), *Strategies against violence: Design for nonviolent social change* (pp. 68–69). Boulder, CO: Westview.

————. (1978b). Dynamics of imaging futures. *World Futures Society Bulletin, 12*(5) : 1–8.

————. (1979a). *Children's perceptions of the changing social order and the future of culture.* Unpublished manuscript prepared for the World Order Models Task Force on Culture in the World System.

————. (1979b). Ethnic separatism and world development. In L. Kriesberg (Ed.), *Social movements, conflict and change* (pp. 259–281). Greenwich, CT: Jai Press.

————. (1980). *Women: The fifth world.* Headline Series 248, Foreign Policy Association. New York: Foreign Policy Association.

————. (1982a, November). *The social imagination and the crisis of human futures: A North American perspective.* Paper presented at the United Nations University Symposium on Crisis and Innovation in the Western World, Milan, Italy.

————. (1982b). *Women's participation in decision making on peace, security and international cooperation.* Unpublished manuscript prepared for the December 1983 Expert Group Meeting on Participation of Women in Promoting International Peace and Cooperation of the UN Branch for the Advancement of Women, Vienna, Austria.

————. (1986). The two cultures of religion as obstacles to peace. *Zygon, 21*(4): 501–518.

————. (1987). Building utopias in history. In R. Walker & S. Mendlovitz (Eds.), *Towards a just world peace* (pp. 213–234). Guilford, England: Butterworth.

Boulding, K. (1964). *The hundred largest world organizations, 1963.* Unpublished manuscript.

————. (1978). *Stable peace.* Austin, TX: University of Texas Press.

Bowker, J. (1986). The burning fuse: The unacceptable face of religion. *Zygon, 21*(4): 415–438.

Brock-Utne, B. (1985). *Educating for peace: A feminist perspective.* New York: Pergamon.

Broido, V. (1977). *Apostles into terrorists.* New York: Viking.

Brown, J. (1981). Image and object. *Journal of Mental Imagery, 5*(1) : 24.

Buber, M. (1947). *Between man and man* (R. G. Smith, Trans.). London: Kegan Paul.

————. (1949). *Paths in utopia* (R. F. C. Hull, Trans.). London: Kegan Paul. (Beacon Paperback, 1958)

————. (1958). *I and Thou* (R. G. Smith, Trans.). London: Kegan Paul.

Bulfinch, T. (1947). *Bulfinch's mythology*. New York: Thomas Y. Crowell.

Burton, J. (1982). *Dear survivors*. Boulder, CO: Westview.

————. (1984). *Global conflict*. Brighton, England: Wheatsheaf Books. (Distributed in the U.S. by the Center for International Development, University of Maryland, College Park)

Carlson, D., & Comstock, C. (1986). *Citizen summitry*. Los Angeles/New York: Jeremy P. Tarcher/St. Martin's Press.

Center for Innovative Diplomacy. (1986). *Bulletin of Municipal Foreign Policy, 1*(1).

Cox, G. (1986). *The ways of peace, a philosophy of peace in action*. Mahwah, NJ: Paulist.

Dag Hammarskjold Foundation. (1981). Towards a new world information and communication order. *Development Dialogue, 2*.

————. (1985). Another development in pharmaceuticals. *Development Dialogue, 2*.

Deming, B. (1968). *Prison notes*. New York: Grossman.

————. (1971). *Revolution and equilibrium*. New York: Grossman.

Dewey, J. (1922). *Human nature and conduct*. New York: Henry Holt.

————. (1934). *Art as experience*. New York: Menton, Balch and Co.

Durnbaugh, D. (Ed.). (1975). *On Earth peace: Discussion on war/peace issues between Friends, Mennonites, Brethren and European churches, 1935–1975*. Elgin, IL: Brethren Press.

Eagle, M. K. O. (Ed.). (1974). *The Congress of Women, held in the Women's Building, World's Columbian Exhibition*. New York: Arno. (Original work published 1895)

Eibl-Eibesfeldt, I. (1972). *Love and hate*. New York: Holt, Rinehart & Winston.

Evans, D. (1982). *Lives of mentally retarded people*. Boulder, CO: Westview.

Feld, W. (1972). *Nongovernmental forces and world politics*. New York: Praeger.

Feld, W., & Coate, R. (1976). *The role of international nongovernmental organizations in world politics*. (Learning Resources in International Studies, Learning Package No. 17). Columbus, OH: Mershon Center, Ohio State University.

Fisher, R., & Ury, W. (1981). *Getting to yes: How to negotiate without giving in*. Boston: Houghton Mifflin.

Fiske, E. B. (1982, April 4). Computers alter lives of pupils and teachers. *New York Times*, pp. 1, 42.

Forsberg, R. (1984). The freeze and beyond, confining the military to defense as a route to disarmament. *World Policy Journal, 1*(2): 285–318.

Freire, P. (1979). *Pedagogy of the oppressed*. New York: Continuum.

Friedman, M. (1960). *The life of dialogue*. New York: Harper & Row.

Galtung, J. (1969). A structural theory of imperialism. *Journal of Peace Research, 6*(3): 67–92.

———. (1980). *The true worlds: A transnational perspective.* New York: Free Press.

Gandhi, M. K. (1948). *The story of my experiments with truth.* Washington, DC: Public Affairs Press.

Gardner, H. (1985). *Frames of mind.* New York: Basic Books.

Gilligan, C. (1982). *In a different voice.* Cambridge, MA: Harvard University Press.

Gilman, C. P. (1979). *Herland.* New York: Pantheon. (Original work published 1916)

Goodall, J. (1986). *The chimpanzees of Gombe, patterns of behavior.* Cambridge, MA: Belknap/Harvard University Press.

Goody, J. (1968). *Literacy in traditional societies.* Cambridge, England: Cambridge University Press.

Gowin, D. B. (1981). *Educating.* New York: Cornell University Press.

Graff, H. (Ed.). (1981). *Literacy and social development in the West: A reader.* New York: Cambridge University Press.

Hammond, Inc. (1954). *World Atlas* (Ambassador). Maplewood, NJ: C. S. Hammond.

Harford, B., & Hopkins, S. (Eds.). (1984). *Greenham Common: Women at the wire.* London: The Women's Press.

Hart, R. (1979). *Children's experience of place.* New York: Irvington.

Hass, H. (1970). *The human animal: The mystery of man's behavior.* New York: Putnam.

Herrick, W. (1981). *Love and terror.* New York: New Directions.

———. (1983). *Kill memory.* New York: New Directions.

Hilgard, E. (1981). Imagery and imagination in American psychology. *Journal of Mental Imagery, 5*(1): 5–66.

Huizinga, J. (1955). *Homo ludens, a study of the play element in culture.* Boston: Beacon.

Huxley, A. (1968). *Brave new world.* New York: Bantam Books.

Jaipal, R. (1983). *Non-alignment: Origins, growth and potential for world peace.* New Delhi: Allical.

Johansen, R. (1986, Fall). The Reagan Administration and the UN: The costs of unilateralism. *World Policy Journal,* 601–641.

Judge, A., & Skjelsbaek, K. (1973). Transnational associations and their functions. In A. S. R. Groom & P. Taylor (Eds.), *Functionalism: Theory and practice in international relations* (pp. 190–224). London: University of London Press.

Keohane, R., & Nye, J. (Eds.). (1970). *Transnational relations and world politics.* Cambridge, MA: Harvard University Press.

———. (1985). Two cheers for multilateralism. *Foreign Policy, 60*: 148–167.

Khadduri, M. (1955). *War and peace in the law of Islam.* Baltimore, MD: Johns Hopkins Press.

Khan, I. (Ed.). (1985). *World Muslim Gazetteer.* Karachi: World Muslim Congress.

Kochler, H. (1982). *The principles of non-alignment.* London: Third World Center for Research and Publishing.

Kropotkin, P. (1903). *Mutual aid, a factor in evolution.* London: William Heinemann.

La Berge, S. (1985). *Lucid dreaming.* New York: Ballantine Books.

Larson, A., & Jenks, W. (1965). *Sovereignty within the law.* New York: Oceana.

Lerner, G. (1986). *The creation of patriarchy.* New York: Oxford University Press.

Lewin, K. (1948). *Resolving social conflicts.* New York: Harper Brothers.

Lovelock, J. E. (1979). *Gaia: A new look at life on earth.* New York: Oxford University Press.

McAllister, P. (1982). *Reweaving the web of life: Feminism and nonviolence.* Philadelphia: New Society Publishers.

Macauley, J., & Berkowitz, L. (Eds.). (1970). *Altruism and helping behavior.* New York: Academic Press.

MacBride, Sean (Ed.). (1984) *Many voices, one world* (abr. ed.). Paris: United Nations Educational, Scientific, and Cultural Organization (UNESCO).

MacPherson, J. (1962). *The four ages of man.* New York: St. Martin's Press.

McWhinney, E. (1984). *United Nations lawmaking: Cultural and ideological relativism and international lawmaking for an era of transition.* New York and Paris: Holmes and Meier/UNESCO.

Macy, J. (1983a). *Despair and personal power in the nuclear age.* Philadelphia: New Society Publishers.

————. (1983b). *Dharma and development.* West Hartford, CT: Kumarian Press.

Maruyamah, M. (1979, September–October). Mindscapes: The limits to thought. *World Future Society Bulletin, 13–23.*

Marx, L. (1964). *The machine in the garden.* New York: Oxford University Press.

Mayer, P. (1966). *The pacifist conscience.* New York: Holt, Rinehart & Winston.

Mazrui, A. (1982). The moving cultural frontier of world order. New York: World Policy Institute Working Paper.

Mendelsohn, E., & Nowotny, H. (1984). *Nineteen eighty-four: Science between utopia and dystopia.* Boston: D. Reidel.

Mendlovitz, S. (1975). *On the creation of a just world order.* New York: Free Press.

Midlarsky, E. (1968). Aiding respnses: An analysis and review. *Merill-Palmer Quarterly, 14,* 229–260.

Mitrany, D. (1966). *A working peace system.* Chicago: University of Chicago Press.

Moskos, C. (1976). *Peace soldiers: The sociology of a UN military force.* Chicago: University of Chicago Press.

Munch, P. A. (1926). *Norse mythology: Legends of gods and heroes* (rev. ed.) (S. B. Hustvedt, Trans.). New York: American Scandinavian Foundation.

Musto, R. G. (1986). *The Catholic tradition.* New York: Orbis Books, Maryknoll.

Nerfin, M. (1985). *An introduction to the third system*. IFDA Working Paper. Nyon, Switzerland: International Federation of Development Alternatives.

Nicol, D. (Ed.). (1981). *Paths to peace: The UN Security Council and its presidency*. New York: Pergamon.

Nordhoff, C. (1966). *Communistic societies in the U.S.* New York: Dover. (Original work published 1875)

Novak, J. D., & Gowin, D. B., (1984). *Learning how to learn*. Cambridge, England: Cambridge University Press.

Noyes, J. H. (1870). *History of American socialisms*. Philadelphia: J. B. Lippincott.

Nuclear Times. (1986, November–December). Citizen diplomacy: The next steps. 12–23.

Ornauer, H., Wiberg, H., Sicinski, A., & Galtung, J. (1976). *Images of the world in the year 2000*. The Hague: Mouton.

Orwell, G. (1949). Nineteen eighty-four. New York: Harcourt, Brace and World.

Palmer, P. (1981). *The company of strangers*. New York: Crossroad.

Pechota, V. (1972). *The quiet approach: A study of the good offices exercised by the UN Secretary General in the cause of peace*. New York: United Nations Institute for Training and Research.

Perez, A. G., & Kinnock, N. (1986). North-South monitor. *Third World Quarterly, 8*(4) : 1367–1418.

Pillar, P. (1983). *Negotiating peace: War termination as a bargaining process*. Princeton, NJ: Princeton University Press.

Polak, F. (1972). *The image of the future* (E. Boulding, Trans. & Abr.). San Francisco: Jossey-Bass/Elsevier. (Original work published 1955)

Pollard, F., Pollard, B., & Pollard, R. (1949). *Democracy and the Quaker method*. London: Bannisdale Press.

Rahman, F. (1966). *Islam*. Chicago: University of Chicago Press.

Reardon, B. (1985). *Sexism and the war system*. New York: Teachers College Press.

Rikhye, I., Harbottle, M., & Egge, B. (1974). *The thin blue line, international peace keeping and its future*. New Haven, CT: Yale University Press.

Rohn, P. H. (1984). *World treaty index* (Vols. 1–5). Santa Barbara, CA: ABC-Clio Information Services.

Roberts, A. (Ed.). (1969). *Civilian resistance as a national defense: Nonviolent resistance to aggression*. Baltimore, MD: Penguin Books.

Rosenne, S. (1965). *The law and practice of the international court* (Vols. 1 & 2). Leyden, Netherlands: Sijthoff.

Ruddick, S. (1985). Preservative love and military destruction: Reflections on mothering and peace. In J. Trebilcot (Ed.), *Mothering and feminist theory* (pp. 231–262). Totowa, NJ: Littlefield, Adams.

Sampson, A. (1975). *Seven sisters*. New York: Viking.

Sauvant, K. P. (1981). *The Group of 77: Evolution, structure, organization*. New York: Oceana.

Schuman, H., Inkeles, A., & Smith, D. (1967). Some psychological effects and non-effects of literacy in a new nation. *Economic Development and Cultural Change*, 16(1).

Segal, H. (1985). *Technological utopianism in American culture*. Chicago: University of Chicago Press.

Selassie, B. K. (1980). *Consensus and peace*. Paris: United Nations Educational, Scientific, and Cultural Organization (UNESCO).

Sharp, G. (1973). *The politics of nonviolent action*. Boston: Porter Sargent.

───────. (1985). *Making Europe unconquerable: The potential of civilian-based deterrence and defense*. Cambridge, MA: Ballinger.

Shore, H. (1981). *Cultural policy: UNESCO's First Cultural Development Decade*. Washington, DC: U.S. National Commission for UNESCO.

Singham, A. W., Hune, S. (1986). *Non-alignment in an age of alignments*. Westport, CT: Lawrence Hill.

Sivard, R. (1986). *World military and social expenditures*. Leesburg, VA: UMSE Publications.

Skjelsback, K. (1974). A survey of international nongovernmental organizations, parts 1 & 2. *International Associations*, 5: 267–270, 6: 352–354.

Smith, A. (1976). *The theory of moral sentiments*. Oxford, England: Clarendon. (Original work published 1759)

───────. (1939). *The wealth of nations*. New York: Random House. (Original work published 1776)

Smith, C. D. (Ed.). (1985). *The hundred percent challenge: Building a National Institute of Peace*. Washington, DC: Seven Locks.

Sorokin, P. (Ed.). (1950). *Explorations in altruistic love and behavior*. Boston: Beacon.

Spufford, M. (1981). *Small books and pleasant histories: Popular fiction and its readership in seventeenth century England*. Athens, GA: University of Georgia Press.

Stang, H. (1975). *Westernness and Islam*. (Trends in Western Civilization Program No. 7.) Oslo: University of Oslo.

Stephenson, C. (1982). *Alternative methods for international security*. Washington, DC: University Press of America.

Stopford, J., & Dunney, J. (1984). *The world directory of multinational enterprises*. Detroit, MI: Gale Research Company.

Straus, M., Gelles, R., & Steinmetz, S. (1980). *Behind closed doors*. New York: Doubleday.

Strauss, A. (1978). *Negotiation—varieties, contexts, processes and social order*. New York: Jossey-Bass.

Tagore, R. (1924). *Nationalism*. London: Macmillan.

Teilhard de Chardin, P. (1959). *The phenomenom of man*. New York: Harper & Row.

Thick Nat Hanh. (1967). *Vietnam: Lotus in a sea of fire*. New York: Hill and Wang.

Tocqueville, A. de (1945). *Democracy in America*. New York: Alfred Knopf. (Original work published 1840)

Toynbee, A. (1972). *A study of history* (Vols. 1–10). London: Oxford University Press. (Original work published 1934–1961)

Union of International Associations. (1972–1973). *Yearbook of international organizations* (Vol. 14). Brussels: UIA.

————. (1983–1984). *Yearbook of international associations*. London: K. G. Saur.

————. (1985–1986). *Yearbook of international organizations* (Vols. 1–2). London: K. G. Saur.

————. (1986). *Yearbook of world problems and human potential*. London: K. G. Saur.

United Nations. (1945). *Charter of the United Nations*. New York: UN.

————. (1986) *Everyone's United Nations: A handbook on the work of the United Nations*. UN Publication No. E.85.I.24. New York: UN.

United Nations Educational, Scientific, and Cultural Organization. (1969). *Birthright of man* (Jeanne Hirsch, Comp.). New York: UN.

————. (1980). *Peace on earth*. Paris: UNESCO.

————. (1983). *UNESCO yearbook on peace and conflict studies*. Westport, CT: Greenwood.

United Nations International Year of the Child Secretariat. (1978, December). *From the world's children to the world's media*. Wallingford, England: New International Publications.

Venkata, R. (1975). *The ways of the peacemaker: A study of UN intermediary assistance in the peaceful settlement of disputes*. New York: United Nations Institute for Training and Research.

Walker, C. (1981). *A world peace guard*. Vedchi, India: Peace Brigades International. (Obtainable from Peace Brigades International, 4722 Baltimore Avenue, Philadelphia, PA 19143)

Watkins, M. (1976). *Waking dreams*. New York: Gordon & Breach.

Webster. (1979). *New collegiate dictionary*. Springfield, MA: G & C Merriam.

Wehr, P. (1979). *Conflict regulation*. Boulder, CO: Westview.

White, L. (1968). *International nongovernmental organizations*. New York: Greenwood.

Wien, B. (1984). *Peace and world order studies: A curriculum guide* (4th ed.). New York: World Policy Institute.

World Futures Studies Federation. (1986). *Reclaiming the future: A manual on futures studies for African planners*. Prepared for UN Development Program. London: Tycooly International.

Yarrow, M. (1978). *Quaker experiences in international conciliation*. New Haven, CT: Yale University Press.

Xiaotaong, P. (1987). *Human identity*. Unpublished report prepared for the Committee for a Just World Peace, World Policy Institute, New York.

Ziegler, W. (1982). *Mindbook of exercises for futures inventors*. Denver, CO: Futures Invention Associates, 2260 Fairfax St.

————. (1987a). *Designing and facilitating projects and workshops in futures invention*. Denver, CO: Futures Invention Associates.

————. (1987b). *Mindbook for imaging/inventing a world without weapons* (5th ed.). Denver, CO: Futures Invention Associates.

Index

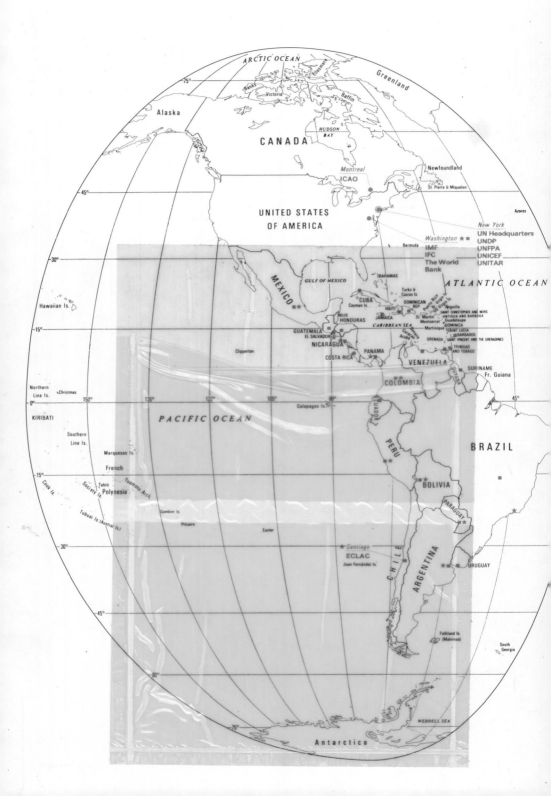